KING'S LYNN & THE GERMAN HANSE
1250 – 1550

Preface

The regional capitals of the German Hanse have understandably attracted historians rather than the mass of smaller towns which belonged to what was an informal urban community, although the latter are now generating more interest. Bruges, London, Bergen and Novgorod, or the four great overseas kontors of the Hanseatic towns, have likewise preoccupied historians far more than their forty-four smaller trading posts scattered across northern Europe. The latter kontors were usually hosted by port towns which were to a greater or lesser extent trading partners of the German Hanse. Scholarly work on England and the Hanseatic towns has given some valuable space to the several English east coast ports north of London which fall into this category. Yet there is surely room for individual case studies of their medieval trade and politics in relation to the German Hanse which can throw more light on both.

The principal aim of this book is to assess the significance of Lynn in Anglo-Hanseatic history when towns and the merchant class were rising in medieval Europe. To understand the origins of today's modern Hanse embracing almost 200 member towns across northern Europe is another.

This study can be seen as a synthesis or project using various secondary sources (English and German) relevant to Anglo-Hanseatic history and Lynn. Some research into local and central government primary sources has also been undertaken. This was greatly facilitated by the late Roger Harrison's compilation of material relating to medieval Lynn taken from the Chancery Rolls. Liam Burrows was generous in sharing his research findings on Lynn customs accounts at the National Archives. The King's Lynn Borough Archives at the Town Hall hold a remarkable collection of medieval records which have informed this study. The staff at King's Lynn Library have been most helpful in securing interlibrary loans over a long period. I also acknowledge my debt to Stuart Jenks, T H Lloyd, John Fudge, Philippe Dollinger and other authors whose work on the Hanseatic towns and England has been so important. From both Volker Henn who read my draft first chapter, and John Alban on the subject of medieval ships, I received good advice. The late Syd Swan gladly assisted me for several years with translations of passages in German texts. Rosemary Bryan and Alison Gifford spent innumerable hours typing the book and took a most welcome interest in its evolution. Rebecca Rees spent some time on the important task of proof reading its final draft. Gillian Floyd gave me insights into

The Lisa von Lübeck in Lynn in August 2009 with the docks behind her.

sailed to England for the first time with Lynn its destination.

Hull (2012), Boston (2015), Ipswich (2017), Yarmouth (2019) and Beverley (2020) have followed Lynn's example by becoming members of the New Hanse which counts almost 200 towns across sixteen European nations. The upsurge of interest in the New Hanse has largely been due to the historic events in Europe after 1989. The fall of the Iron Curtain and the reunification of Germany combined with the EU membership of the Baltic states were critical factors. Towns in several Baltic and eastern European countries have joined German and Dutch counterparts to relaunch what is seen as a shared and dynamic Hanseatic community. Although all these member towns do possess a Hanseatic past and identity to varying degrees (a necessary membership qualification), the New Hanse cannot be interpreted as a direct descendant of the medieval German Hanse. A significant number of these towns were not members of this Old Hanse but its trading partners whose relationship with German merchants was not always harmonious. This includes the above six English towns and the Scottish cities of Edinburgh and Aberdeen which have also become members of the modern Hanse.

The book comprises five chapters running in chronological order save that the first is concerned with the question 'What was the German Hanse?' Six key interlocking aspects are examined to foster an understanding of its character and firmly locate the chapters following in their wider European context. Lynn's early engagement with the Hanseatic towns is examined in the second chapter. It discusses when and why German merchants arrived in the Wash ports to trade, particularly those from the Baltic called Easterlings. Lynn and Boston had the earliest and strongest connections to the Germans from the Baltic and North Sea coastal towns before London became dominant in Anglo-Hanseatic commerce. The third chapter follows the voyages of English ships and traders into the Baltic from the late 14th century and the impact they made in Prussia. Lynn merchants were in the vanguard of English mercantile ventures to the Baltic lands as the island kingdom sought export markets in the East. The fourth chapter traces international conflict in Norway and Iceland as well as the Baltic, through the 15th century, which disrupted England's trade with the Hanseatic towns, and culminated in an Anglo-Hanseatic Sea War. The Treaty of Utrecht (1474) brought an Anglo-German peace settlement. The fifth chapter begins with the foundation of the Hanseatic kontor at Lynn in 1475 and takes discussion of Anglo-Hanseatic commerce to circa 1550. That the German diplomats at Utrecht had insisted on a trading post being granted at Lynn confirmed the importance of the Norfolk town in the Hanseatic world. A short conclusion precedes a postscript on Lynn's Hanse House since 1751 which brings this study to an end.

The medieval names of Hanseatic towns are used throughout the book but their modern designations can also be found. I prefer 'Lynn' rather than 'King's Lynn' in the text, as in local parlance, and because the town was 'Bishop's Lynn' until 1537 when Henry VIII ended the overlordship of the Norwich bishops. The medieval sources frequently refer to the Wash port as simply 'Lenne' or 'Lenn'. The town's name is a survival from the Celtic past, with Lyn or Lenn meaning pool or lake, as in Lincoln and Dublin. It should finally be noted that Lynn's Parish and Priory Church of St Margaret's became a Minster Church in December 2011 but appears as St Margaret's Priory Church.

A note on terminology is necessary. For a long time English historians have usually applied the label 'Hanseatic League' to describe that large group of German towns whose role in Europe's medieval economic development was formative. One notable exception is T. H. Lloyd's *England and German Hanse 1157-1611* (1991). Though the term 'Hanseatic League' remains current in England, the author prefers 'German Hanse' for reasons which will become clear.

Notes

1. Norfolk Record Office, 'With Ships and Goods and Merchandise', *King's Lynn and the Hanse. A guide to an exhibition of facsimile documents* [NRO 1998], 14.
2. Harrison, R., The Chancery Rolls: The Close Rolls 1256 – 1377 (King's Lynn 1994), 661.

What was the German Hanse?

I

Although the German Hanse of the Middle Ages has generated more interest and even fascination in Europe in the last forty years, as reflected in the growth of the New Hanse founded in 1980, historians have also been asking more searching questions. In late medieval Hanseatic documents, it sometimes described itself as "a firm confederation of many towns and villages to guarantee a prosperous progress of the commercial activities by sea and land". [1] The same records also refer to the towns "van der Dudeschen hense" (1358), or towns of the German Hanse, though the merchants were mainly north German, with the notable exception of Cologne and its Rhineland satellite towns. But its origins were in groups or hanses of German merchants seeking to secure trading privileges abroad rather than in the towns themselves. It evolved into an urban community from the 1350s when the combined power of the towns was needed to protect German foreign trade. There was, however, no sharp break in Hanseatic history. The towns continued to act on behalf of their merchants. The German Hanse was a loose urban association without a hierarchical structure (in which members elected officials to ensure conformity) as is usually the case with an urban league. Nor was it a guild for the same reason. There were guilds in the Hanseatic towns to support bands of merchants journeying to and from overseas locations such as Novgorod, Bergen, Bruges and London.

Hanses or groups of traders travelling abroad for their mutual protection were common enough in medieval Europe, and the German Hanse had its beginnings in this world of commercial adventure and risk, but by the 15th century the towns exercised far more control than previously. In a letter from Lübeck to the English government in 1469 it was made clear that the "Hansa Theutonica" was "not controlled by the merchants" but the lords or rulers of the member towns "by whom its affairs are directed". [2] This German urban community is still extremely difficult to grasp or tie down. It did not have a founding charter or constitution even though Bremen asked Cologne to search the archives for one in 1418! It lacked a bureaucracy or armed forces. There were no common finances, bank or seal, nor a chief executive until Dr Sudermann in 1556. Nor was there a membership list and, anyway, it was not fixed. A town could leave the community, or be excluded, whilst another could apply to join. Jenks comments

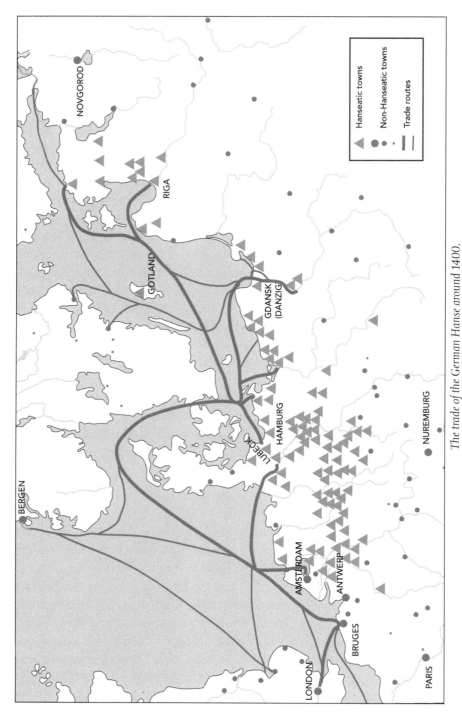

The trade of the German Hanse around 1400.

Reproduced from Braudel, F., Civilisation & Capitalism 15th - 18th Century [London 1984]. The Wash ports on the far left.

on its character thus:

> Consequently, what we think of as the 'Hanse' is actually a continuously shifting coalition of towns with roughly compatible overall goals, but, at any given moment, widely differing interests and tactics. In fact, the Hanse was a bit like a kaleidoscope: the slightest twist in international affairs instantly produced a completely new constellation of towns. This is not to say that chaos reigned. All Hanseatic towns had long-term interests and trading partners, with whom relations ranged from intimate co-operation to bitter, even violent rivalry. Generally speaking, Hanseatic politics turned on the question of whose economic interests were affected by a given development. [3]

It is therefore almost impossible to list all the Hanseatic towns at any one time, but membership usually consisted of almost 100 larger and about 100 smaller ones, with the latter usually represented by the former on a regional basis. The smaller towns did not play a forward role in the community but were numerous and part of its economic and political network. There was more trade between the member towns than they had with foreign countries.

The German Hanse was a remarkable and unique organisation in medieval Europe, both for its longevity (400 years or more) and geographical extent, from Smolensk to London, from Tallinn to Bruges, from Lübeck to Venice. Professor Friedland observed:

> It has been said that by the Hanse the face of Europe was turned from the Mediterranean to the North and, by this, later on, the eyes of Europe were turned in the north-western and western directions towards Atlantic trade and the traffic system of modern centuries. [4]

The German history magazine *Geoepoche* subtitled a recent edition (no. 82) on 'Die Hanse' (1150-1600) as 'Europe's Secret Superpower'. Its heartland was the coastal cities of the German North. German traders from the North Sea ports of Hamburg and Bremen were sometimes known as Westerlings to distinguish them from the Easterlings out of Lübeck and other Baltic havens. The Baltic was the Ostsee or East Sea as opposed to the West See or North Sea. The English word 'sterling' referred to the nation's currency having its origins in the silver coinage used by the Westerlings and Easterlings.

To learn more about the German Hanse this chapter investigates six of its key interlocking aspects. These aspects (or what might also be termed dimensions) are discussed in an order which hopefully has some logic and allows this German urban community to be seen as a multifaceted whole.

II

Lübeck and the German west Baltic towns as well as Hamburg should come first because they were the heartland of the German Hanse. Lübeck took the lead. It was in the far north of the Holy Roman Empire which was a vast Central European federation of German speaking territories controlled by princes, and included fifty imperial free cities such as Lübeck, with the Emperor or Kaiser at the summit as overlord. Save for Danzig, Königsberg, Riga and other eastern towns, the Hanseatic cities fell within its borders. Charlemagne had been crowned by the Pope in Rome as the first Holy Roman Emperor in 800 AD and the Empire endured until Napoleon abolished it in 1806. It was both the successor of the Roman Empire and 'Holy' as defender of the Roman Catholic

Lübeck's seal (1256) showing a seafaring trader and an overland merchant in partnership on board a ship.

Reproduced from Friedland, K. & Richards, P., Essays in Hanseatic History (Dereham 2005).

Church which was itself a powerful force. The Empire's major actors (urban, princely, ecclesiastical) organised frequent local and regional assemblies, whilst the Imperial Parliament or Reichstag was the ultimate or central body, to resolve political and other issues to maintain its integrity.

Lübeck's geographical location ensured that it would be in a strong position to influence the development and nature of the German Hanse. Ellmers advances the city's central role in its origins through the linking of the inland towns of western and central Germany to the Baltic trade. His argument depends on the "iconographic interpretation" of Lübeck's first civic seal. [5] It was cut in 1223 but the design was deliberately kept in 1256 and 1281 to demonstrate that the city had been the birthplace of the German Hanse. The seal shows a ship or cogge of the 13th century with a seafarer and a merchant from the interior as his partner in the expansion of Baltic commerce. It highlights Lübeck's position on the Baltic which allowed the two to join forces for their mutual economic benefit. Yet the migration of Saxon and Westphalian traders to the Baltic coast in the 12th and 13th centuries was the forerunner to German commercial expansion rather than the foundation of Lübeck itself. Their capital investment fuelled the growth of Lübeck and other new German towns along the Baltic's southern shore as more colonists from the West were attracted to the East. The overland route between Lübeck and Hamburg gave this new urban network additional momentum by effectively connecting West and East European markets.

Lübeck became an imperial city after being granted independence or self-government by the Holy Roman Emperors Frederick Barbarossa and Frederick II in 1188 and 1226 respectively. Due to the fact that these Kaisers had their strongholds in Prague and Central Europe, it was difficult to enforce their hegemony in the North. Charles IV visited Lübeck with a large entourage in 1375. Having refused to assist the Hanseatic towns in their recent conflict with Denmark, he was not promised any material aid for his own schemes. Barbarossa had been the last emperor to come to the Baltic town in 1181! Over these 200 years Lübeck had become wealthy and large but only an informal capital of the emerging German Hanse with no real power to discipline member towns. The city had asserted leadership by seeking trade agreements abroad for merchants from all the Hanseatic towns. Lübeck appointed ambassadors to the courts of the kingdoms and city states of western and southern Europe (including the Roman Papacy). It was the diplomatic capital of the German Hanse. Lübeck directed negotiations with homeland and foreign princes to solve the problems of German traders overseas. Not until 1418 were Lübeck and the towns in its region (Hamburg, Stralsund, Wismar, Rostock and Stettin) formally charged to manage the affairs of the community. This included a brief to settle the conflicts within Hanseatic towns particularly when their autonomy was threatened by overlords as in the case of Rostock.

Disastrous fires in Lübeck in 1251 and 1276 led the council to order that brick buildings must replace wooden ones. From the market-place new brick merchant houses combining domestic and commercial functions soon ran down the gentle hill to the Trave. Here riverside brick warehouses were erected for the salt and corn and other commodities which enriched the city's merchants who numbered at least 500 in the 14th century. Lübeck's population around 1300 has been estimated at 15,000 but growth was reversed by the Black Death. Following that continental wide epidemic (1348 − 50) its population recovered and was approximately 25,000 in 1466 which made it bigger than Hamburg but smaller than Cologne.

III

Lübeck was the first German seaport on the Baltic having been founded in the 1140s by Count Adolf of Holstein who annexed the territory of the pagan Wends. The Danish hold on the city was undone in 1227 when a coalition of north German princes defeated King Valdemar at the battle of Bornhoved. In 1241 Lübeck sealed an alliance with Hamburg which was another imperial city whose broad hinterland via the Elbe and proximity to the North Sea promoted the partnership. This event has been seen by some as the origin of the German Hanse but such urban pacts were not unusual at this time. Together the two cities controlled commercial traffic between the Baltic and the North Sea, though merchandise had to be taken overland by wagon, at least for most of the fifty miles between them. The wagons travelled in convoy and armed horsemen were employed to protect it (the fee to join the convoy was called 'a hanse'). Herring, wheat, rye, linen, iron and furs were transported from Lübeck to Hamburg and then by sea or overland to western Europe. Wine, fruit and cloth were amongst the commodities going in the opposite direction. There must have been a limit on the movement of bulk loads like fish or rye because of the high costs of such road haulage. The opening of the Stecknitz canal in 1398 facilitated trade between the two cities because goods could now be conveyed by water, though road traffic remained important.

Lübeck and Hamburg were largely protected from raids by pirates because of their location up river. Their alliance was partly designed to deter highway robbers and the neighbouring territorial gentry who interfered with road traffic by building fortified towers to intimidate and tax it. Some of these wooden towers were burnt down. Yet Lübeck, Hamburg, Bremen and Lüneburg also agreed mortgages with regional landed magnates to acquire territory which helped to protect trade routes. In 1359 Lübeck negotiated a mortgage with the Dukes of Saxony-Lauenburg to control the town of Mölln to the south on the river Stecknitz which connected the city with the prized salt mines at Lüneburg. Scott concludes: "Mortgages were a convenient means of reaching an accommodation with neighbouring princes who might otherwise prey upon the cities' merchants". [6] It was possible for a Hanseatic town and the prince in its hinterland to cultivate a close partnership or power sharing as Wismar shows. This Baltic town remained the official capital of the Mecklenburg princes until 1358 and was under their jurisdiction for a long period. However, Lübeck played a leading role in Wismar's foundation, and its merchants rather than their resident prince joined the German Hanse.

Hamburg built a tower and small fort at the mouth of the Elbe in 1310 to serve as a navigational aid and look-out for pirates. It exported grain and beer to England and Flanders on its own account and 500 breweries operated in the city by the 15th century. In 1369 this great 'brewhouse' of the German Hanse exported one third of its beer to Amsterdam. Brewing was a key industry in other Hanseatic coastal towns with Bremen, Wismar, Lübeck and Rostock exporting beer to the Low Countries and Scandinavia. The addition of hops after 1300 acted as a preservative to assist its successful shipping overseas. Barrels were rarely returned to their town of origin but re-used for various purposes in the places to which they were despatched. Trade in beer, salt, pitch, fish, furs and most other commodities depended on the manufacture of enormous numbers of barrels. In 1375 the barrel used in Rostock was adopted as the standard beer measure in the Hanseatic towns to facilitate trade. The popular name of this Baltic port town was 'the maltings' of the Hanse. Hops, wheat and barley were grown in the hinterlands of these German coastal towns to supply their many maltings and breweries.

During the 13th century German colonisation of the southern Baltic coast resulted in the foundation of towns immediately to the east of Lübeck which acted as a kind of urban patron. These towns were usually based on existing settlements with Slavonic inhabitants. Rostock (1218), Wismar (1226), Stralsund (1234) and Greifswald (1250) are good examples. Over 100 towns on the Baltic were granted Lübeck Law or the same civic constitution and legal system as the city on the Trave, though not all local authorities implemented it. In Lübeck the city council sometimes operated as an 'Oberhof' or court of appeal hearing cases of property and other disputes in the Baltic towns. In 1259 Lübeck, with Rostock and Wismar, agreed a pact to secure trade routes against pirates; in 1283 Greifswald, Stralsund and Stettin (Szczecin) joined them. The common commercial interests which pulled these German towns together were also illustrated by the monetary union formed in 1379-81; Hamburg, Lübeck, Wismar, Lüneburg, Rostock and Stralsund were all members. These towns became known as the Wendish sector of the German Hanse (the Wends had been the original Slavonic settlers). Their relations were not always harmonious. In 1284 Stralsund complained about Lübeck's attempt to monopolise the lucrative herring trade to England.

A rediscovered manuscript in Low German apparently taken from Lübeck to Russia in 1945 has recently been published in Germany: *Der Bardewiksche Codex des Lübischen Rechts von 1294*. This digest or collection of rules came out of Lübeck to develop law and order in its commercial and cultural exchanges with the growing new German Baltic towns to strengthen the connections between them. The large number of Lübeck law books dating from the 13th century are testimony to the city's prosperity and civic pride as well as regional dominance.

To Lübeck's south and west were at least twenty-five Saxon towns which played a less important role in the emerging German Hanse, save for Bremen, a river port which tended to independent action. The city was officially re-admitted to the community in 1358, having apparently been excluded in 1285 as a result of its refusal to support the blockade of Norway, although its merchants had remained in the Hanseatic urban network. Dollinger quotes the Bremen council which was grateful to be granted "the honour of sharing in the privileges and charters" of the Hanseatic community from which they had in the past been "deprived".[7] Hamburg and Bremen were nevertheless economic competitors, and the former may have preferred the permanent exclusion of the town on the Weser.

Old merchant house now a restaurant at Stralsund whose traders sailed to the Wash ports before 1400.

The alternative to the land or isthmus route between Lübeck and Hamburg was the voyage around the Jutland peninsular which the Germans called the Umlandfahrt. It took several days and risked rough weather conditions as well as the tolls of the Danes who for long struggled with the German towns for mastery of the Baltic. This sea passage was increasingly undertaken by Danzigers because transport costs for bulk cargoes of timber and corn from the eastern Baltic to western Europe were greatly reduced. Lübeck was consequently becoming less central to the Hanseatic trading network by 1400. However, the overland route between Lübeck and Hamburg continued to be used by merchants, the former city providing various commercial services which counteracted the advantages of the Umlandfahrt. Lübeck had also secured the sea route to the northern Baltic lands and Russia through establishing a community at Visby, on the island of Gotland, and a trading post at Novgorod. Its merchants were using Visby as a stepping stone to northern Russia as early as the 1160s. Reval (Tallinn) in Estonia was another chief entrepôt for Lübeck in its Russia trade and, in turn, the Hanseatic metropolis was Reval's most important foreign business centre. Rye, furs, flax, lard and other commodities from Reval were shipped via Lübeck to Bruges and Antwerp as well as overland to Nüremberg and other European cities.

A privileged geographical location with access to east and west European markets was not the sole reason for the medieval growth of Lübeck and the Wendish towns. The herring fishery of the western Baltic was at first of enormous importance to them. The south-western region of Sweden or Scania was then part of the Danish Kingdom with its shores attracting thousands of small boats in the late summer and early autumn every year. According to *The Chronicle* of Saxo Grammaticus the herring swarmed so thickly off this coast around 1200 that a man could wade into the water and catch them by hand! Grain, salt, cloth, furs, spices, pottery and beer were brought to the region by German (and later Dutch and English) traders to exchange for the cured herring at the Scania fairs. Hanseatic and other towns were granted a 'vitte' or plot where their fishermen and merchants could live and work. The Lübeckers imported wine to satisfy demand at the local wine shops. The Baltic towns settled on the Falsterbo peninsula where Germans and Danes had churches and cemeteries as well as warehouses. Here their coopers made the barrels to transport the herring salted and packed by Danish and some German women. The mix of salt and blood of the fish provided an air tight seal. In the 15th century the herring were repackaged into other barrels with salt water and tasted better to fetch a higher price. Catholic Europe relied heavily on fish to replace the meat deemed unholy to consume on certain weekdays and during festivals.

The military victory of the Hanseatic towns and their allies over Denmark in the 1360s, confirmed by the Treaty of Stralsund in 1370, ensured their domination of the Baltic and Scania, at least for the foreseeable future. English and Dutch merchants travelling there found their freedom to trade severely restricted. The Lübeckers purchased large quantities of herring from local fishermen and transported salt supplies for preserving the fish from Lüneburg's mines and south-west France. By 1368 they sent at least 250 ships to Scania every year and, by 1400, no fewer than 500; the majority were small craft but others were large vessels capable of holding '400 Tonnen'.[8] The Scania fishery was still buoyant through the 15th century despite fears that the herring were deserting the Baltic. In 1410 the fish did not appear off Scania and poor catches were reported in 1411, 1412, 1416 and 1425. That Prussian merchants stopped travelling to Scania for most of the 1420s and 1430s is instructive. Yet over 20,000 traders visited Scania in 1463 to buy salted herring at the fairs for distribution across Europe. And in the summer of 1486 "a vast amount of herring was caught in Skania" according to *The Danzig Chronicle*.[9] Historians cannot agree when the herring finally migrated from the Baltic to the North Sea, but the Scania fishery declined in the 16th century, to impact adversely on the Hanseatic towns. Recent research on the salted herring fisheries in the western Baltic (1200-1650) has found indications that overfishing was a factor in the collapse of the Sound fishery circa 1580.

IV

A second key aspect relating to the formation of the German Hanse and European economic development is further German colonisation of Slavonic territories east of Lübeck, largely as a result of continental population growth in the 13th century. The six Prussian towns which belonged to the community by the late 14th century were Danzig (Gdansk), Elbing (Eblag), Königsberg (Kaliningrad), Braunsberg (Braniewo), Kulm (Chelmno) and Thorn (Torun). To the south of these towns Cracow (Krakow) and Breslau (Wroclaw) were both members until the late 15th century. Though Thorn was the commercial headquarters of these Prussian cities in the 14th century, its merchants trading with western Europe via the Vistula, it was Danzig which achieved ascendency by the 1380s. Its extensive hinterland secured by the Vistula river system included Prussia's landed estates and the forests of eastern Europe. Wax, pitch, iron, copper and timber (for barrel staves, gates, furniture, ship masts) went from Danzig to Lübeck, with cloth and salt going in the opposite direction (a ship took four days and a wagon two weeks). Lübeck merchants had a warehouse and economic privileges in Danzig from 1298 to emphasise the substantial commercial traffic between the two cities by sea and land. The Prussian port town also had important sea links with the Livonian (Latvia and Estonia) Hanseatic towns to the north and to Königsberg overland. Only three of these Livonian towns were prominent members of the German Hanse; Riga, Reval (Tallinn) and Dorpat (Tartu), with the German populations in a minority save for Riga. Riga was founded in 1201 and became a member town in 1282. In 1939 a German cogge dating from the early 13th century was excavated there. Visby on Gotland was a significant Hanseatic town until the early 14th century and other Swedish towns had German residents. The Prussian and Livonian towns constituted another Hanseatic sector or power bloc far to the east of the Wendish towns. They were not autonomous urban centres which could independently seek membership of the German Hanse. Although members of that community in their own right, these new towns were under the suzerainty of the Grand Master of the Teutonic Order, the only territorial prince admitted to membership. He negotiated with the other Hanseatic towns and foreign princes on behalf of the Prussian towns whose growth he promoted.

The Teutonic Knights were a German Order of warrior monks founded in the Holy Land around 1190, by crusaders from Bremen and Lübeck, who opened a hospital there. The Christian West was not only challenged by the Ottomans in the Holy Land, but also by the pagan tribes of eastern Europe. When the Pope and German Emperor endorsed Polish requests for reinforcements to conquer eastern Europe for Christendom in 1226, it was to the Teutonic Knights that they turned. From the 1230s they proceeded to wage war on Baltic pagan tribes (including the Prussians) and allowed to retain conquered land to create their own state. Prussia functioned both as a buffer against Russian expansion and the base for German colonisation eastwards. For Lübeck and the Wendish towns an alliance with the Teutonic Order was essential. Its Grand Master had made Marienburg (now Malbork in Poland) his headquarters in 1309 which prompted a great construction programme over the following decades. The resulting monastic buildings and arsenal as well as the 'parliament house' which comprised this fortress overawed visitors. Up to 1,000 horses were also stabled at Marienburg for deployment in both war and peace. Around 1400 there were probably no more than 800 Teutonic Knights who built other castles to defend their Prussian and Livonian territories. On military campaigns they were reinforced by fellow knights from western Europe as well as mercenaries. In 1410 the Teutonic Knights were defeated at the Battle of Tannenberg (seventy miles south-east of Marienburg) by a combined Polish and Lithuanian invasion force, led by King Ladislas. He had converted to Catholicism as Jogaila of Lithuania in 1386, and later married Jadwiga, the heiress to the Polish Crown. The Knights then survived a long siege of Marienburg but further setbacks followed in the Thirteen Years' War (1453–66). As a result of the Treaty of Thorn (1466) the former strong and independent Teutonic Order was obliged

Marienburg Castle on the Nogat river was the headquarters of the Teutonic Knights in Prussia. Reconstruction was necessary after the Second World War. Now Malbork Castle in Poland.

to accept dependence on Poland, involving the surrender of West Prussia and Danzig, whose German citizens now forged a connection with the Polish Crown. The Grand Master had moved his residence from Marienburg to Königsberg (now Kaliningrad in Russia) in East Prussia in 1457. The Teutonic Order was disbanded in 1525 as the Lutheran Reformation in Germany embraced it. East Prussia was transformed into a secular state and the last Grand Master converted to Protestantism.

Christian crusades in eastern Europe were regarded as Holy Wars prosecuted with the enthusiasm and even fanaticism often associated in the West today with Islam. From the 1220s Lübeck operated as a crusader port town supporting the Teutonic Knights who led expeditions from there to the eastern Baltic territories. Every Easter the city sent ships and provisions to Livonia with novice Christian soldiers representative of all layers of its society. The German communities in the towns of the eastern Baltic were small and such expeditions brought both protection and colonists. Some Christians questioned the morality of using warfare to convert pagans. The Knights defended their missionary role in eastern Europe, although accusations that they were more interested in land than people damaged their reputation.

The annual Christian crusades or 'reisen' against the pagans of eastern Europe became part of the calendar of the continent's aristocracy. English nobles participated. In 1392 Henry Bolingbroke (later Henry IV 1399-1413) sailed from Lynn to Danzig with about 150 retainers and servants to assist the Teutonic Knights. Three ships were fitted out in the Wash haven and loaded with barrels of fresh water, crabs, lobsters, stockfish, fruit, spices, beer, six dozen plates and a banner bearing the arms of St George. Special cabins and a chapel had to be erected for the comfort of the aristocratic party. The vessels set sail on 24 July 1392 and with a favourable wind reached Prussia in just eighteen days. Unfortunately, when Henry and his little army arrived in Danzig, they discovered that the Teutonic Knights had no military campaign to prosecute. A Prussian chronicle claimed that there was a dispute over the right to carry the banner of St George, the patron saint of both England and the German Order. However, Henry had already seen action as an eager crusader in Lithuania in 1390 and enjoyed good relations with the Grand Master, having left the Wash port of Boston with three ships that July. At the end of 1390 Bolingbroke rested and feasted back in Prussia before departing Danzig in March 1391, with two German chartered vessels, and returned to Boston via Hull. His decision to sail from Lynn in July 1392 might have been because the town was a centre of the cult of St Margaret of Antioch who was popular amongst crusaders and venerated by the Teutonic Knights. In September 1392 Henry decided to travel with around fifty friends and servants from Danzig to Prague and Vienna on the way to Venice where his party embarked for the Holy Land. The aborted military campaign in the Baltic lands had been transformed into a grand diplomatic tour and pilgrimage.

V

A third aspect to help explain the nature of the German Hanse is the establishment of four big trading posts across northern Europe by merchants from the member cities. They negotiated commercial privileges and business centres at Novgorod (Russia), Bergen (Norway), Bruges (Flanders) and London from foreign rulers impressed with German economic strength. These four great kontors or trading posts were more or less independent until 1358 when the first Hanseatic assembly in Lübeck asserted overall control because of their huge significance for the German towns. Each kontor (the title was not commonly used before 1500) was governed by an alderman and a council with its own seal and articles of association or statutes. They imposed discipline and insisted on celibacy and non-fraternisation with native populations, save for Bruges. There were forty-four smaller foreign trading posts or branches of these four principal kontors which played a supportive role in keeping the wheels of Hanseatic international commerce turning. The Bergen and Bruges kontors figured in the medieval trade and politics of the Wash ports of Lynn and Boston which hosted Hanseatic communities tied to the London kontor.

Novgorod was the ancient Viking capital of northern Russia and an important market for furs and wax in the 12th and 13th centuries attracting both Scandinavians and Germans. The latter agreed a commercial treaty with the local Prince in 1191 (with Gotland merchants) and Novgorod became their first foreign kontor in 1269 when the Russians granted permission. It operated as an autonomous merchant community. Appeals against the commercial and social judgements of the Novgorod alderman had, however, to be heard in Lübeck. No fewer than 160 merchants buying furs were at Novgorod in the winter of 1336-37 to emphasise the scale of the trade. The kontor was known as St Peter's Court or the St Petershof (after its brick church which was also used as a warehouse). Other warehouses and houses were made of wood; there was a hospital, prison, bath house and brewery too, to serve a German community of about 100. A wooden palisade surrounded the trading post whose gates were closed at night with guard dogs ready to greet any intruders! Only the riches that could be generated from the Russia trade overcame German dislike of this harsh and dangerous environment. Yet some German apprentices lived in Russian households to learn the language so good relations between foreigners and natives could exist.

Furs, pitch, wax, honey and timber were traded by the Russians for cloth, grain, beer and manufactured goods, although the Germans had sometimes to pay in silver (a remarkable wood carving at St Nicholas Church in Stralsund portrays such transactions). Furs packed in barrels for the journey to Lübeck or Bruges included sable, marten, ermine, lynx, otter and squirrel in what was a lucrative trade. The skins were brought by Russians to the St Petershof where the Germans inspected them before purchase; this was a privilege much resented in Novgorod. Relations between the Russians and Germans deteriorated in the course of the 15th century and violence erupted on occasions. The latter accused the former of attacking their baggage trains from Novgorod to the coast. Dorpat (Tartu), Reval (Tallinn) and Riga were the Hanseatic towns closest to Novgorod which acted as conduits for Russo-German commerce. In a 16th century Low German song, Tallinn was commonly known as 'the house of wax and flax', Visby on Gotland as 'the house of pitch and tar', and Riga as 'the house of hemp and butter'.[10]

In the 13th century increasing numbers of foreign merchants came to Bruges to purchase English wool and Flemish cloth transforming it into Europe's business capital. The Zwin was a bay springing from a storm tide in 1124 which linked the city to the North Sea. It was the port for several large Flemish towns (including Ghent and Lille) which produced the fine cloth in demand across Europe. Bruges also manufactured luxury cloth on its own account. Flanders became a magnet for traders from Italy, Spain, France, England and the Hanseatic towns. In 1277 the first Genoese ships moored in Bruges and Venetian galleys arrived in 1314 in convoy from the Mediterranean. The Germans had already secured trading privileges and houses there from the Flemish Countess Margaret II in

1252. Although mainly lodging in hostels or commercial inns across Bruges, they were mostly to be found in the vicinity of the Carmelite Friary, and they held meetings in its refectory. It was there in 1347 that the German merchants agreed the statutes to regulate their affairs to suggest a united German Hanse did not exist in Bruges before. They were divided into three groups or thirds; those from Lübeck, the Wendish and Saxon towns; those from Westphalia and Prussia; and finally those from Gotland, Livonia and Sweden. Each regional group elected two aldermen to their new governing body and the Bruges kontor was now effectively in place. The Flemish spoken in Bruges was intelligible to Low German merchants whilst French was the language adopted by Italians and Iberians.

During the 1330s and 1340s the population of Bruges was at least 50,000 and, although the plague years (1348-50) probably killed about 10 per cent of the inhabitants, it soon recovered. There was significant migration from Flanders. The teeming bands of merchants and mariners must have made Bruges the most international city in Europe. The numerous hostellers not only provided foreign traders with accommodation but often operated as their bankers and warehousemen. Prostitution was also big business in Bruges whose city council used fines or licences for brothels to benefit its treasury! In 1440 a festive procession in Bruges in honour of the Duke of Burgundy involved foreign merchants, including 136 richly attired Hanseatic men on horseback. By 1457 the city had allowed the Germans to control the district around the Carmelite Friary where one of their houses was "magnificently" extended in 1478 to serve as their headquarters.[11] This kontor or 'Osterlingenhuis' remains standing, although partly demolished. About 700 German traders and servants were living and working in Bruges in the 15th century, only the Italians being more numerous, but the latter did not act as a single group or hanse. To Flanders the north Germans brought forest products (timber, furs, wax, pitch), fish, corn and iron to exchange for the cloth made in the Flemish towns. Dyestuffs, spices, figs, rice, salt, wine and luxury goods from southern Europe were also available for export. The Bruges kontor managed German trade to Lisbon, Bordeaux, La Rochelle, Nantes and Bourgneuf. In the city itself the Germans merchants integrated with the local community and wills show the extent of their charitable activities.

Bergen in Norway was a thriving port town where wind dried cod or stockfish from the Lofoten Islands in the far north, along with fish oil, furs and timber, attracted German, English and Dutch traders. The Norwegians were more dependent by the late 13th century on the Hanseatic towns whose merchants imported cloth, salt, pepper, grain, beer and wine. Their cogges sailing from the Baltic in April and May could enjoy a favourable easterly wind to take them through the Sound (the narrow channel between Denmark and Sweden) and north around the southern coast of Norway to Bergen. The same ships could carry their return cargoes from Bergen to the Baltic in the summer as the prevailing wind changes to west or southwest. So the Bergenfahrer (Bergen travellers) had an ally in Mother Nature.

The King of Norway granted the Germans commercial privileges in 1278, 1285 and 1294, but they could not send ships north of Bergen for fish. A trade embargo was used by Lübeck and the Wendish towns in 1284 to secure Norwegian concessions after one of their ships had been attacked. The Bergenfahrer based in Lübeck were allowed to establish a kontor in Bergen in the 1360s, known as German wharf or 'Tyskebrugge'. Smaller Hanseatic trading posts in Norway were located at Tonsberg and Oslo. The Black Death in 1349 killed around 50 per cent of Norway's population and many survivors from rural districts migrated to the coastal towns. Home agriculture was badly affected and the nation made even more reliant on food imports by Hanseatic merchants. The 'Tyskebrugge' was safeguarded by another treaty between Norway's King and the Germans in 1378. In 1408 St Mary's Church was assigned to the Germans; its stone walls protected it from the fires which periodically consumed Bergen's wooden buildings. There were big fires in 1413 and 1476 when the kontor itself was burnt down. Bergen residents hosted the homeless Hanseatic traders who were able to keep their businesses going. German and English merchants temporarily forgot their economic rivalry and fought these conflagrations together.

The Hanseatic quarter in Bergen consisted of twenty-two wooden buildings divided into tenements running down long plots to the harbour where the fishing boats from the Norwegian North moored. The Germans were associated with local churches and undertook charitable works. They were not allowed to marry Norwegian women to avoid later disputes over the ownership of a merchant's assets, although love affairs were not uncommon, and illegitimate children are mentioned in wills. There were also brothels adjacent to 'Tyskebrygge'. The latter had a militia which wielded considerable local power demonstrating the weakness of the Danish-Norwegian authorities. Over 2,000 Hanseatic men lived in Bergen in the summer, including bakers, tailors and other artisans, out of a total town population of 8,000. Even in the winter there were at least 1,000 resident Germans. Young apprentices from Lübeck and Rostock had to endure brutal initiation ceremonies before being accepted as 'Hanse Brothers'. The prospects of fame and fortune in their home towns springing from mercantile success in Norway kept up recruitment. The Germans were again forced to leave Bergen in 1426, only to receive renewed commercial privileges in 1455. Their kontor did not close until 1764 when Norwegians took full charge of it. It might be noted that by 1680 the Bergen trade accounted for no more than two per cent of Lübeck's exports.

The German trading station in London was located on the north bank of the Thames near London bridge where a large building was occupied by Cologne merchants. This Teutonic Hall was established by 1175 when they secured a charter from Henry II (1154-89) gifting commercial privileges. Successive English kings confirmed these economic liberties for the Germans who were mainly Rhinelanders importing wine. Edward I (1272-1307) demonstrated how much English monarchs valued the presence of foreign merchants, not least as a source of taxation and loans, when he introduced the Carta Mercatoria in 1303. They were granted the same freedom to trade and travel with exemption from local tolls enjoyed by English merchants but were required to pay some additional custom duties on imports and exports. German merchants in England had helped to pave the way for the Carta Mercatoria. Just before its suspension in 1311 (it was restored in 1322) they secured from Edward II the confirmation of their royal charters before 1303, and particularly important was that granted in 1260 by Henry III, which endorsed the existing tax concessions for all German merchants in England based in London. Were Cologne men the sole beneficiaries or those from other German cities too? In 1266 Henry III granted Lübeck and Hamburg traders in England the same commercial advantages as the Cologne merchants as well as their own hanses. Thus it seems improbable that the Lübeckers and Hamburgers in 1266 were part of "a wider community" because otherwise "why was such independent action necessary".[12] The modern merchants of Hamburg's Chamber of Commerce organised until recently an annual dinner and celebration of the grant of their hanse in London in 1266 (2004-2016). It has been succeeded by the Hanseverein Hamburg with an annual lecture and Hansepreis (award ceremony).

The first written reference to a united German Hanse or merchants 'de hansa Alemanie' in England came in 1282 when they concluded an agreement with the City of London. Cologne and the north German towns were clearly in partnership. Only through such an alliance could they exert sufficient influence to sustain their privileged position in the English capital. In 1317 Edward I ratified all the previous charters granted to the Hanseatic towns and ordered that further taxation should not be imposed on German merchants in England without their consent. This charter cost them £100. It was a royal declaration that the Hanseatic community based in London had a special position in the kingdom. The legal basis of the commercial liberties enjoyed by the German Hanse in England in the 14th and 15th centuries "was completed in 1317".[13] These concessions were jealously guarded by the Germans who were more successful than other aliens in medieval England in retaining such trading rights. In 1427 they were obliged to pay an annual lump sum to the Lord Mayor to guarantee their "ancient rights" in the City of London.

The London kontor was an autonomous entity. It was governed by a twelve strong council which included the headman or alderman elected annually on New Year's Eve, with its membership representing the several Hanseatic regions. The alderman oversaw a court to hear cases between members and also cases between Germans and Englishmen when the former were defendants. An English alderman was a member by royal appointment from 1426 at the invitation of the Hanseatic community in London, though this apparently formalised an existing arrangement. He acted as a mediator between the Germans, the Crown and the City. Hanseatic merchants were amongst the richest of all the foreign traders in London and well known to government officials and courtiers. Their ability to supply armour and fine jewels from Europe ensured they had a warm welcome in such circles. From 1282 the Germans had the honour of maintaining one of the City's seven gates (Bishopsgate) which they rebuilt in 1479. The German church, All Hallows, was just outside their walled compound and shared with the other residents of Dowgate ward. Hanseatic merchants were buried in the churchyard and most left legacies to the Church. Across Europe they were usually buried where they died but would be commemorated in their home towns to sustain family identity and status.

The London kontor expanded from around 1250 as the Germans acquired the freehold of adjacent plots between Thames Street and the riverside. It was bounded by Dowgate on the west and All Hallows Lane on the east. The heart of the trading post was the original Teutonic Hall (remodelled later) which was a large stone building at right angles to the Thames. On the first floor was the meeting and dining room of the community and well-furnished merchant offices. The ground floor was used to store beeswax, furs, linen, wood, fish and other goods. The southern gable of Teutonic Hall overlooked the river where there was a quay with a crane and warehouses nearby. The kontor buildings appear to have run in three long blocks (divided into storage spaces probably for individual merchants) from Thames Street to the waterside.   This impressive Hanseatic headquarters in England's capital city was surrounded by a high wall and distinguished by a tall tower with a blue cupola.

Hanseatic merchants sat with their friends in the garden and did business "while the younger members of the kontor waited on the company".[14] The same author says that the rules of strict celibacy and non-fraternisation with the English were enforced. Yet the male colonists found their sexual pleasure in the bathhouses and taverns outside. The alderman did try to impose disciplined social behaviour on his compatriots, along with good and honest commercial practice. There was a ban on bringing women and "loose fellows" into the trading post, playing football in the yard and picking fruit in the garden. No doubt the young journeymen were the ones seen to be most likely to transgress. They served an apprenticeship of two years to learn English and local business methods but would only be elevated to merchant status by demonstrating their skills and, perhaps, good behaviour. On Thames Street was a tavern famous for Rhenish wine and offering ample opportunity for Anglo-German encounters.

As the number of east and north German merchants increased the London kontor became known as 'The House of the Easterlings' or 'Esterlinges Halle'. In 1384 a survey of its properties provides the first reference to 'le Steelyerde', or the Steelyard as the trading post came to be called. The Germans rented a plot on the river called 'stielwharf' and this may have been significant in the English renaming. More probable is that the designation 'Steelyard' derived from a mistranslation of the Low German 'Stalhof'. Hamburg

'Haus der Osterlinge' or House of the Easterlings at Bruges.
Reproduced from Lübeckische Geschichte (Lübeck 1997).

and Lübeck men referred to 'Der Londoner Stalhof' which had nothing to do with steel. 'Stal' referred to the lead seal attached to cloth whose quality had been checked for sale in the yard or 'hof'.

The London Steelyard was a secure compound with its gates closed at night, but on a few occasions it came under attack. Wat Tyler and his peasant army during the famous Peasants' Revolt of 1381 is one example. His rebels pursued "the hated foreigners" presumably into the kontor and murdered those who could not pronounce the words "bread and cheese" with the "pure English accent".[15]

In October 1493 it was besieged by a London crowd unhappy about German commercial privileges and their apparent refusal to accept the King's embargo on trade with the Low Countries. It was then invaded and warehouses plundered and set on fire, but the Easterlings drove out the attackers and shut the gates! The Lord Mayor arrived to prevent further trouble taking eighty of the rioters prisoner with their leader sent to the Tower.

The Hanseatic Steelyard in London.
Detail from an engraving by W. Hollar (1647).

English monarchs continued to regard the Hanseatic community in London as an economic benefit to the nation. At the coronation of Henry VI in 1429 the capital's foreign traders followed the Lord Mayor on horseback including Germans and Italians.

Wheat, rye, ropes, masts, pitch, tar, flax, hemp, linen, wax, fish and wine were imported by Hanseatic traders in London who mainly exported wool and cloth. The Steelyard's crane by the riverside loaded and unloaded numerous ships from Europe. Although Westphalian, Saxon, Wendish, Prussian and Livonian merchants were all represented in London, the largest group or hanse was from Cologne, reflecting its greater share of Anglo-Hanseatic trade. The Steelyard has been described as a small piece of Germany in England; it was certainly a symbol of the wealth and power

15th century coloured glass from Cologne now in Thorney Abbey near Peterborough (The Pieta).

Research suggests it was taken from the London Steelyard around 1600 and probably purchased on the open market by the Duke of Bedford.

of the Hanse in England. This community was not constant in membership but it was considerable: "There were meeting rooms and houses and a great hall for the 400 German merchants who lived here".[16] Others rented rooms in the City because the Steelyard could not accommodate all the German traders based in England's capital.

Queen Elizabeth I expelled the Germans from their Thameside trading post in 1598, only for James I to return it to them in 1606, although the Hanseatic towns no longer enjoyed commercial privileges. The Steelyard proved an attraction for Londoners into the 1660s. On 2 May 1665 civil servant and diarist Samuel Pepys had supper with his wife and friends at the Rhenish winehouse there. It was destroyed in the Great Fire of London in 1666 but the greater part was rebuilt by the Hanseatic towns. Not until 1853 did German ownership come to an end when the Steelyard was sold for £72,500 and demolished for the construction of Cannon Street Railway Station. The foundations of the original 12th century Teutonic Hall were uncovered by archaeologists in the 1980s. In more recent times the Thames embankment behind Cannon Street Station has been renamed 'Hanseatic Walk'. The parish church of All Hallows (adopted by the Germans) was consumed by the Great Fire of London in 1666, rebuilt soon after, but demolished in 1964.

VI

A fourth important factor in the formation and success of the German Hanse relates to sea transport. The ability to move beer and grain efficiently as demand rose in an expanding Europe cannot be separated from the history of ship building. The German towns bordering the North Sea and Baltic were in an ideal geographical position to dominate sea traffic between East and West, but they needed development of the cogge. Vessels of this description were sailing from Bremen in the late 12th century carrying crusaders to the Holy Land. In the course of the 13th and 14th centuries the cogge became northern Europe's principal merchant ship for transporting bulk cargoes (grain, beer, fish, wax, timber). It appears on the early seals of Hanseatic towns but marine archaeology from the 1940s in the Netherlands and later in Germany has allowed us to learn much more about the construction of medieval cogges.

The ship excavated in the Weser at Bremen after 1962 is today the central exhibit at the German National Shipping Museum in Bremerhaven. Dendrochronology proves that the vessel was constructed in 1379-80. It was clinker built with overlapping oak planks nailed together and the seams between them caulked with moss held in place by iron clamps. The cogge had a flat bottom to facilitate movement in shallow harbours. Its broad hull was reinforced by five strong deck beams passing through the side planking. Decks had probably been installed in the 13th century to protect various cargoes of up to eighty-four lasts. Cargoes were measured in lasts and one last was equivalent to two tons. Even a small cogge of fifty lasts was able to carry the same load as a convoy of fifty wagons pulled by 200 horses.

The *Ubena* of Bremen and the *Kieler Hansekogge* constructed in the 1990s are both replicas based on the medieval vessel discovered in the Weser at Bremen in 1962. The cogge was a tubby shaped and sturdy ship usually of oak or elm. High in the water, it offered further shelter for cargoes, although slow (five knots in a good wind) and cumbersome to navigate. Fittings for occasional oar propulsion were retained for a long time. The larger cogge towed an auxiliary craft or tender which served as a lifeboat as well as being used to help manoeuvre it in harbours.

The cogge acquired castles at both bow and stern which provided good platforms for archers to repel pirates (crossbows were firmly attached to the vessel and on the crow's nest). The adoption of a sternpost rudder around 1250 made it easier to handle by the steersman on the quarterdeck. The single big square sail could be increased by bonnets or cloth strips sewn to its bottom. It was usually tanned red to resist mildew and could be raised by a winch which was also used to haul the anchor. The spruce or larch mast may have doubled as the centre post of a derrick to load and unload bulky goods when harbour cranes were absent.

The *Kieler Hansekogge* is approximately 7.5 metres in width and 23.5 metres in length, with a depth of roughly two metres below the waterline. In the late 14th century this was the normal size of the larger vessels which needed a crew of about twenty men. A bigger 14th century cogge was discovered off Wismar on the Baltic coast and a replica constructed in 2004 called the *Wissemara*. In the 15th century the cogge was transformed or replaced by the building in Hanseatic ports of hulks, and later caravels, which carried at least 300 tons of freight. Fudge has summarised:

> The Hanseatic kogs, hulks, and later caravels were the main carriers in this long distance trade. It is not easy to distinguish precisely one type from another, though prior to mid-century kogs were single-masted klinker-built vessels. Generally they were smaller than the later types, which featured

The Kieler Hansekogge in Lynn's river on 7 August 2004 after crossing the North Sea for the first time.
A replica built at Kiel of a ship constructed in 1380 at Bremen where it was excavated in the 1960s.

> forecastles and aftercastles, as well as sternpost rudders. Three masts eventually became more common, and a typical hulk of the later fifteenth century may have had a keel length of about seventeen metres and a beam of almost six.However, much larger caravel-built vessels were being constructed in Danzig by the 1480s. Up to a dozen or more partners shared ownership of the large Hanseatic ships, which, when they did leave port for England, the Lowlands, or the Bay, were crewed by Hansards.[17]

The term 'carvel' was applied in the 15th century to skeleton-built ships which appear to have had Portuguese origins but were being constructed in northern Europe by the 1430s. Clinker built cogges or hulks could suffer from weakness or lack of rigidity the larger the ship. With the carvel method very large ships with three masts could be built because the internal heavy ribs gave them greater strength. Their ability to carry more cargo also reduced shipping costs. The *Lisa von Lübeck*, a representation of a late medieval ship, or caravel, sailed across the North Sea to visit Lynn in 2009.

The word 'skipper' had its origins in the Low German 'schip here' or the proprietor of the ship in which he sailed. Ship ownership in Hanseatic and

The Lisa von Lübeck a representation of a 15th century vessel of the kind which visited the Wash ports arrives in the Great Ouse at Lynn in August 2009.

English towns became divided into shares to spread the risks. Although three or four German merchants were probably the principal shareholders for any one cogge, the ship's captain and the craftsmen who built it were also likely to be in the consortium. By the 15th century it was common for the ownership of a Hanseatic ship to be divided into thirty-two or even sixty-four shares for the largest vessels. A merchant might have shares in several cogges. The Knights of the Teutonic Order owned four ships outright and had shares in many others. When calculating the size of the Hanseatic fleet around 1500, Dollinger refers to a source which estimated 1,000 ocean going vessels equivalent to 60,000 tons, which would have made 'the Hansa' Europe's leading naval power "outranking Holland and England and also perhaps France and Spain".[18]

The visit of the *Kieler Hansekogge* to Lynn in August 2004 generated much public interest and a dozen local residents were fortunate enough to join the crew to sail from the Great Ouse into the Wash, then up the Witham to Boston. It was clear that the ship could accommodate far more people than a crew of twenty. Pilgrims, family members, artisans and apprentices were often passengers on the medieval cogges. Both English and German merchants could be found on vessels they partly owned, or had chartered, but less frequently by 1400. The captain and helmsman were the key characters on board, with their own sleeping quarters and, in the case of the Bremen cogge of 1380, a toilet. A boatswain and shipwright were also important crew members and a cook was mentioned on a Lübeck vessel in 1224. For baking bread and cooking meat and other food the medieval cogges had brick ovens. On short sea voyages drinking water was storied in large jugs but in barrels in the bigger ships on longer journeys.

A priest usually went with the ship equipped with a portable altar to say mass and reassure the crew and passengers exposed to the elements. He was also a scribe to keep records. Sea journeys were long and monotonous so chess and dice were amongst the games played to pass the time. Sailors and some passengers were also armed to defend the ship against pirates. Vessels were frequently named after the Christian Saints, such as 'St Nicholas', to protect their crews from the perils of the sea. On voyages the coast was hugged and high church spires were essential seamarks or navigational aids. A map of 1539 shows towers topped by fires along the German Baltic coast to assist ships in the autumn and winter months. There is no reference to a compass on board a Hanseatic cogge until 1433 and sea maps only came into use during the 15th century. To arrive safely in port after a long and perhaps perilous voyage from Lynn to Danzig (with a valuable cargo) was a cause for celebration and parties were held on the ship. Minstrels might come on board and the crew was joined by family and friends as much beer was drunk. Brotherhoods of sailors in the Hanseatic towns gave solidarity and pride to the poorer communities from which they came. Urban and rural labourers as well as the coastal fishermen of northern Germany enrolled as mariners and probably 600 lived in Lübeck alone.

VII

A fifth aspect of the German Hanse to highlight naturally follows from discussion of the cogge. As its merchants developed overseas markets and negotiated commercial privileges in several European countries, with the four great kontors and smaller trading posts abroad connected to home ports by the cogge, it was inevitable that the German towns would become embroiled in international politics. It was a political problem overseas which resulted in the decision to call an assembly at Lübeck in 1356. German privileges had been infringed in Flanders and the Hanseatic cities imposed a trade embargo on Bruges in the 1350s until these rights were fully restored in 1360. This demonstrated that their community could attain a degree of common action sufficient to impose its own terms in international affairs. For Braudel the German Hanse had been created in 1356 with the first assembly, which emphasised Lübeck's pre-eminence too:

> Beginning in 1227 (with the victory over the Danes at Bornhöved), the city's success was sealed with the granting to the Hanseatic merchants of privileges in Flanders in 1252-3, a whole century before the first general

Diet of the Hansa which brought together its representatives in Lübeck in 1356, only then creating the Hanseatic League. But well before this date, Lübeck had been the standard-bearer of the Hanseatic League recognised by all as the capital of the merchant confederation. The city's arms — the imperial eagle — became in the fifteenth century the arms of the League itself.[19]

In February 1356 there had indeed been an assembly of the towns in Lübeck to discuss the position of German merchants in Flanders. Though this can be argued to be their first one, it is not known who was present. It was followed by another meeting of the representatives of the Hanseatic towns in Bruges in June 1356 to confirm the statutes or constitution agreed by the German community there in 1347.

It has already been seen how these German towns were cooperating before the 1350s to advance their common interests but a formal community with periodic assemblies only begins then. Henn maintains that a united German Hanse only came into existence in the 1350s and 1360s when the towns whose merchants occupied the four great kontors asserted their authority through their first assembly. Bruges (1356), Novgorod (1361), Bergen (1365) and London (1375) were all obliged to surrender their autonomy. Towns in the Hanseatic regions realised the need for joint action to ensure German commercial interests in Europe were protected. From the mid 14th century "the Hanseatic community understood itself as the German Hanse and was regarded as such from the outside and strictly speaking Hanseatic history only begins from now on".[20] The governing bodies of the four great kontors now looked to the Hanseatic assembly for guidance or as a court of appeal. Documents refer to these foreign trading posts as "the merchants' staples upon which the German Hanse primarily was founded and built".[21] The meeting in June 1358 at Lübeck is recognised as the first assembly because it included all the towns involved in the four big overseas kontors. Although assemblies were occasionally held in Cologne, Hamburg, Lüneburg, Stralsund and Danzig, the usual venue was Lübeck. Of the seventy-two such meetings held between 1356 and 1480, no fewer than fifty-four were in the city on the Trave. Lübeck took the lead by paying messengers to deliver invitations to attend, providing the delegates with the written resolutions to take home, and covering all the other expenses falling on the host. When serious internal political divisions prevented the city from acting as the capital of the German Hanse (1408 to 1416), its members turned to Hamburg to take charge on a temporary basis.

To host a Hanseatic assembly enhanced a town's prestige and standing as well as offering an opportunity for its merchant families to display their wealth.

Delegates from the more important towns arriving in Lübeck were welcomed by trumpeters and drummers, together with jugs of wine (those from Riga in 1511 for example after a journey taking several weeks). Assembly proceedings were recorded in Low German from 1369 which was the official written language of the community. There are Hanserecesse or minutes for forty-three such general meetings. However, attendance was often low, with towns reluctant to participate because of the costs and hazards of travel. In 1383 the Prussian towns were admonished by Lübeck for failing to appear at the assembly of that year. Nor did the Westphalian towns make regular appearances (Soest, Dortmund and Osnabrück did not all send delegates until 1418). Probably the highest attendance at an assembly was at Lübeck in 1477 when thirty-eight towns were represented. Regional princes and non-Hanseatic towns could attend but not participate in decision making.

Usually a town sent two delegates to an assembly from its governing body or council, including the mayor (who was normally a merchant). Companions would travel with them. In 1518 for example forty-one delegates arrived in Lübeck from twenty-two cities; Danzig and Cologne both sent two councillors accompanied by a civil servant. Smaller towns sometimes squabbled over the seating arrangements which indicated the status of individual members. The mayor of the host town chaired the Hanseatic assemblies and gave speakers the floor. The agenda comprised international matters, the condition of the roads, taxes on trade and internal disputes between community members. How to combat Baltic piracy was also a major issue in the 1370s and 1380s. An edict had to be unanimous and further ratified by local councils in due course, but it could be ignored by a member town unless it corresponded with its interests. Sometimes the delegates of one or more towns gave provisional approval to a particular proposal but insisted on consulting their home towns before a final decision was taken (this procedure was called 'ad referendum'). An assembly did possess the power to exclude any town from the community failing to comply with its economic or political strategy. The word 'Verhansung' was coined to describe this act.

Looper has persuasively argued that the Hanseatic assemblies were the hubs of an urban information system through which member cities acquired the knowledge to adopt their most beneficial economic policy at any one time. On its edicts he concludes: "For now it may be sufficient to say that the cities used these protocols as sources of information to establish their own course and conduct". These transactions were "not considered as decision lists that ought to be implemented".[22] The emphasis is on the German Hanse as an informal urban network dedicated to economic rather than political goals and serving the merchant. Regional meetings of the towns were held to agree a course of action in preparation for a Hanseatic assembly.

A dissertation by Proost on the Rhineland river town of Emmerich (today twinned with Lynn) allows further insight into the nature of the German Hanse. In the 1350s its privileges in Flanders were finalised as German control of international commercial activity in the West tightened. It appeared prudent for the smaller towns of the Low Countries and Lower Rhineland to seek membership and Emmerich was one of several to take that step. Its exact date of entry into the community is uncertain but it sent delegates to a regional assembly in Cologne in November 1367. It was also entitled to send councillors to a Hanseatic assembly in Lübeck. The trouble and expense of travelling long distances encouraged the smaller towns to permit the larger ones in their region to represent them. Emmerich was listed amongst the participants at a Lübeck assembly in May 1407, but a local document refers to an agreement which proves that Zutphen's councillors represented "Embrick", which had paid twenty-six French crowns to defray expenses for food and travel of these gentlemen to "Lübecke" where the towns of the "Henze" were gathered.[23] It was not until October 1601 that men from Emmerich were present at an assembly in Lübeck, although they were still obliged to consult Zutphen before reaching decisions. Those affecting river and overland trade in Germany were clearly of the greatest interest to the smaller Hanseatic towns which also acquired some protection from the oppressive influence of local landowners through membership of the community.

The smaller Hanseatic towns in Rhineland and Westphalia were tied in varying degrees to Cologne, that large industrial town and river port, which headed a third sector of the German Hanse (in addition to the Wendish and Prussian sectors). Nearby Dutch towns in the eastern Netherlands on the former Zuiderzee or river Ijssel were also members of the German Hanse before 1400. Kampen, Elburg and Harderwijk attended their first Hanseatic assembly in 1367. Stavoren, Deventer, Zwolle, Zutphen, Nimwegen, Arnheim and Groningen were members too. Around 1440 Kampen and Zwolle applied for 'readmission' to the community, or probably confirmation of their membership, though the reason is unclear. It appears to be linked to the emergence of the towns of Holland (to the west) as trading rivals of the German Hanse rather than simply business partners. Kampen and the towns in its region connected Rhineland river traffic and western Europe to the Baltic so needed to maintain good relations with both sides in what was as intermediary role.

Occasional assemblies in Hanseatic towns were not just long business meetings because banqueting and dancing permeated civic life at this level. Delegates were leading citizens who often had relatives in many other cities and family reunions were common. The Lübeck assembly of 1518 lasted five weeks. The host city employed bands or minstrels to entertain their wealthy and distinguished guests at the Town Hall. Lüneburg was incorporated into the German Hanse in 1371. It hosted a Hansetag in 1412 when twenty-three towns attended. The city council rebuilt its banqueting and dancing hall in the Town Hall around 1450 with the fireplaces making it possible to hold events in winter. Benches were placed along the walls for the spectators and five Gothic chandeliers provided for radiant illumination of these grand occasions. Salmen continues:

Many of the 'Hansetage' held in close succession between 1412 and 1619 in Lüneburg found their social high point in this banqueting hall. The many licensed minstrels, recorded in the Lüneburg council's offical archives, who came from other towns in the Hanseatic League, contributed musically to the festivities, as did the 'figellatori' and the 'pipere und trumpere des Rades to luneborgh' (pipers and trumpeters of the Lüneburg town council). The former are recorded from about 1335, the latter from about 1430. In 1443 there were five Ratsmusiker, from 1546 seven, of which three were 'Spellude' (wind players), three 'Gigerden' (string players), and one a lutanist. Due to several subsequent building alterations, it can no longer be determined where they were positioned in the dance hall of the 'Gewandhaus' or cloth hall.[24]

Cologne, Lübeck, Danzig and Reval were amongst the other Hanseatic towns where public dance halls were enlarged in the 15th century to enrich the social life of their merchant rulers and important guests. Salmen's work is an antidote to the stereotyped image of Hanseatic traders as dour and blunt men without interest in the arts and music.

VIII

The first Hanseatic assembly in Lübeck in 1358 may have established the German Hanse as an international power, but the struggle for mastery of the Baltic between Denmark and the German cities had not been concluded. King Valdemar Atterdag of Denmark occupied Scania in 1360. He sacked the Hanseatic city of Visby on Gotland in 1361 to threaten the shipping routes from Lübeck to Russia. Two thousand farmers and peasants were massacred. He was trying to break the constraints on Danish trade imposed by the Hanseatic towns, although his great ambition was to build a Baltic empire. The Germans targeted Danish ships and coastal towns but their naval counter attack failed through the strategic errors of its leader, Johann Wittenborg, mayor of Lübeck, whose siege of Helsingborg in 1362 ended in defeat. This Danish fortress overlooked the narrow channel called the Oresund Strait and known in English as the Sound. Its sister fortress two nautical miles away to the west directly across the Oresund (Shelly Sound) is Kronborg castle. So the Danish Kings kept a stranglehold on seaborne traffic entering and leaving the Baltic and imposed tolls on the numerous cargo ships.

In 1367 a meeting at Cologne comprising seventy-seven German and Dutch towns resolved to fight the Danish King to the death and funds were raised for a second assault on his country. A war chest was created through the Pfundzoll or special tax on all ships and merchandise leaving or entering Hanseatic harbours. Each city or port authority was responsible for collecting it. The allocation of the revenue was to be determined by a Hanseatic assembly where Lübeck and the Wendish towns were the most influential. This Cologne confederation was in effect a political

Kronborg castle in 1582.
It was remade by Dutch builders (1574-85) financed by the toll on ships passing through the Sound. From: Theatrum Urbium by Braun-Hogenberg.

league which included non-Hanseatic towns and was disbanded in 1385. The German Baltic towns and several Dutch ports had been partners because their commercial interests dictated access to the Baltic and Denmark's defeat.

Unexpectedly, perhaps, King Valdemar abandoned his kingdom to look for allies overseas. The seaborne forces of the Hanseatic and Dutch cities proceeded to conquer Scania and Copenhagen as well as pillaging Danish settlements around the Baltic. The King sued for peace in 1369 and signed the Treaty of Stralsund in 1370 which at least temporarily turned the Baltic into a German lake. It advanced Prussian economic interests represented by the Teutonic Knights through safeguarding the sea lanes between East and West. The West itself, particularly England, France and Flanders "had all to recognise that a new power had arisen in the North of Germany".[25] The emergence of the German Hanse as a European power can to some extent be traced to the Treaty of Stralsund as the major gains that could spring from common action fully dawned on the member cities, though they had several aristocratic and urban allies in the war against Denmark. Neither German nor Danish parties at Stralsund could or even wanted to create a lasting peace but rather diplomacy had been used to reduce or manage conflict and violence in the Baltic.

The Treaty of Stralsund protected German communities in Sweden where there were Hanseatic kontors at Stockholm, Kalmar and Malmo. Another short-lived trading post was established in 1378 in Copenhagen. Of great significance was the fact that the Cologne confederation secured the conveyance of the Danish fortresses on the Sound which commanded the passage of shipping between the Baltic and North Sea. However, the Hanseatic towns found these five castles difficult and expensive to manage; in 1385 they were returned to Queen Margaret of Denmark who had already invaded Scania. The Germans wanted to avoid a war and accepted her offer to restore their commercial privileges in Norway and Denmark. The Queen had rescinded them in 1380 on the death of King Haakon. Margaret was the daughter of Valdemar Atterdag (who had died in 1375) and inherited her father's imperial ambition to become another thorn in the flesh of the German Hanse.

At this time the control of the Baltic by the Hanseatic towns was challenged by a band of pirates known as the Vitalien Brothers led by Gödeke Michels and Klaus Störtebeker. They caused enormous economic damage by attacking the shipping of the Germans and other nationalities. The Danish islands provided convenient shelters for the pirates. To strike back against these sea robbers the Hanseatic cities equipped warships crewed by mercenaries and funded by a special tax on members. This had been agreed at an assembly at Lübeck in 1377, but the Prussians amongst others were reluctant to pay. Initially in the service of the Duke of Mecklenburg in his Scandinavian campaign against Queen Margaret of Denmark, the Vitalien Brothers were allowed to use Wismar and Rostock in his province as bases! Queen Margaret was blamed by the German Hanse for this upsurge in Baltic piracy because her Scandinavian expansion policy undermined international peace and demanded she pay compensation for its vessels lost at sea. From 1381 to 1385 piracy was so pervasive in the Baltic that even Wismar and Rostock decided to ignore their ducal overlord and join Lübeck to eradicate it. In 1384 Queen Margaret herself despatched nine Danish ships to reinforce the Hanseatic fleet assembled to fight the pirates. She had also sought the permission of Richard II (1377-99) to charter three Lynn warships to strengthen her own fleet. Piracy in the Baltic abated when Queen Margaret and the Hanseatic towns made peace over Scania in 1385, but her attempts to conquer Sweden after 1390 unleashed the sea robbers once again. The German Hanse despatched one fleet of forty ships with 3,500 armed men to fight them. Lübeck told Riga that their fleet was "300 sails strong" and they had "seized" English ships and stolen the cargoes.[26] When the Vitalien Brothers captured Visby on Gotland shock waves were sent through the Hanseatic world. In 1398 the Teutonic Knights and Prussian towns sent eighty-four ships and 4,000 men to retake Visby and 400 pirates sailed away from their nearby harbour. In 1408 Gotland was transferred by the Grand Master to Queen Margaret who had already conquered mainland Sweden.

The Vitalien Brothers were eventually driven into the North Sea by the

Teutonic Knights and 'the combined fleets' of Lübeck and the Prussian towns which ensured "that by 1400 the Baltic was entirely free of them".[27] Using Rostock and Wismar as bases these 'likendeelers' (those who divided their booty equally) had already plundered Bergen and attacked ships belonging to Norfolk ports fishing off Norway. The Vitalien Brothers now launched assaults on Hanseatic shipping in the North Sea from East Frisia where Emden was their headquarters. In the spring of 1400, the so-called peace ships from Lübeck and Hamburg assailed the pirate retreat there and killed at least eighty men. This was followed in 1401 by another counter attack by a small fleet under the Hamburg merchant and councillor, Nikolaus Schoke, who captured Störtebeker. Pirate chieftains including Störtebeker and many of their band were beheaded in Hamburg in October 1401. Recent research reported in a Lübeck newspaper has questioned whether Störtebeker existed [Lübecker Nachrichten 8 September 2019]. Instead, there was a Johann Störtebeker from Danzig who was a merchant and ship's captain active in the Baltic after 1401. Pirates continued to pose a threat to Hamburg's shipping until a fleet commanded by the city's mayor and merchant, Simon of Utrecht, conquered Emden and the pirate stronghold of Sibetsburg in 1433.

IX

A sixth and final aspect of the German Hanse which must be examined is the exclusive small groups of merchant families who governed the towns. In Lübeck the Society of the Circle or 'Zirkelgesellschaft' was its first lay religious fraternity founded in 1379 (with close ties to the Franciscan Church of St Catherine which still stands). Herein business information and transactions took place. No fewer than 6,400 wills of the city's merchant rulers before 1500 survive and reveal its tight upper crust social networks. Intermarriage consolidated this oligarchy and by 1380 most of the members of the city council were related. The Veckinchusens were such urban lords. The family moved from Westphalia in west Germany to the eastern frontier region of Livonia, but its members spread throughout Hanseatic Europe, to Reval (Tallinn), Dorpat (Tartu), Riga, Lübeck, Cologne and Bruges. The brothers Hildebrand and Sivert Veckinchusen lived in Lübeck and Cologne as well as Bruges in the 14th and early 15th centuries running their own businesses (sometimes with partners). Pan European trade in furs through their urban network was extremely profitable before success turned to failure for Hildebrand by over speculation in several commodities. He had thrice been alderman of the Bruges kontor but found himself in a local prison for debtors by 1422 and returned to Lübeck, a ruined man, in 1426. Success and failure in high-risk business ventures undertaken by both Sivert and Hildebrand ensured an often difficult life for their wives and families. Sivert had fled from

Lübeck to Cologne in 1409 to avoid civil strife but times were hard; he could not even afford to buy his wife a new wardrobe and "spoke enviously" of a friend whose wife was kept "in the latest fashion".[28] Anger Mändes, Von Soests, Von Suchens and the Giszes were other well-known families whose kinsmen might be found in a number of Hanseatic towns. However, such great families were unlikely to endure beyond three or four generations, and new blood was needed to reinforce the Hanseatic urban patriciates.

Georg Gisze was based for some years in London where his portrait (oil on wood) was painted in 1532 by Hans Holbein (1497-1543). The artist had recently returned to London from Basel. He set up a workshop close to the London Steelyard whose German occupants were immediately attracted by a man from their homeland who could satisfy the novel craze for portraits. For Holbein the wealthy Hanseatic merchants were an ideal clientele. He painted at least seven of them but Gisze's portrait was the first and most detailed. It shows an elegantly dressed Georg in his upstairs office at the Steelyard and offers a unique glimpse into the interior of a German kontor. The wall of his office is panelled and behind him are shelves with books and boxes as well as letter racks. There are keys on hooks. The rich young man holds a letter from his brother in Danzig which he opens with a silver coin. On the table in front of him is a fine vase with three pink carnations which flowers symbolically associated with lovers and three years later he was to marry Christine Kruger. The room was destroyed by the Great Fire of London in 1666.

Gisze (1497-1562), the youngest of seven sons, came to England in 1522 to represent the family firm whose headquarters were in Danzig. His father was a member of Danzig town council, although the family had its origins in Cologne. Georg was involved in the stockfish trade importing cargoes in Hamburg ships to sell in London and exporting cloth back to Hamburg. Gisze and his colleagues commissioned Holbein to design one of the nine pageants through the city for the coronation of Ann Boleyn in 1533. He also executed two large moralising paintings on fine linen cloth for their Teutonic Guildhall as well as the 'Steelyard Portraits'. Portraits of these German merchants abroad were usually completely frontal or full faced emphasising a sense of duty, or even piety, perhaps because they were designed "to be sent home as a complete record of their appearance" in London or Bruges.[29] Holbein's genius in his portrait painting was to convey an amazingly true likeness of his subject.

A network of family firms with bases in the major member cities was at the heart of the German Hanse as a continental wide organisation and fostered its unity. Sons, uncles, nephews and cousins from exclusive merchant families, from Danzig, Lübeck, Cologne and Hamburg, were trusted servants in Bruges, Bergen, Novgorod or London. This was particularly important when credit was being

The portrait by Hans Holbein of the Hanseatic merchant Georg Gisze in the London Steelyard (1532).

To the left of the quill on the table is his stamp or merchant mark with a bone handle and a metal seal matrix.

arranged over long distances. Strict qualifications for citizenship kept them a class apart in their home towns. In Danzig's law book called the *Willkür* nobody could become a citizen unless he produced evidence showing that he was "free born within wedlock". In the absence of documentation two reputable citizens had to declare on oath that the new citizen was a free man "of German type and tongue". He was also expected to possess weapons to defend his town and own a certain amount of property as well as being married. All persons coming from other Hanseatic towns could become Danzig citizens "without further ado".[30] Foreigners in Danzig had formidable obstacles to overcome to enjoy the same status. Southern Germans, Italians, Englanders, Dutchmen, Flemings and Jews appear to have been excluded from citizenship. Only the citizens of

Danzig and other Hanseatic cities could benefit from the privileges granted to German merchants abroad. The social and cultural cohesion of these Teutonic urban rulers was sealed by their common language. This was Low German which was "the language of a power elite and a wealthy elite, implying membership of a defined social and professional group".[31] It was the official language of the German Hanse but its merchants were not averse to learning foreign languages like Russian and French when useful. Their diverse geographical origins were reflected in several Low German dialects which were nevertheless more or less understood by many in Flanders, The Netherlands and England. Plattdeutsch or Low German is still spoken in Schleswig Holstein where Kiel and Lübeck are the largest towns and recognised as an official language.

The merchant oligarchies in Hanseatic towns were minorities remote from their numerous neighbours who laboured in the markets and by the waterside. The social topography was similar to that of Lynn or Bruges, with the merchant class clustered around the market places and city centres, but the middling and lower classes further out. In Lübeck and other Hanseatic towns artisans rented accommodation from the merchants in the side streets where wheelwrights, coopers, potters, tanners and weavers worked. Urban revolts against "unaccountable patricians" by tradesmen and artisans were common at the turn of the 14th century.[32] Opposition to random taxation and excessive expenditure often sparked trouble. Two revolts of the butchers at Lübeck in 1380 and 1384 were generated by overstrict market supervision, and compulsion by the Town Hall, but both failed. The fact that the 1384 uprising was led by an ambitious merchant called Paternostermaker reminds us that such dramatic events cannot simply be seen as class warfare. Lübeck was again the storm centre from 1408 to 1416 when social unrest and conflict "shook the Hansa to its foundations" but "ended in almost total victory for the patricians".[33] Popular opposition to the local oligarchs in a number of German cities was eventually defeated and victory loudly proclaimed by delegates at the 1418 Hanseatic assembly. Lübeck and other towns sometimes prohibited public access to important streets when they hosted these periodic general meetings.

In the new medieval towns of northern and eastern Germany the authority of their merchant rulers was given formidable architectural expression in the construction of large brick churches, town halls and gabled houses. In German the town hall is the 'Rathaus' (literally: 'Advice' or 'Counsel House'). Here were located the council chamber, court room, market hall, banqueting and dancing saloons, along with the municipal archive for important documents. There might also be a prison, street tavern, wine cellars and a balcony overlooking the market place for civic minstrels to soothe buyers and sellers (the music in today's supermarkets is not an original idea). The town halls were the powerhouses of

The Lübeck Rathaus as it appeared in the 1930s just before the Second World War.

the Hanseatic cities surpassing in size and splendour all other urban structures save for the churches. Representations of Lübeck and other German towns in engravings or hand-coloured woodcut prospects in the 1490s defined their status and civic might. Secular and ecclesiastical Gothic style brick buildings of the 14th and 15th centuries remain prominent in the Hanseatic cities of northern Germany. Gabled brick houses constitute the distinctive urban fabric associated with Bremen, Hamburg, Lübeck, Rostock, Wismar and Stralsund, but much of it has been reconstructed in the wake of the Second World War. This is not to forget that in the medieval centuries the labouring populations of the Hanseatic towns lived in humble dwellings and cellars which have long disappeared. In the Baltic coast town of Wismar in 1475 there were almost 600 houses but nearly 1,500 huts and basements. The wealthy merchants did undertake charitable works, including hospitals to accommodate the very poor, the old and the sick (at Lübeck in 1286 the well-known Heilige Geist Hospital was built). The local monasteries helped to look after the old and sick. Hostels in the towns catered for the pilgrims visiting the Baltic shrines.

Lübeck's Rathaus was erected sometime before the 1230s when it was rebuilt. It was enlarged by the addition of a banqueting and dancing hall (1298-1308) and further extended in the 1340s and 1440s. Part of this Town Hall was destroyed in the Second World War. Salmen tells us more:

Lübeck afforded itself a town hall, enlarged in a number of stages from the early 14th century onwards, which also featured a 'Hansasaal'. Besides rooms for the market, for town council meetings and public assemblies, there was on the first floor, even before 1400, a hall of about thirty metres in length, without any sight-obstructing pillars, which had been added on to the south side of the 'Burgersaal'. This was called the 'Danzelhus'. Here too, as in Cologne, the room capacity was apparently not great enough, for between 1442 and 1444, this dance house was extended by a building that contained open halls for commerce downstairs and a further large banqueting hall upstairs. In this imposing town hall, integrating three hall buildings in a uniquely concentrated construction programme, the most important aspects of a city government were accommodated: administration, commerce (drapers' hall), and organised festivity (dance hall).[3]

Lübeck's Rathaus became the centre of a great deal of merriment as well as business when the mayor hosted a Hanseatic assembly. The 'Hansesaal' or Hanse Hall where the towns met no longer exists. Delegates celebrated mass at the beginning and end of the grand event at the Marienkirche which was badly damaged by bombing in 1942 and later restored. This magnificent Gothic brick church influenced the design of about seventy churches in German towns to the east of the Trave. It accommodated the mayor's chapel where the council met and above which was Lübeck's archive and treasury. Council resolutions were announced to the parishioners in its nave. The adjacent Rathaus was the principal symbol of Hanseatic hegemony but the Marienkirke expressed civic pride and faith topped by very tall spires on its twin towers. The 15th century city gate or Holstentor is another strong symbol of medieval Lübeck's prosperity and civic dignity. Today Lübeck is a World Heritage City and sometimes referred to as 'The Queen of the Hanseatic League'. Its mayor or 'Bürgermeister' is President of the New Hanse formed in 1980 with almost 200 member towns across northern Europe today.

X

This chapter has hopefully helped to answer the testing question 'What was the German Hanse?' It was without doubt a success story. No other urban consortium in medieval and early modern Europe could match it for its longevity and geographical scope. This final section will discuss how and why it began to unravel. The German Hanse remained a loose urban organisation despite the periodic assemblies introduced in the 1350s to attain the highest possible level of cooperation in domestic and foreign affairs. In 1407 Lübeck complained to Stettin about the lack of solidarity amongst the Hanseatic cities which lost them respect in foreign countries and jeopardised their hard-won commercial privileges. This reflected the reality that Hanseatic towns completed with one another as well as non-Hanseatic towns for commercial traffic much to Lübeck's chagrin. In 1474 Breslau decided to leave the German Hanse because the benefits of membership were finally outweighed by its trade with the southern German towns and desire for greater freedom.

There was no executive body to impose a common policy on the member towns whose differences became more marked in the 15th century. Smaller towns were moreover constantly in danger of losing their autonomy to regional princes. At Lübeck in 1518 it was agreed not to invite twenty-two towns to future assemblies, either because of such princely influence or civic unrest, though they could remain within the Hanseatic network. Dollinger tells us that thirty-one towns were excluded from the German Hanse at this assembly because they had virtually opted out of the community through failure to participate or were "no longer able to keep the deliberations of the diet secret from their territorial rulers"[35] Amongst those towns to forfeit membership were Stettin, Berlin and Cracow. At the 1518 assembly thirty-five towns were represented from all the Hanseatic regions as well the Teutonic Order and the Dukes of Schleswig and Mecklenburg.

Without its independence it was pointless for an urban community to be a member of the German Hanse. The territorial princes in Germany tried to exert greater control over the towns for which nothing was more important than their autonomy. In 1431 at Lübeck thirty-one towns assembled to agree mutual support against such external threats.

At Lübeck in 1450 there was an attempt to form an urban union or tohopesete when the towns pledged military action if they were attacked. But there was no grand scheme to transform the German Hanse into a confederation and its internal cohesion weakened over the next century. In 1556 the German towns elected Dr Heinrich Sudermann of Cologne as Syndic or Law Officer to uphold their interests at home and abroad. This involved them making contributions to pay for his services including diplomatic missions as well as for the upkeep of the kontors around Europe. A written agreement by sixty-three towns to forge a stronger community or confederation (Hansische Konföderation) followed in 1567, but it failed to overcome internal divisions. To retain influence and commercial privileges overseas proved increasingly challenging for the Hanseatic towns. They enjoyed some degree of cooperation to resist the threat posed by the German territorial princes. In 1615 Solms-Rödelheim successfully commanded their mercenary soldiers against Duke Friedrich Ulrich during the battle for the city of Braunschweig.

The three main urban power blocs or sectors of the German Hanse found their differences overriding their common interests before 1500. Lübeck with the western Baltic and Saxon towns, the Prussian and eastern Baltic towns headed by Danzig, and Cologne and the Westphalian towns were finding it hard to reach a consensus on major issues. The English kingdom played a part in dividing them. As Lübeck detached itself from commercial dealings with England in the later decades of the 15th century, the result of Anglo-Hanseatic trade disputes and conflict examined in chapter four, its relationship with Cologne became strained. It was broken with the commencement of the Sea War between England and the German Hanse in 1469. Cologne's appeasement policy towards London was unacceptable to Lübeck and the Rhineland city was excluded from the community in 1471. Commercial intercourse between the Rhineland and England had been important since the 12th century; the lucrative trade in wool, cloth, wine and manufactured goods was too much to sacrifice when the Baltic was of peripheral concern to Cologne. Unlike Lübeck and Danzig, which were mainly port towns dependent on maritime economies, Cologne was an industrial city requiring export markets, albeit its popular name was the 'wine cellar' of the Hanse.

Western Europe was critical to the economic growth of Prussia whose grain and forest products were exchanged there especially for cloth and salt. Though Prussians were unhappy when English and other aliens set up businesses in Danzig and other towns from the 1380s, they resisted Lübeck's attempt to control trade with the West, and its anti-English policy. Prussia under the Grand Master of the Teutonic Order had anyway a poor record when it came to Hanseatic solidarity and respecting collective decisions. Riga and other east Baltic towns linked to Danzig were also trying to break from the trade protection favoured at Lübeck. Danzig had, moreover, replaced Lübeck as the main Hanseatic trading partner of England's east coast ports by 1400. In response to the commercial competition from unfolding overland routes in Europe "the Danzigers energetically expanded their seaborne traffic to western markets". In the final quarter of the 15th century they also secured "a foothold in the Icelandic fisheries" and "extended their long-distance carriage trade to Iberia"[36] In the 1460s Danzig and West Prussia became part of the Polish Kingdom further detaching them from Lübeck. The centrality of Lübeck and the west Baltic towns in northern Europe commerce was likewise challenged by the extension of overland trade routes. The Anglo-Hanseatic Sea War (1469-73) firmly shut western Europeans out of the Baltic and encouraged the growing redirection of West-East traffic through the Low Countries, via the Frankfurt and Antwerp fairs into the heartland of Europe. South German cities benefited too from their position between north-west Europe and Italy by offering alternative land access to and from central and eastern Europe. Around 1500 the Fugger banking and mining family of Augsburg was powerful enough to compete with Lübeck for trade in northern Europe and "even posed a serious threat to Hanse firms in the Baltic itself". [37] The firm even had a bank in the North German city!

A sure sign of the reorientation of European commercial networks was the closure of the Hanseatic kontor in Bruges and its transfer to Antwerp in the 1520s. Some German merchants had already made the move. Access to the western Flemish port from the sea was hampered by the silting of the Zwin inlet. As the European centre of finance and business Bruges had been the cornerstone of the trading empire of the German Hanse. In Lübeck itself there were Italian bankers in the 15th century, but the city was not able to develop into a European banking hub to rival Bruges or Venice.

Braudel highlights the "elementary kind"of capitalism practised by Hanseatic towns as a likely explanation for their relative decline because its merchants made "little call on credit", with silver coin for a long time "the only currency allowed."[38] They forbade the use of credit in trade with Novgorod in 1295 and this was extended to Flanders in 1401. Lindberg says that Dollinger believed these anti-credit policies were designed by the Hanseatic towns to achieve a monopoly in the East-West trade: "As a result, a large part of the trade in the Hansa area was carried out in the form of expensive and inefficient barter trade"[39] German traders abroad were not in fact against using credit. The bans on credit transactions in Russia and Flanders sprang from quarrels with their hosts over commercial activity to protect Hanseatic interests. What can be said is the Hanseatic merchants formed small business partnerships with one another which were safe and secure but not capable of raising capital for big projects.

At Antwerp the Hanseatic towns erected an impressive Renaissance style merchant headquarters in the 1560s. From the Brabant city German merchants from Cologne in particular were better placed to distribute English cloth in central Europe. Its golden age was, however, brought to an abrupt end. In November 1576 Spanish troops ran amok in Antwerp destroying property and plundering merchant houses. Thousands died in a city which had become enmeshed in the religious conflict unleashed by the Reformation. The English Merchant Adventurers based in London who exported unfinished and undyed cloth to the continent had already departed Antwerp. Political instability in the Low Countries forced them to seek a safer urban location for their wares and shock waves were sent through the Hanseatic world when they moved to Hamburg in 1567. Via the Elbe the port town was the gateway to much of Germany and central Europe. To allow the English to trade in a chief Hanseatic city by invitation from its rulers on preferential terms was met by disbelief in Lübeck. For Hamburg's councillors its commercial regeneration was the priority but the disintegration of the German Hanse was inevitably accelerated. Lübeck's policy of severely restricting the freedom of foreign merchants in the Hanseatic territories militated against the economic interests of the member towns. English merchants had to leave Hamburg for Emden and then moved to Stade near Hamburg in 1587 before returning to Hamburg in 1611.

Hanseatic command of the economy of northern Europe had been facilitated by the absence of strong nation states to challenge the community, though Queen Margaret's attempt to unite the Scandinavian countries had posed a major threat. They remained formidable opponents. Christian IV of Denmark and Norway (1588-1648) was a determined adversary of the German towns "harming Hanseatic trade and politics with all his might".[40] Sweden became an even more powerful enemy. Its overlordship of northern Europe in the 17th century was a consequence of that complex religious and political conflict known as The Thirty Years' War (1618-48) which devastated a large part of the continent. The Swedes occupied the Hanseatic cities of Wismar, Rostock and Stralsund. The events of the Thirty Years' War "finally proved that the Hanse had no place in the modern world".[41] Its towns did not suffer much damage but the community was badly fragmented and communication between them extremely difficult. At the 1629 Hanseatic assembly the delegates agreed that the remaining member towns should be represented by Hamburg, Bremen and Lübeck. The latter failed in their attempts to organise a Hanseatic assembly in 1651, 1662 and 1668 but succeeded in 1669. However, only six towns responded to the invitation to Lübeck: Danzig, Rostock, Brunswick, Hildesheim, Osnabrück and Cologne. Stralsund and Wismar questioned the usefulness and purpose of another assembly! The rebuilding of the London Steelyard after the Great Fire (1666) was an important agenda item but only Hamburg was prepared to pay a significant amount into the fund required. Lübeck found no support for its proposal to reconstruct the Antwerp kontor with the towns pleading poverty.

The Hanseatic assembly in 1669 did not generate any firm action plan to secure the renewal of the community and the poor attendance reflected the loss of the spirit of urban cooperation of the past. It proved to be the final meeting of the German Hanse. Lübeck, Hamburg and Bremen continued their association as Free and Hanseatic cities, or the remnant of the German Hanse, into the 18th and 19th centuries before integration into the German Empire in 1871. Lübeck was deprived of its historic independence and free status in 1937 by Hitler's regime.

The strength of the German Hanse was fatally sapped by the decline of the four great kontors which had been the economic engines of its wealth and power. The significance of the closure of the Hanse House at Bruges has already been emphasised. In the 15th century the English exploitation of Icelandic and north Atlantic fisheries, closely followed by Hamburg and Bremen, undermined the Bergen kontor. In 1559 the German artisans there were "obliged" to accept Norwegian citizenship "if they wished to remain in the town".[42] The St Petershof in the Free City of Novgorod was closed by the Russians in 1494, after its annexation by Ivan III in 1478, and Ivan IV sacked the town. The German kontor was reopened in 1514 but it was never to regain its former importance. The Bruges and London trading posts were more central to Hanseatic interests than Bergen or Novgorod as both cities were hubs of Europe's economy. In London the City denied German traders access to Blackwell Hall where foreigners were supposed to buy cloth. The closure of the London Steelyard by Elizabeth I in 1598 reflected the rise of English nationalism fostered by the sea power which had defeated the Spanish Armada in 1588. The Germans returned to London but without the tax advantages and share of English cloth exports they had previously enjoyed. The widening of England's trading horizons from the late 16th century drove the expansion of its merchant fleet for voyages to Asia and America as London and Amsterdam became centres of a new world economy. The North Sea was no longer the 'Atlantic of the Middle Ages' nor the Baltic lands Europe's only expanding frontier. But England's economy still greatly depended on cloth exports to Europe in the early 17th century and continental politics preoccupied Tudor and Stuart statesmen. Danzig and Lübeck prospered in the 16th century, largely due to the grain trade from the Baltic as Europe's urban populations grew apace. At the same time the Dutch rather than Hanseatic merchants were capturing more of the Baltic corn and timber trade with Amsterdam soon to be known as "the Cornbin of Europe".[43] Danzig needed the freight space of the Dutch fleet to conduct at least half of its seaborne commerce by the 1580s.

Notes

1. Henn, V., 'The German Hanse and its Kontors'. A paper delivered at the Hanseatic History and Archaeology Symposium in King's Lynn (2009),1.
2. Dollinger, P., *The German Hansa* (MacMillan 1970), 412.
3. Friedland, K. & Richards, P. eds., *Essays in Hanseatic History* (Dereham 2005), 96.
4. Friedland, K., *Lectures 1970-2009* (Kiel 2010), 87.
5. Lloyd, T.H., *England and the German Hanse 1157-1611* (Cambridge 1991), 6.
6. Scott, T., *Society and Economy in Germany 1300-1600* (Basingstoke 2002), 143.
7. Dollinger, *The German Hansa*, 403.
8. Grassmann, A. ed., *Lübeckische Geschichte* (Lübeck 1997), 199.
9. Dollinger, *The German Hansa*, 394.
10. Pullat, R., *Brief History of Tallinn* (Tallinn 1998), 66.
11. Friedland, & Richards, *Essays*, 84.
12. Lloyd, *England and the German Hanse*, 19.
13. Ibid., 50.
14. Nash, E.G., *The Hansa: Its History and Romance* (London 1920), 171.
15. Zimmern, H., *The Hansa Towns* (London 1899), 183.
16. MacGregor, N., *Germany: Memories of a Nation* (London 2014), 233.
17. Fudge, J., Cargoes, Embargoes and Emissaries: *The Commercial and Political Interaction of England and the German Hanse 1450-1510* (University of Toronto), 43.
18. Dollinger, *The German Hansa*, 144.

19. Braudel, F., *Civilisation & Capitalism 15th -18th Century* (London 1984), Vol.3, 102.

20. Henn, *The German Hanse and its Kontors*, 7.

21. Ibid., 8.

22. Brand, H., *The German Hanse in Past and Present Europe* (Groningen 2007), 189.

23. Proost, M., *Die Bedeutung der Stadt Emmerich während der Hanzezeit* (Münster 1964-65), 38-40.

24. Friedland & Richards, *Essays*, 73.

25. Zimmern, *The Hansa Towns*, 68.

26. Bjork, D.K., 'Piracy in the Baltic 1375-1398', in *Speculum*, vol. 18 (Cambridge, Mass 1943), 62.

27. Dollinger, *The German Hansa*, 80.

28. Gies, J. & F., *Merchants and Moneymen: The Commercial Revolution 1000-1500* (London 1972), 209.

29. Foister, S., *Holbein in England* (Tate Publishing 2006), 66.

30. Keyser, E. *Die Baugeschichte der Stadt Danzig* (Köln 1972), 357.

31. Braudel, *Civilisation & Capitalism*, 103.

32. Scott, *Society and Economy in Germany*, 215.

33. Dollinger, *The German Hansa*, 139.

34. Friedland & Richards, *Essays*,70.

35. Dollinger, *The German Hansa*, 316.

36. Fudge, Cargoes, *Embargoes and Emissaries*, 168.

37. Lloyd, *England and the German Hanse*, 364.

38. Braudel, *Civilisation & Capitalism*, 105.

39. Lindberg, E., 'Club Goods and inefficient institutions: why Danzig and Lübeck failed in

40. the early modern period', *Economic History Review* (August 2009), 626.

41. Postel, R., 'The Hanseatic League and its Decline'. A paper read at Central Connecticut State University, CT (20 November 1996), 7.

42. Lloyd, *England and the German Hanse*, 363.

43. Secretan, V., Bryggen: *The Hanseatic Settlement in Bergen* (Bergen 1982), 26.

44. Braudel, *Civilisation & Capitalism*, 207.

Easterlings in England's Wash Ports

I

By 1200 Lynn had become a significant English port and market town, having grown rapidly over the century since Bishop Losinga of Norwich recognised it as a settlement on his Gaywood estate. He had endowed the Benedictine monks of Norwich Cathedral with the lordship, though their Priory Church of St Margaret was only built and rebuilt through the wealth of Lynn's mercantile community. The Norwich bishops became determined to retain their grip on the booming town. They founded a second town and market in the 1140s on the Newland to the north of the first and assumed the lordship of both centres (now Bishop's Lynn) in 1205. When Lynn received its first royal charter of borough freedom in 1204, granting its merchants a degree of self-government, it was already the fourth or fifth port of the Kingdom. According to King John's (1199-1216) levy on the value of imports and exports going through England's main ports (Bristol excluded) in 1203-05, only Boston, London, Hull and Southampton yielded more. The high status of the Norfolk town in 1205 was also confirmed by the stationing of royal galleys in its river and a mint appears to have been set up nearby. The development of larger sea going ships in the 12th and 13th centuries advantaged estuarine harbours like Lynn and Boston over inland ports on the same river systems which became less accessible. Thus, Lynn benefited at the expense of Cambridge and Boston took Lincoln's waterborne traffic. Ship building was also well established in the Norfolk port by the 14th century as the royal galley launched there in 1337 tells.

Lynn's prominence in the Middle Ages depended on an extensive hinterland captured by the river Great Ouse and its tributaries, which included several counties at the heart of the nation. Although historians have seen the river's diversion from both Ely and Wisbech to Lynn around 1250 as the turning point in the history of this Wash haven, it is probable that the changes were effected by 1150, not long after Bishop Losinga founded Lynn's Benedictine Priory. Boats could travel between Lynn and Cambridge as early as 1169; in 1227 and 1274 Huntingdon men complained that their market was vulnerable to the competition of St Ives which was easier to reach from Lynn. Stamford at the

River communication with several eastern and midland counties gave Lynn its rich and extensive hinterland.

From *The Making of King's Lynn (Chichester 1971).*

head of the Welland navigation was a major collecting point for wool sent by river to Lynn and Boston for export and lead was reaching the Wash ports from Derbyshire via the same route by 1184. The impressive extent of the hinterland of the Norfolk haven is emphasised by the King's order in 1266 for its merchants to send thirty-six tuns of wine for his army in Kenilworth (Warwickshire). Apart from the Great Ouse and Nene river systems, there were smaller subsidiary waterways extending Lynn's hinterland still further into Norfolk, Suffolk and Cambridge. Overland or road transport was also important in directing traffic to the town as the number of stone bridges over the Fenland rivers by 1400 demonstrates. Corn carts arrived at its quays from as far away as Bury St

Edmunds and Peterborough for return loads of salted fish and forest products (timber, pitch, wax and furs).

That Lynn's lines of communication to the midland counties by water were important was shown in 1373. A petition to Parliament argued that the town should once again become a staple port because of the various streams running through Cambridge, Huntingdon, Bedford, Buckingham, Northampton, Leicester and Warwick. Wool and other goods could consequently "be conveyed more easily and cheaply to Lynn than to any other port".[1] The petition from the merchants and landowners of these several English counties was granted. Wine, timber, dyestuffs, wax, pitch and herring were amongst the commodities sent in return up river to the midlands. In 1725 Thomas Badeslade prefaced his proposal for improving the Great Ouse by quoting an "ancient author" who compared this river with the Milky Way, "by reason of those accommodations of merchandise, food, and necessary provision, which are constantly carried up and down it; and Lynn sits at the door of this river, as it were the turnkey of it".[2] Lynn's privileged geographical position was reinforced by its location on England's east coast, facing continental Europe across the North Sea, with London and Scotland within fairly easy reach by ship too. In 1318 three merchants from England's capital had sent a ship to the Wash port to fetch fish and other goods but on the return journey it was robbed by Flemish pirates off the Norfolk coast. In the late 14th century large quantities of raw hides were brought from Newcastle to feed Lynn's leather industry, but this traffic was taken by London. Coal from Newcastle, fish, beer and wine were the primary commodities in its buoyant coastal trade.

Fenland reclamation by lay and ecclesiastical owners in the 12th and 13th centuries began to contribute significantly to the nation's food supply. In 1250 Matthew Paris made his famous observation that the Fens had been transformed from a haunt of "devils" to fertile meadows and fields. Such economic development boosted the Wash ports. Lynn was the natural geographical outlet for increasing amounts of corn, wool, hides and ale from its broad hinterland; its merchants returned wine, fish, salt, cloth and building materials up river. The Fenland estates of the Bishop of Ely represented a considerable inland economy sending foodstuffs overland by cart to London but numerous boats to Lynn. At Lynn the bishop's men sold corn and wool to English and European merchants before buying the timber and other commodities needed on Ely's estates. The fact that Fenland religious houses like Ely, Ramsey, Sawtry and Peterborough owned property in the town implies that it was conveniently accessible by water. Lynn's coastal and overseas traffic before 1300 was impressive enough to attract increasing numbers of home and foreign merchants. Owen charts the rapid rise of the town to national prominence after 1200 as its trade continued to grow apace:

> Once the royal records are available, the volume of information about
> goods passing in and out through Lynn seems to be inexhaustible. The
> picture of trade alters as the medieval centuries pass, but certain facts
> remain constant. Furs, hawks, iron and other raw ores, brass, millstones,
> worked marble, wax, timber of all kinds, wine, dye stuffs, spices and fish
> come in from abroad, corn and ale, lead, wool, and later cloth, come in
> from the hinterland and are shipped abroad, or coastwise to the north or
> to London.[3]

Merchants from overseas frequenting Lynn included men from Holland,
Gotland, Norway, Flanders, France, Spain, Italy and northern Germany. John
Hispania or Spain was town mayor five times between 1280 and 1296 indicating
some became permanent residents. The medieval town took on a cosmopolitan
character as ships from all over Europe crowded its river and foreign sailors
thronged its streets and taverns.

It is no surprise that German merchants from Europe's East were visiting
Lynn in the course of the 13th century, following traders from the Baltic island
of Gotland. Even in the 12th century there were references to Easterlings (the
men from the East or the Baltic) visiting the Wash ports. A John Estreys is named
as one of the witnesses to the grant of the recently built St Nicholas Chapel to
Norwich's Cathedral Priory in a bishop's charter of 1165 for example. King
John in 1214 and King Henry III (1216-72) in 1224 gave German vessels royal
permission to sail to Lynn. Stavoren and Cologne traders were amongst those
favoured from "the land of the Kaisers".[4] Importing fish and forest products,
north German merchants were drawn to the international fairs of the eastern
counties, along with Italian, Spanish and Flemish men. Boston, Lynn, Stamford,
Northampton and St Ives were the places to buy the highly valued English wool.
Easterlings or Germans continued to enjoy royal protection for their journeys to
English fairs, including Lynn, in the 1230s and 1240s. In 1237 Henry III granted
a charter to the Gotlanders excluding them from customs on their imports and
exports as well as freedom from tolls in England. Lübeck had set up a trading
post on Gotland by 1160 and secured control of its overseas commerce making
it probable German merchants were the main beneficiaries.

The Wash ports functioned as gateways into England's economic heartland
for European merchants because of their position at the head of river systems
giving access to inland towns. Hanseatic men had both warehouses and houses
at Huntingdon by 1347 accessible by water from Lynn. The dates of the
important East Anglian fairs were a key factor in determining their shipping
calendar as well as the weather. Kings amongst other grandees purchased their

furs from the fairs, with the royal tailor at Lynn in 1245 and Boston in 1250, to deal with Gotland and Norwegian merchants. Up to the 14th century Germans were prominent in the trade between England and Flanders. In 1267 Lynn and Hanseatic merchants chartered a ship in the Norfolk haven to export wool and lead to Flanders purchased in the fair at Bury St Edmund's. This Suffolk market town had a prosperous abbey being over forty miles from Lynn via the Little Ouse and Lark. Stourbridge Fair at Cambridge was probably the greatest mart in eastern England connected by the Cam and Great Ouse to Lynn. In the late 13th and 14th centuries shipowners from Holland and Zeeland were often intermediaries between German merchants and eastern England. Their vessels were small but carried the cargoes of several traders who spread commercial risk by using more than one ship from Boston and Lynn to the continent. Dutch and Flemish ships also imported millstones from the Rhineland into Lynn where the Holy Trinity Guild enjoyed a monopoly of their sale.

Part of a 13th century bede roll of deceased members of the Guild of the Holy Trinity contains names indicating both the European and homeland origins of those who had settled in Lynn: "There is not better demonstration of the multifarious origins of the trading community at Lynn".[5] Siward de Lubyk, Ricardus de Almania, Hermannus Flicke and Stephanus de Colonia are examples of German names. There are in addition at least thirteen men carrying the surname 'Estrensis' (including Folcardus the servant of Bernard Estrensis). 'Estrensis', or variations on it, is clearly a reference to Easterlings or a locative surname. This Great Guild was not only the largest and wealthiest of Lynn's religious guilds, but also its merchant guild which managed municipal and commercial activities. There was a degree of German integration in the town's merchant community which evolved as a consequence of its early overseas trading with the Hanseatic towns as described by Professor Friedland in *Die Hanse*:

> In the course of the next decades the 'Hanse' became fixed in the awareness of the European economy as a comprehensive community of German overseas merchants. Initially in the West on the English East Coast, in Lynn and in Boston, where merchants, particularly from Baltic harbours, maintained establishments. There they legitimised themselves, vis-à-vis municipal authorities, as a fraternity of the German Hanse (*fratres de hansa alemannies in Anglia existentes*, Lynn 1302) living here in England, referring to the German Hansa as a community trading in Boston just as in Flanders (1316/17) or identified themselves as "the Cologne merchants of the German Hanse" (1325).[6]

Yet Germans in Lynn and Boston were not always able to trade without undue interference. In 1291 Thomas Hauteville attempted to collect from them lastage or local tolls claiming the right in East Anglian ports as the King's hereditary falconer! Probably not for the first time, the Germans successfully resisted Thomas, on the grounds that royal charters gave them exemption from such taxes. Henry III had confirmed their commercial privileges in England in his charter of 1260. The incident also reveals the impressive scale of Anglo-German trade through Lynn before 1300:

> The volume of trade they were already doing before the end of the thirteenth century can be inferred by the attempt of Thomas de Hauteville, in 1291, to extort lastage from one hundred and forty of their ships laden with wool, leather, skins, fur, lead, tin and copper. The customs accounts, especially those already printed by Gras or abstracted by German scholars, bear this out.[7]

German vessels from the Baltic may sometimes have been using the Umlandfahrt or sea route around the Jutland peninsula before 1300 rather than their cargoes being taken overland from Lübeck to Hamburg for shipment abroad. The English east coast havens were premier destinations. If Hamburg was known as 'the brewery' and Lübeck as 'the trading chamber' amongst Lynn's Hanseatic trading partners, then the Norfolk port might aptly have been called 'the warehouse on the Wash'.

II

Shifting sandbanks have always made navigation of the Wash difficult for vessels sailing to Lynn or Boston. Hanseatic merchants had a similar problem approaching their north German harbours but acquired the expertise to deal with it. Naish suggests that they jogged the Wash ports into action to assist shipping from the continent. Birch branches or tall beacon poles were driven into the sand to mark the channels into Lynn and Boston in the 13th and 14th centuries, though it is not known who was responsible for them. In Lynn it was likely to have been the Holy Trinity Guild. Sometimes hermits lived in isolated places near the entrance to harbours and tried to help mariners. In 1349 a petition was sent to the Bishop of Norwich on behalf of John Puttock who lived in a hut on the Great Ouse estuary where he built a high cross no doubt for navigators. The towers of St Nicholas and St Margaret would also have been useful seamarks around 1300. Fires or lamps on top of high structures guided vessels arriving at night. Ships from the north German seaports entering Lynn's river would have flown pennants denoting their home town and a long Hanseatic wimple (white over red) from the mast. Vessels from Lübeck always flew the red and white ensign to announce that they had come from a city whose overlord was the Holy Roman

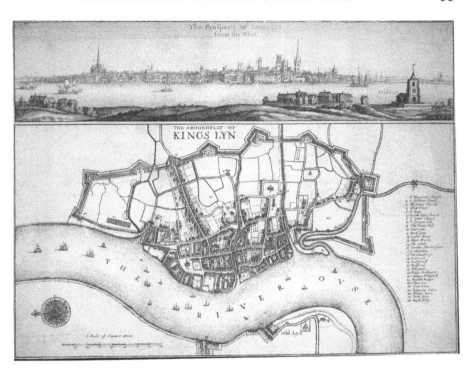

A groundplat and west prospect of Lynn executed circa 1660 by W. Hollar is the earliest known survey of the town.

Emperor. All Hanseatic ships carried the Christian cross at the top of their mast to signal their good and peaceful intentions.

The archaeological excavation in 1964 at Thoresby College in Queen Street provided physical evidence of where ships moored in 13th century Lynn. It revealed the first medieval timber wharf to be discovered in England and proved that the east bank of the Great Ouse had moved sixty yards westwards after 1300. A slate tablet in Thoresby College courtyard marks the location. Icelandic coarse cloth called wadmal was recorded in Lynn customs accounts in the early 14th century and a fragment was found on the site in 1964. It was probably used to wrap more expensive goods imported by German merchants. The Union of Norway and Iceland in 1262 involved all exports from the north Atlantic island being transported first to Bergen where Lübeck men were already prominent. Lynn's main wharfs before 1300 were almost certainly in this southern part of the town before more were constructed to the north of the Purfleet. The Purfleet itself was an important waterway as the regular orders by Lynn's authorities over a long period for those responsible to remove rubbish indicate. Archaeological excavations undertaken in Baker Lane in 1968 and 1969 revealed a timber wharf some distance from its south bank underneath what is now a car park. They demonstrated that merchant properties backed onto the Purfleet too. It

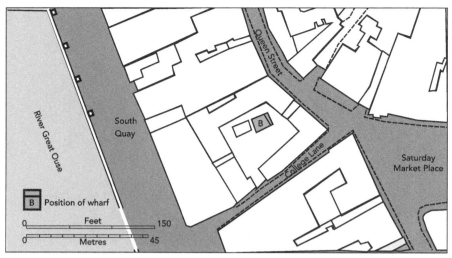

Diagram showing the position of the medieval wharf excavation at Thoresby College in Lynn.
Redrawn by Kate Lee. From Carter, A. & Clarke, H., Excavations in King's Lynn 1963-1970 [London 1977].

was then a somewhat broader waterway which functioned as a safe anchorage with public quays to accommodate foreign vessels. Hanseatic cogges sailing to Lynn from Bremen would have disembarked continental pilgrims here bound for Walsingham (England's Nazareth) in north Norfolk. Pilgrim badges were discovered in the Purfleet mud around 1900. English pilgrims could pay for passage to the shrine of St James at Compostella in Spain on German ships leaving the Norfolk port to load Iberian or French wine and salt. That it was also a favourite pilgrimage for some Lynn merchants is suggested in the will of William Lok in 1408.

The diversion of the Great Ouse from Wisbech to the Norfolk port via the Well Creek around 1150 was the result of the silting of the Ouse/Nene estuary at the nearby Cambridgeshire town. To the south the Great Ouse had simultaneously been redirected from Ely and Littleport to join with the Wissey and Little Ouse via Brandon Creek to form a combined stream north to Lynn. New quays or wharfs would have been necessary at Lynn to take advantage of greater commercial opportunities and to contain the flow of the bigger river. This emphasises the importance of investment in infrastructure if English and Hanseatic ports were to attract shipping. At some point in the 14th century, however, the Thoresby College wharf was abandoned due to silting and rubbish dumping, thus obliging its reconstruction further west. Such wharfs might also be described as revetments or retaining walls. It is clear that there was an element of deliberate in-filling at Lynn as the river moved slowly westwards requiring new quays for larger vessels with a deeper draft. A similar process took place in London, Bremen, Lübeck and other North Sea and Baltic harbours. Deck

beams protruding through the hull of late
medieval ships acted as buffers against
quays and appear to have been wrapped
to protect them. What has not yet been
found along Lynn's medieval waterfront is
evidence of cranes but costly mechanisms
to lift heavy goods would only have been
built on public quays. Town merchants had
their own private wharfs where cranes were
probably simple hoists which have left no
trace.

That the east bank of the Great Ouse
was moving west in the 13th and 14th
centuries is confirmed by the medieval
parts of Clifton House in Queen Street, an
exceptional merchant house, embracing
several centuries of town development.

*Clifton House from the west with its Tudor
tower dominant.*

The original medieval house was a stone
hall at right angles to the street built before
1300 and perhaps the first to the west of the
former river bank (now Queen Street). No

*The medieval tiled floor and vaulted undercroft
are on the south and north side of the property
respectively.*

doubt it also needed a new quay against the Great Ouse. Further land acquisition
from the river allowed the house to be extended westwards. Throughout was laid
a floor of Westminster tiles (so named after the tiled floor in Westminster Abbey)
highlighting the high status of the property and today the largest in situ medieval
tiled floor in any English secular building. Probably in the 1340s a northern
extension (or new house?) to this already remodelled merchant house was
constructed; the amazingly well-preserved brick vaulted undercroft with stone
columns supported a timber framed superstructure overlooking the Purfleet.
Brick was not widely used in Lynn until the 15th century and the undercroft is
the earliest example of it being found in the town's domestic architecture using
a large brick "probably imported from Holland".[8] Similar vaulted undercrofts in
medieval English and Hanseatic towns were designed for the sale and storage of
commodities such as wine and entered from the street. At Clifton House steps
up to the blocked door on the street are visible. With the Great Ouse lapping
against its quay to the west, and the Purfleet or main harbour immediately to
the north, no other merchant premises in Lynn could have been better situated.

Ballast to give ships stability was also unloaded from Hanseatic and English
bottoms arriving at Lynn and used as building material. Cobbled beaches found
in the vicinity of Baltic harbours were a primary source of ballast in the Middle

Ages. Rock analysis shows that the remaining fabric of the medieval town wall at Lynn contains numerous examples of water-worn cobbles with such origins. Imported cobblestones were used for other building projects as a recent archaeological survey at St Nicholas Chapel shows. Particular kinds of granite and limestone from Baltic lands are also found in the town's ancient buildings. Stone from Iceland and Norway arriving in Lynn as ballast was likewise taken for buildings and pavements. Ballast not re-cycled for construction would have been stockpiled on Lynn's quays for further use by vessels departing the port. The tiles (possibly meaning bricks) imported by Dutch ships into the Wash ports in the 15th century had served as ballast too. Sand from beaches and rivers was another kind of ballast occasionally used in Hanseatic and English vessels.

III

Simon Staveren despatched a declaration to Lübeck's council in November 1271 (now in the city's archive) which offers hard evidence of the presence of an organised group or hanse of German merchants in the Wash ports in the 13th century. He is described as an Alderman of the Holy Roman Empire at Lynn where he is a 'burgess' or citizen and a merchant. The occasion was the levy of a tax (probably a fifteenth on merchandise) by King Edward I due in April 1272. Staveren had sealed "a recognizance" for £200 to cover the new aid on the wool sixteen Lübeck merchants had bought at Boston fair in June 1271.[9] He claimed that his actions were to protect the liberties of all Lübeck merchants trading in England in case some failed to pay the royal collectors. Staveren asked the Lübeck council to make him "an extraordinary" repayment for his work so that he could be "content". Arnold Scutetmand, Bardewic Monacus, Cunrad Fot, Henry Hoppermann and Bertram Morweghe were amongst the sixteen Lübeckers trading in 1271 at Boston whom he represented.

It is likely that Simon Staveren's (aka Symon de Lenn) home town was Hamburg and business took him to Stavoren (hence his locative surname) on the Zuiderzee which was an important harbour for trade with England. The Dutch town was closely associated with Lübeck and Hamburg but not a full member of the German Hanse until later. He imported English wool and other commodities in exchange for forest products from the Baltic which had probably arrived there from Hamburg. Ships from Stavoren were frequently at Lynn in the 13th century and in 1249 Simon was designated as a German merchant licensed to trade in wool in England. He had been based at Teutonic Hall in London where he must have known Arnold fitz Thedmar (1201-74) who was Alderman of the Germans there. Staveren was clearly attracted to Lynn 100 miles north of the capital and had sufficient status to become a member of the Great Guild to share the economic and social privileges of its merchant rulers.

It seems that the acquisition by foreigners of citizenship in England's towns was not incompatible with the royal trading rights German merchants had already secured. Simon's intimate knowledge of Anglo-German commerce surely led to his elevation as Alderman of the Holy Roman Empire at Lynn which may have been "the headquarters" of Lübeck and Hamburg traders in England.[10] His predecessor was Gottschalk. The latter was at St Ives fair in 1270 and described as Alderman of the Germans at Lynn as well as a burgess there. How long the north German merchants had been established in the town is unknown, but Gottschalk may have been their first representative in the Norfolk haven. He is named as 'Godescalk Estrensis' in a contemporary membership list of the Holy Trinity Guild.[11]

One of the sixteen merchants listed in Simon Staveren's declaration in 1271 was Bertram Morweghe (or Morneweg) who "possibly" started his successful career as a merchant in Lynn.[12] In Lübeck he was amongst the citizens who rebuilt the well-known Holy Ghost Hospital where his image can be seen today in its Chapel. His son, Hermann, was one of the city's richest men of his time. It should be emphasised that Lübeck men were found in Europe's East and West well before 1300, making their fortunes and reputations. In Russia and England (in Novgorod and Lynn) they

Bertram Morneweg's image (around 1300) in the Holy Ghost Hospital at Lübeck. His early career as a merchant included time in the Wash ports.

acted as a group or hanse with an alderman elected to oversee their interests. Their association was sealed by an oath encouraging English or Flemish merchants to accept them as legitimate business partners. For young Hanseatic traders mobility over long distances across Europe was normal often as the agents of fathers or uncles.

Journeys by sea or overland became less frequent as merchants grew older and content to conduct business from their home city.

Gottschalk and Staveren must have convened meetings of German traders in Lynn to tackle commercial issues and taverns may have served that purpose. Unlike Boston, the Norfolk port had no Hanseatic kontor until 1475. Its friary buildings would have been modest before 1300, but large enough to accommodate town meetings by the later 14th century when the Carmelites hosted them. Queen Isabella and her household lodged on occasions in the 1340s at Lynn's Franciscan house with which she had a connection. The Guild of St Francis founded in 1454 included both friars and townspeople who held meetings in "the monastery of the Grey Friars".[13]

The Franciscans had settled in Lübeck in 1225 and their site was extensively developed under the patronage of its merchant rulers whose funerals and family chapels were found in the imposing brick friary church of St Catherine. It seems almost certain that the Lübeckers in Lynn and Boston transmitted their religious enthusiasm for the Franciscans from the Baltic to the Wash. In 1287 one Easterling at least was an early benefactor of their Lynn house. This was Bernard Le Estrensis who owned property in the town and was a member of the Great Guild. The funerals of Hanseatic traders dying in Lynn were probably held in the Franciscan church as was the case in Boston. The cloister walks of the Franciscans throughout Europe were the sites for lay burials. Drowning at sea was always a danger and memorial services for Hanseatic sailors losing their lives in this way were no doubt held at the friary churches in the Wash ports.

A drawing of the Greyfriars Tower (1801).
Ship ballast probably from the Baltic was used as a building material circa 1400. It survived the Henrician Reformation because of its usefulness as a seamark.

Lynn merchants often preferred the friaries as their final resting place rather than the Priory Church of St Margaret. Their younger sons occasionally chose to become friars. Friars acted as confessors for merchants whose business dealings could easily transgress the moral teaching of the Church, particularly against excessive profits and usury. Substantial donations for building or maintaining friary churches might improve the chances of a merchant entering Heaven rather than Hell! The presence of the many friars in the Wash ports bear testimony to their place in England's premier urban league. The four great orders, Dominican (Black), Carmelite (White), Franciscans (Grey) and Augustinians were all established in Lynn by 1260.

Hanseatic influence in Lynn by the 14th century becomes more tangible in

St Margaret's Priory Church from the northwest in 1985.
Here is the Saturday Market Place where an annual medieval fair attracted foreign merchants.

the two impressive Flemish brasses in St Margaret's Priory Church. The life-sized and youthful effigies of local merchants Adam Walsoken and Robert Braunche with their wives are depicted. They are probably the largest medieval memorial brasses in England and amongst the most important and masterly of their kind from this period in Europe. Of latten plates (an alloy of copper and zinc) fitted together, the design is that of the Tournai School of engravers in Flanders. This was also the source of those commissioned by Hanseatic merchants in Bruges for transport to Lübeck and other north German towns. Tournai brasses are admired for their intricate design and expert execution, with bold stylised figures, usually with staring eyes, and

Drawn detail from the monumental brass (1349) of Adam Walsoken and his wife in St Margaret's Priory Church showing an early representation of an English windmill.

"fiddle-bow" lips. Flemish incised marble slabs and brasses were carried by ship from Bruges to Lübeck and Lynn. No other English east coast port in the 14th century imported more such remarkable artefacts.

There were at least four Tournai brasses in Lynn by the middle decades of the 14th century but two disappeared in the 18th century, that of Robert Attelathe (died 1376) with his wife (Joan) in St Margaret's Priory Church, and William Bitering with his wife (Julianna) in St Nicholas Chapel. There had been eleven brasses in the Priory Church in 1724. Braunche, Walsoken, Attlathe and Bitering all knew one another; they were members of the Great Guild and town council and elected as mayor more than once. Adam Walsoken died first in 1349. Braunche, Attelathe and Bitering would have marvelled when they saw his wonderful Flemish brass in the choir of St Margaret's. This must have motivated them to commission similar memorials. These lay burials were in the chancel. Here the marble slabs with their brasses were usually laid flat on the floor so not to obstruct Church ceremonies as a raised tomb would have done.

The Braunche brass is the best known because it portrays a peacock feast. This Lynn merchant supposedly entertained Edward III in 1349 whilst mayor and the grand event was recorded on the brass. It is however unclear whether the King visited Lynn when Braunche was mayor casting doubt on this interpretation. The male figures moreover appear to wear the armour of the nobility (possibly with the exception of one or two guests) suggesting this cannot be a civic occasion.

There are nine men and three women at the table, with a crowned figure at one end of it, and the scene includes musicians and servants. It seems likely that the peacock feast shown on the brass was mythological and never actually happened but shows Braunche wanted to be associated with the aristocratic culture of the 14th century.

The peacock feast at the base of the Branche brass.

Lynn's great merchants were indeed associates of Edward III who visited the town on several occasions. They were acting as royal officials and bankers when the King pawned the crown jewels to raise funds to fight the French. From 1339 the 'magna corona' was in Trier (near Cologne) in the hands of Archbishop Baldwin before being passed to Hanseatic merchants in 1343. Tidemann Lemberg from Dortmund and other German bankers took over the loan and as security received Edward III's crown which was probably stored in Bruges. It was not until June 1345 that it was returned to the King in London but how far he had settled his huge debt is unknown. Lynn merchants were involved in the proceedings because William Melchbourne brought the great crown back to England. He was rewarded by Edward III in 1347 for "redeeming" it with an annual pension of £20 to be paid out of the customs revenues at Boston.[14]

Braunche (who died in 1364) and his two wives are the principal subjects of the peacock brass. He was twice mayor and is dressed as a wealthy merchant of the time; he wears a long close coat slit from the waist downwards with tight sleeves; Braunche's hair is worn long and flowing. His pointed shoes are fastened on the instep with a latchet and he treads on a dragon representing the evil conquered by the prayer in which Braunche is engaged. On either side his wives, Letitia and Margaret, are both clothed in the high fashion of women in the reign of Edward III. The upper part of their robes closely fit the figure, whilst the lower part is loose, and falls in elegant folds with richly embroidered borders.

The monumental brass (1364) of Robert Braunche and his two wives in St Margaret's Priory Church.

Both Flemish brasses in St Margaret's

View of St Margaret's medieval nave from a 1740s reprint of an earlier engraving (circa 1670) probably by Henry Bell.

The spire on the south-west tower fell during the great storm of 8 September 1741 and destroyed most of it.

are valuable cultural artefacts highlighting the faith and fashion of the governing body of Bishop's Lynn in the 14th century. Its wealthy merchants were clearly 'Hanse minded' following German practice in having these arresting and very expensive memorials manufactured abroad. Such brasses were intended to enhance their civic status and motivate the pious to pray on behalf of the deceased in Purgatory (where the shriven soul might be purged of remaining sins). They were also family memorials which would have had a more profound impact on the viewer in the 14th century than today. The wide engraved lines were emphasised with black mastic and the brasses were lavishly gilded to make them even more magnificent. That Braunche's brass carries the royal coat of arms (of Edward III) suggests that Lynn's merchant class aspired to become aristocrats or knights and they owned suits of armour inherited by their sons.

Lynn's 14th century merchant rulers were wealthy and influential men whose ships engaged in international trade in corn, fish, salt and wool. This commercial world embraced Bruges where they became acquainted with German merchants and Flemish brasses. Lynn shipowner John Wesenham and his partners raised 20,000 florins in Bruges in 1345 from English and Hanseatic merchants to help him enter the inner circle of royal financiers. Lynn's exquisite and famous 'King John Cup' was possibly acquired in that city of wool, luxury trades (including books) and bankers. The English colony in Bruges had its beginnings in the early

14th century and was established by the 1330s (with fifty or sixty merchants and some accompanied by their womenfolk) when the Flemish city was Europe's main market for the golden fleece of the island nation. Its wool was exchanged for Mediterranean spices and dyestuffs. English merchants rented property rather than living as guests of the hostellers as favoured by the Germans. They leased a Weigh House from the city to weigh their goods in what was called Engelsestraat (English Street) as it is still known today. This English community held meetings in the refectory of the Carmelite Friary which was also used by Hanseatic and Scottish merchants.

Of additional interest in St Margaret's Priory Church is the domed or standard chest in the nave. Of pine, it has a lime lid. Research on existing records and visits by Gavin Simpson and others have identified 130 such imported chests concentrated in East Anglia and Kent.

The King John Cup was made in the 14th century and is exhibited at King's Lynn Town Hall.

It shows a contemporary hunting scene with hawks and falcons on the gauntleted fists of fashionable ladies. It was probably in the possession of the Holy Trinity Guild before 1548 when it appears in the town records.

They were made from very large pine trees which were not found in England in the Middle Ages. Dendrochronology has confirmed the 15th century as the period of manufacture; the documentary sources and the pine strongly indicate a Baltic origin. The chests must have come from Danzig into England through the east coast ports. Lynn's waterways reached far into its region and such chests were purchased by Cambridge colleges at Stourbridge Fair. They were used as packing cases for fragile or expensive items on the long sea journey from East to West. English customs accounts of the period refer to the import of Danzig chests and, in 1402, a chest of hats was amongst the cargo of a Prussian ship arriving in Lynn. They were purchased for the safe keeping of valuable possessions in merchant and ecclesiastical households as well as Town Halls (clothes, linen, candles and books). The import of the chests through Lynn by Hanseatic merchants is confirmed by the national customs records for 1464/65 when they were usually filled with wooden dishes or platters on which food was served. An inventory compiled for St Margaret's Priory Church in 1454 lists eleven such Hanseatic (?) chests and the surviving one in the nave might be from this collection. Their manufacture had commenced around 1400 but for how long is unknown. Danzig chests helped to furnish Lynn's more prosperous households in the 16th century. In 1589 the shipmaster Robert Ladimans' inventory of goods and chattels included "an old danske chest" and "an old danks chest" in his chamber and little parlour respectively.[15]

IV

At the commencement of the 14th century Hanseatic trade through Lynn was growing largely at the expense of Flemish and Norwegian merchants. In the 13th century Lynn merchants had sent corn and cloth to Bergen in exchange for fish, furs, hunting birds and whetstones (used as ballast). Royal officials visited the annual fairs of the Wash ports to purchase Norwegian furs, with the Arctic squirrel a favourite. In 1245 King Haakon of Norway sent Henry III six gerfalcons caught in Iceland by his servants who had endured great hardships. This bilateral trade was buoyant and once in 1255 "no less than eleven" Norwegian ships were in the Norfolk harbour "loading up with corn".[16] Another major return cargo was Grimston ware pottery from the kilns at Pott Row near Lynn which has been excavated at several sites in Bergen. Vessels from Bergen and Trondheim in Norway as well as from Lynn itself were still importing fish, timber, skins and butter to the Wash ports around 1300. However, German merchants based in Bergen were taking a larger share of this traffic, and more forest products were being shipped to England from the Baltic rather than Norway.

When twenty-two German cogges moored at Lynn with stockfish in 1302 it was a strong indicator that its Hanseatic trade was becoming "considerable".[17] Then Lynn men tried to break into or re-enter the profitable fish trade at Bergen where the Lübeckers had established an economic foothold. The Germans declared a commercial boycott of the Norfolk port complaining about restrictions imposed on alien merchants in the town rather than the events at Bergen. Six Hanseatic vessels from Lübeck, Wismar and Stralsund visited Lynn in 1303 in defiance of the boycott because their captains or owners presumably preferred business to politics! As a consequence these German traders were summoned to appear before senior members of the Hanseatic community in England at Boston fair, being obliged to pay recompense, or face expulsion from it. This incident testifies to the difficulty the Hanseatic community in England had in controlling all the merchants from Germany visiting the island kingdom. In 1310 the Hanseatic boycott of Lynn was ended when the town agreed to a restoration of the trading rights enjoyed by the Germans. They were allowed to rent or buy houses whilst other foreigners were obliged to lodge with native burgesses. It is useful to detail what else the Hanseatic merchants could and could not do as confirmed in 1310:

Grant by the Mayor and burgesses of Lynn, with the assent of the

community, to all merchants of the Hanse of Germany, that they shall
have for the future all their old liberties in buying and selling except to
their own fellows domiciled in Lynn, to whom they ought not to sell.
Restrictions are placed on the length of time during which they can stay
without payment at any quay, and arrangements are made for the hearing
of disputes between them and the merchants of Lynn by two burgesses
and two of their own merchants to be chosen by the alderman of the
Hansa.[18]

Hanseatic merchants acting as a group or hanse with their own alderman
or governor were again established in the Wash haven. How many were
"domiciled" is unknown. The same Hanseatic ships and skippers were probably
regular visitors to Lynn providing the opportunity to foster good relations with
their English hosts. Lynn's merchant rulers realised that trade with the Hanseatic
towns was far too important to lose. This contrasted with the experience of other
foreign merchants who complained of severe maltreatment in the Norfolk ports.
Norwegian ships and goods were regularly arrested in Lynn whose merchants
reported the seizure of their own cargoes in Bergen. Edward II set up a royal
commission in 1313 at the request of Norway's King to investigate the grievances
on both sides. English penetration of the herring fisheries around the coasts of
Norway was clearly a factor.

V

The fish trade was at the core of the medieval economy in northern and western
Europe. It was central to the diet and a principal protein source for all social
classes. The archaeological excavations at Lynn in the 1960s revealed how much
cod and other fish fed the rising populations of England's medieval towns. Lynn
had its own fishing community at the North End where small boats sheltered in
the mouth of the river Gay. The town must have been supplied by the local fleet
and fish brought coastwise from other ports (haddock, plaice, cod and oysters).
Its fishermen also supplied the King's household and armies in Scotland and
France in the 14th century when their catch was clearly substantial. But Lynn's
role as a major English distribution centre for fish involved significant imports
from abroad. Salted herring from the Scania fishery was shipped to the Wash
ports in big quantities from the late 13th century by merchants from Lübeck,
Stralsund and Dutch towns. German and English ships brought stockfish (wind
dried cod) from Norway to Lynn and Boston in increasing amounts by the early
14th century. Fish had become Lynn's chief import by 1320 and numerous
barrels were sold at the town's annual fairs for carriage up river. Boats loaded
with dried and salted cod were "constantly" leaving its harbour for the inland

shires.[19] In 1325 King Street was known as 'Le Stocfisrowe', probably because merchants specialising in herring and dried cod lived there.

Fish cannot be separated from salt which was 'the white gold' of the medieval centuries. Around the Wash it was produced in great quantities in the 12th and 13th centuries by the evaporation of sea water in large pans boiled over peat fires until the salt crystallised. It was needed for the preservation of fish and meat as Europe's population increased. In the 13th and early 14th centuries Lynn and Boston had the lion's share of the English export and coastal trades in salt. Ships came to load it from Scandinavia and Germany as well as London. What proportion of the total export trade in salt from the Wash ports was accounted for by Hanseatic merchants is difficult to estimate, although the Scania fishery in the Baltic demanded huge quantities. Lübeck, Wismar and Stralsund men were prominent participants in the traffic. Salt was occasionally used as ballast in German ships returning to the Baltic or Hamburg from Lynn and Boston. A salt industry comparable to that around the Wash did not grow up on the shores of the Baltic because of its low salt content. However, the salt industry on the Wash shores was being undermined in the 1320s and 1330s by production on the Bay of Bourgneuf, in south-west France, where the natural evaporation of sea water made the salt cheaper. Old maps of La Rochelle indicate how the salt marshes surrounding the town were exploited for their 'white gold'. In the 14th century 'Bay salt' was even being shipped to the Wash ports by traders from Holland and Zealand, but Lynn men were soon involved. In 1338 the Bitering brothers were fetching Bay salt from France for re-export to north Germany in Hanseatic bottoms. Using alien vessels for ventures of this kind was not uncommon for

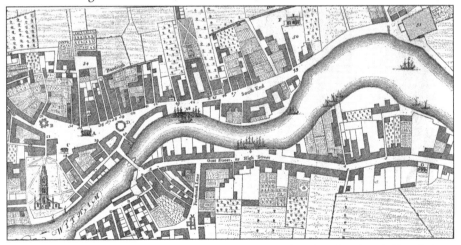

Part of a survey of Boston (1741) showing the Parish Church and market place (left) with the main quay (centre) and the medieval guildhall nearby (marked N.). In the top right hand corner the plot numbered 51 (a bowling green) is the approximate location of the Hanseatic kontor abandoned by 1500.

Lynn merchants when "the salt runs" were at their peak.[20] The Hanseatic towns regarded south-west France as their main foreign source of salt by 1350 and sent a fleet southwards every year to buy it. Salt, mostly from France and Portugal, was Reval's (Tallinn) major import. In the decade 1426-36 the annual average of "big ships" arriving from the West was fifty-seven "of which at least nineteen were salt ships".[21] Other Hanseatic fleets brought large quantities of French wine and salt to Lübeck, Riga, Königsberg and Danzig; the latter port saw sixty ships arrive in 1468 "with salt and wine cargoes from the Bay".[22]

Modest quantities of grain were also shipped to England from the 1230s by German merchants, from Hamburg, Lübeck, Stralsund and Danzig, with Hull and Lynn the main destinations. They established "a foothold" in the English corn market by the early 14th century and their position was "consolidated" in the 1320s.[23] In 1324-25, a peak year for the trade at Lynn and Hull, of the ships arriving in the Wash port, thirty-seven brought grain and seven carried grain only. Such cargoes consisted mostly of rye rather than wheat. The Baltic origin of these food supplies is clear because the rye was usually found alongside furs, wax, bacon, herrings, wine, carp, potash and wood. It was normally transported in sacks but sometimes in barrels or even loose. The import of rye from the Hanseatic towns into English east coast ports increased when home harvests were poor. English merchants were also importing some grain from Denmark and Prussia in the 1320s and, in the years leading up to the Black Death, there are "plenty of indications that English merchants took part in the grain trade with the Baltic region".[24] In March 1417 Henry V wrote to the Grand Master of the Teutonic Order requesting his help in "the exportation of corn from Prussia into England" because heavy rain had badly damaged the 1416 harvest.[25] Hybel concludes that cheap grain from eastern Europe helped to feed England's growing urban populations, particularly when home harvests were poor, though the amounts imported were not large. The importation of wheat from southern Europe was necessary in the Great Famine (1315-17) when the Baltic region was also adversely affected by harvest failure.

In the immediate aftermath of the Black Death (1348-49) the export of grain was prohibited despite the dramatic fall in England's population due to the plague. In January 1350 a royal command was addressed to the mayor of Norwich and copies sent to Lynn and forty-four other ports to the effect that no corn or animals could be exported without the king's permission "as by the frequent exportation of corn and animals a great scarcity of those things has arisen in the realm".[26] In June 1350 a similar royal directive was sent to Lynn's mayor only not to export corn out of the port "upon pain of the forfeiture of the corn and of the vessels" in which it was loaded.[27] On 4 December 1351 there was another governmental ban on corn being exported because of the scarcity of corn in the kingdom following the bad crop and by its export from England. The decimation by the plague of the rural labourers needed to bring in the harvest was another factor threatening famine in England. Urban unrest or the fear that it could be triggered by food shortages was surely in the minds of England's governors. Public anger over corn exports which threatened food shortages had resulted in major riots in Lynn and Boston on the same day in 1347 (16 June) followed by "further disorders" in the Norfolk port on 18 and 19 June.[28] At Lynn popular discontent was targeted at the export of grain by local merchants to Bordeaux which cargoes the King had licensed.

In years of good harvest Lynn and other east coast ports exported grain to the Low Countries and other parts of Europe as well as coastwise to London. The Wash port sent shipments to Flanders and Scandinavia during the European famine of 1224-26. Wheat despatched from Lynn to Bordeaux and south-west France in the 14th century paid for the import of considerable quantities of wine. Thomas Melchbourne had several royal licences to export corn to Norway, Holland, Flanders and Gascony. His commercial and political activities can be followed for over thirty years after 1319 "during which time he dealt in cloth, stockfish, ale, wool, but above all in corn".[29] William Melchbourne and John Wesenham were likewise leading Lynn corn exporters and fish importers in receipt of royal licences. The latter experienced a roller-coaster career as a financier to Edward III (1327-77) in return for commercial privileges. Siglan Susse was another king's merchant (apparently a Gotlander) who had settled in the town by 1307. Over the next twenty years or more he imported timber and herring from Norway and supplied the King with provisions for his army. All these Lynn traders enjoyed royal patronage and occasionally foreign merchants too. In 1343 protection and safe conduct were extended to three Germans to ship a cargo of wheat to Flanders "which the King has granted licence for the said John atte Wolde to take to those parts from the port of Lynn".[30]

The Great Ouse and its tributaries ensured that the Norfolk haven was the destination of boats bringing corn from eight counties, with Cambridge, Huntingdon, Crowland and Peterborough amongst the inland 'granaries'.[31] Lynn was probably England's east coast port most heavily engaged in the grain export trade because of this extensive agricultural hinterland. The sacks of grain and barrels of flour stored in the town's many granaries and buildings temporarily used as such attracted the royal purveyors from the 1290s. Herring, salt, malt and beans were also found in Lynn's many warehouses to make it one of England's premier entrepôts. Its main competitor in the grain trade on the east coast was Hull whose merchants dealt in large amounts of wheat and rye. For the King's purveyors the Wash ports and Hull were the principal sources for supplying foodstuffs to the royal household and armies in France and Scotland.

Of all the commodities sought by Hanseatic merchants in the Wash ports, English wool and cloth were the most important. The Ancient Custom on wool was fixed in 1275 at half a mark (six shillings and eight pence) a sack for English and foreign exporters as Edward I tried to pay off his debts. In 1303, however, the New or Petty Custom was imposed on aliens alone, applicable to all merchandise imported or exported, including wool at the rate of three shillings and four pence a sack. Foreign merchants now paid a custom duty on wool of 10 shillings a sack (from 1311-22 the New Custom was inoperative). Lynn's tron or wool weighing machine had been made in London following a writ of Edward I in 1298 and tested at the King's Exchequer before being delivered "to the men of Lenne".[32] The tron was probably located in the Wool Hall in Woolpack Street (St Nicholas Street) where the trading took place on the first floor. In 1374 a town merchant called John Kepe was appointed the wool tronager in "the port and staple" of Lynn and held this royal post until his death in 1406.

It is estimated that approximately nine million sheep were shorn on English farms every year in the 13th century to fill the wool sacks sent abroad. To facilitate the collection of the customs duties on wool exports, Edward I designated thirteen coastal towns as head ports responsible for the administration of stretches of England's coast. The places selected on the North Sea were Newcastle, Hull, Great Yarmouth, Ipswich, London, Sandwich, Lynn and Boston. In the 13th and into the 14th centuries the Wash ports together must have accounted for the lion's share of English wool exports to Europe, with the textile towns of the Low Countries taking most. Of all their major export trades in the 13th century, that in wool was the greatest for both Lynn and Boston. For Lynn wool exports amounted to a "considerable trade", not just "with Flanders, Zealand and Brabant, but with the Baltic countries, particularly Norway, almost totally dependent at this time on British corn, and with Gascony".[33] At the beginning of the 14th century between 1,000 and 2,000 sacks of wool were exported from Lynn every year and Italians, Scandinavians, Flemings and Germans came to purchase it. Home merchants were involved too. English ships with wool cargoes sailed to the continent in convoy for mutual protection against pirates and storms. Lynn merchants were also exporting substantial quantities of rabbit and calf skins to Flanders and the Baltic. In the town the skinners and fur dressers were located in the appropriately named Skinners Row (St James Street).

Although Italians had succeeded Flemings as England's main foreign wool exporters by 1300, the Germans were more prominent in the Wash ports. The Lübeck men in Lynn and Boston in 1271 already noted were without doubt buying wool for export to Flanders. Cologne and Westphalia merchants took wool from London and the east coast ports to Germany where Dortmund, for example, had a cloth industry of its own. Lynn was a key location and market for the Germans involved in the English wool export trade:

> Although the clerk who kept the Lynn account for 1287-8 was not much concerned to record the nationality of exporting merchants it is quite clear that the most important group in this port was German. Twenty-three Germans exported 543 sacks out of the 1407 sacks of wool and there is little room to doubt that much of the remainder was also taken by Germans. Many of these were also exporting through Boston in this same year. From other sources it is known that Germans were burgesses of Lynn and it seems likely that many of them made the town their headquarters in England.[34]

Lübeckers and Westphalians sometimes used ships from Holland and Zeeland to export wool from Lynn to the Low Countries, but the boycott of the port by the Hanseatic towns in 1303 reduced the traffic. This encouraged local exporters to assert themselves and Lynn men had a substantial share of it in the early 14th century. The Melchbourne brothers, with John Wesenham, could be counted among "the great merchant capitalists" of the kingdom dealing primarily in corn and wool.[35] Thomas Melchbourne had been elevated into high civic office as mayor and parliamentarian before becoming a king's merchant and farmer of the customs for the whole realm as Head of the English Wool Company. John Wesenham also became a royal official as a collector of the customs and the royal butler amongst several other appointments. In 1380 he received an annual life pension of over £46 from the King "as reward for his services".[36]

Lynn's exclusion from the wool staple towns in the 1350s and 1360s undermined its exports before a revival in the 1380s, when about 2,000 sacks a year were sent abroad to match early 14th century totals. The principal destination was Bruges and the Flemish cloth towns from where dyestuffs for England's cloth industry could be purchased. Lynn's wool export trade was however only modest in the 1390s and fell away from the 1440s. Norwich was another important wool market which attracted Hanseatic merchants who accessed the city by water from its outport of Yarmouth. Though the Germans had for a time become the leading alien group in England's wool export trade in the early 14th century, it later fell into native hands through the royal staple system which eventually concentrated business in Calais, and the former were eventually "ousted completely".[37] Of the provincial ports on England's east coast in the 14th century, only Hull could rival or surpass the Wash and East Anglian ports in the overseas trade in wool.

The leading sector of national economic development by 1380 was the manufacture of textiles in several English regions. They became a commodity which figured prominently in Anglo-Hanseatic trade networks being used for clothes, bedding, wall hangings, tablecloths, sails, sacks and shrouds. It seems a recovery in sheep numbers from the 1330s after disease had taken a toll on flocks boosted both the wool and cloth trades in English towns. Lynn and Boston were the natural outlets for the woollen cloth produced in Lincoln and the east midland towns, the older textile centres, before Yorkshire and East Anglia took precedence by 1400. French merchants imported large quantities of woad or blue dye (the plant was ground into powder) to the Wash ports before 1300, serving their customers in Northampton, Huntingdon, Bedford, Stamford, Leicester and Coventry.

Not much of the cloth passing through Lynn was produced in the town itself. Although borough records refer to weavers, fullers and dyers in the early 14th century, Owen concludes that nothing "suggests" the existence in the town of any "large-scale" cloth manufacture.[38] Some Lynn merchants specialised in cloth sales and purchased significant quantities in other towns for dyeing in their Wash haven where woad was plentiful. Worsteads from east Norfolk were exported from Lynn by English and foreign merchants who presumably purchased this durable cloth in Norwich. So successful was Lynn's cloth market around 1300 that a royal ulnager or inspector was posted at the port to ensure that the cloth was of the correct length and width. English and German merchants exported cloth from the Wash harbours to Scandinavia, the Baltic and continental Europe in increasing amounts from the late 14th century. By 1450 cloth was England's major export but most cargoes were now shipped to Europe through London. Its merchants were drawn to the markets in western and central Europe accessed via the Brabant fairs and many were based in Antwerp where there was an 'English House'. Flanders produced high quality cloth which had been imported into England by Flemish and German merchants, but this trade diminished as the homeland industry expanded. English cloth had never been welcomed in Flanders itself.

The cloth custom had different rates for English and foreign merchants from its inception in 1347. Hanseatic traders had secured total exemption from it by 1358, only paying on cloth the New Custom of 1303. As national cloth exports rose quickly from the later decades of the 14th century, the English were in the ascendancy, but Germans and Italians were taking a large share of this profitable trade. About 90 per cent of all Hanseatic exports from England in the 15th century was accounted for by cloth. The cloth manufacturers in the English regions took the advice of German merchants to ensure their product met the needs of particular markets in Europe. The cloth sold in the Wash ports and Hull was designed to satisfy the preferences of consumers in Hamburg or Danzig or Lübeck. A standard cloth for assessment purposes was twenty-four yards in length and one and a half to two yards in width. All cloths were converted by royal custom officials to these dimensions before being taxed and exported.

VI

Lynn in the early 14th century was one of "the most cosmopolitan" of England's ports as reflected in its variety of imports and exports.[39] The substantial amounts of woad brought to the Wash harbour from northern France testified to the demand from cloth manufacturers in its broad hinterland. The French merchants had been allowed to have their own warehouses and hostels in England from 1237. Wine from the Rhineland and particularly Bordeaux was also imported in impressive quantities in the early 14th century before 'The Hundred Years' War' (1337-1453) with France reduced this traffic.

Hanseatic and Netherlandish ships arrived in Lynn in the 1320s with full cargoes of herring or Baltic staples (wax, pitch, iron, furs, ash and wood cut into various sizes), but they also carried canvas, bricks, millstones, copper, steel, spears, onions and garlic to demonstrate the increasing variety of imports. Noteworthy, in addition, are the shipments of silver coins (in barrels or sealed leather bags) unloaded at the Norfolk port to mirror its commercial pre-eminence. The English population was approximately three million around 1380, dependent greatly on a silver currency, but there were insufficient coins in circulation to sustain economic activity without resort to extensive barter and credit. German traders were almost certainly importing silver bullion into Lynn at this time when new mines were opened in central Europe. In 1390 the want of coinage in the kingdom was attributed to the vast sums sent to the Papacy in Rome and to alien merchants taking it out. At the same time England's foreign trade provided much of the silver coin needed to keep the wheels of the national economy turning.

In the early 14th century (1303-07) corn and ale together were Lynn's biggest export contributing "more than 47 per cent of the total of £12927".[40] Cloth came second, with salt in third place, but the latter declined as the more cheaply produced French salt captured north European markets. Ale exports still loomed surprisingly large into the 1320s despite bad harvests which caused England to import cereals. Lynn was the principal port for Zeelanders and Hollanders sailing to England to fetch ale having acquired royal export licences. Cloth accounted for nearly 50 per cent of Lynn's exports by the 1320s and this upward trend continued in the following decades. Small quantities of lead and coins or sterling were also to be found in the holds of the ships which departed the Great Ouse (it appears some of the money or coins which had been imported were being re-exported). It is difficult to know the amounts of various commodities arriving in Lynn being re-exported from the extant custom records. English port towns usually allowed foreign merchants up to forty days to sell their goods and Lynn was no exception. In 1309 its mayor had secured the agreement of the Bishop of Norwich to permit alien traders to stay in the town for forty days to deal. In 1453 Parliament enacted a measure to make foreign merchants pay a special tax if they resided in the country longer than six weeks.

Who were the Easterlings and Dutch and Scandinavians sailing their ships to Lynn in the early decades of the 14th century? Many senior merchants based in comfortable counting houses in Lübeck or Bergen sent their several ships overseas in the hands of trusted master mariners. There were also independent traders who captained their own vessels in what appear to be joint enterprises with the crew. Examining the taxed goods imported by foreign traders into Lynn (29 September 1324 to 28 September 1325) Gras notes: "The extent to which the owners or masters of ships were also the merchants is surprisingly large". The sailors, too, frequently traded "on their own behalf".[41] Throughout his study of England's medieval customs system shipmasters and merchants seem regularly to be one and the same.

VII

The character of the Hanseatic presence in Lynn changed after 1353 when it was excluded from the English staple ports and inland towns appointed by Edward III to facilitate tax collection on wool and other exports. Germans who dealt in wool and stockfish, particularly from Lübeck, decamped to Boston. When Lynn became a staple port in 1373 and a separate customs district again, no longer lumped with Boston by the royal officials, Prussians had replaced Lübeckers. Before 1353 the ships of Lübeck and the Wendish towns were more common in Lynn than those from Danzig and the eastern Baltic, but the latter soon began to appear in greater numbers. Forest products from the East rather than from Norway indicated a decisive shift in the nature of Anglo-Hanseatic trade. Lynn was trading more with the eastern than the western Baltic towns using both German vessels and its own fleet built by an upcoming merchant class. Shipping between the Norfolk borough and other North Sea havens such as Hamburg, Bremen and the Dutch ports remained significant, but Baltic commerce was becoming more lucrative. Some Baltic goods (timber, pitch, wax) were re-exported by Lynn merchants to Gascony whose wine was normally transported to England in exchange for wool and cereals.

The late 14th century was a watershed in England's economic history which was to accelerate Anglo-Hanseatic commercial interdependence. Raw wool exports continued to be buoyant into the 1350s and 1360s and, though there was a marked decline by the 1390s, they remained sizeable into the 15th century.

Yet the national textile industry was developing apace from the late 14th century and more of England's wool was being used at home and more cloth exported. English merchants now ventured into the eastern Baltic with cargoes of cloth to exchange for forest products. Lynn and Hull men were prominent because they imported more timber in exchange for cloth than the other English east coast ports. Baltic oak was particularly in demand for ship building (Scandinavian soft wood was less useful). Tar and pitch from the East were required for both new vessels and repairing old ones. Another by-product of the wood trade was potash used for dyeing cloth and exported from Prussia to Flanders and England. The growth of Anglo-Prussian trade from the later 14th century was to have unfortunate political consequences. The English began to claim similar economic privileges in Baltic port towns as the Germans enjoyed in Lynn or Boston. This issue of reciprocity aggravated a series of Anglo-Hanseatic disputes into the 15th century.

Before more English merchants began to sail to the eastern Baltic towns with cloth to exchange for timber and grain, they had encountered German resistance to their activities in Norway and Scania. The great importance of the herring fishery off southern Sweden was emphasised in chapter one. Once the Hanseatic towns had completed their military victory over Denmark with the Treaty of Stralsund in 1370, they tried to squeeze out the English and other nationalities from Scania, or to strictly limit their freedom to operate there. Lübeck, Rostock, and Wismar had also become dominant in Bergen which was Europe's biggest fish market. The death of Edward III in 1377 offered an opportunity for English merchants to retaliate because new monarchs had to confirm Hanseatic privileges in England. Why should the Germans retain their trading advantages in London and the east coast ports when they opposed English enterprise in Scania and Norway? The Crown agreed to suspend their commercial rights which had been conferred by ancient royal charters. The Parliament of 1378 saw the first official acceptance of the principle that the Hanseatic franchises in England should depend "on the enjoyment of similar rights by English merchants in northern and eastern Europe".[42] It seemed the English kings could no longer guarantee the German Hanse immunity from its parliamentary opponents. A political impasse was the result. A Hanseatic assembly at Stralsund in 1378 informed Richard II (1377- 99) that it would impose a trade boycott on England unless German franchises were restored. Another at Lübeck in 1379 threatened to end Anglo-Hanseatic commerce! The question which remained unanswered was the freedom of English merchants to trade in the Baltic and access Danzig and Riga as well as Scania. Neither the English nor the Germans wanted to seriously damage international trade which enriched both. At another Hanseatic assembly in June 1380 the English were assured that they were at liberty to trade with the member towns but no specific privileges were conceded. In turn, the King conditionally restored Hanseatic privileges in England, with royal proclamations going to the east coast ports in September 1380 regarding "the merchants of the Hanse in Almain". Collectors of the petty customs in London, Lynn, Yarmouth, Boston and Hull were ordered that they must again allow the Germans to enjoy their former economic liberties "as in the times of the King's forefathers" and he had "delivered to them his charter confirming the same". [43] Lynn merchants were now embroiled in international politics to an extent unknown before their penetration of the Baltic in the late 14th century.

VIII

Understanding of Anglo-German medieval history can be enhanced if Boston is considered, that Lincolnshire port at the north-west corner of the Wash, and amongst the nation's premier harbours. Its importance was guaranteed not only as the outport of Lincoln at the mouth of the river Witham, but also by being at the head of an extensive system of inland waterways. The re-opening of the Foss Dyke in 1121 (a canal eleven miles long) was a key factor because it linked the Witham at Lincoln with the Trent. This gave traders river access to Nottingham, York and Hull. The Wash ports of Lynn and Boston both exploited the great geographical advantage of being connected by waterways to broad hinterlands. Enormous amounts of wool from England's northern counties found their way to Europe from the 12th century through Boston's international fair first mentioned in 1125. It opened on St Botolph's Day on 17 June for eight days but was extended several times after 1218. Boston's success as a medieval "boom town" is "best illustrated" by the extension and growth of its fair even lasting until October by the early 14th century.[44] A remarkable congregation of English and continental merchants enjoyed free trade in wool, salt, fish, wax, cloth, lead, timber, furs, leather, spices and wine. Debts were paid and credit advanced, but the fair suffered a disaster in 1288 when robbers set fire to it and nearby houses.

German merchants from Cologne were in Boston from the early 13th century importing wine and manufactured goods in exchange for wool. The French brought far more wine into the Wash haven than other foreign traders which around 1300 "probably" imported more gallons than any other provincial port.[45] The summer fair had acted as the commercial magnet for ships from Europe, though foreign merchants visited the Lincolnshire port less frequently from the 1340s as its wool trade diminished. That its opening was postponed to August is significant. By 1416 it was claimed in London that Boston's fair had ceased for many years, but England's urban marts had almost all been in decline, no longer hubs of the national economy.

Hanseatic merchants had established a trading post in the town by 1259.

St Botolph's Parish Church rises above the Lincolnshire town with the main medieval quay to the right.

Thompson tells us they "had a house in Boston very soon after their recognition and grant of privileges by Henry III."[46] It was located by the river Witham at South End. Boston boasted a Hanseatic kontor well before Lynn and was "the chief provincial centre" of German merchants in England into the late 14th century.[47] Its key connection with the Hanseatic towns in the 14th century was through the Bergenfahrer (mostly Lübeck 'Bergen Travellers'). They shipped grain and beer from the Baltic to Bergen and controlled most of its enormous fish trade. The Bergenfahrer turned Boston into their main distribution centre in England for stockfish. German vessels arriving in the Wash harbour from Bergen carried train oil (from seals and whales), timber, pelts and hides too, but barrels of stockfish filled most holds. In the year from Michaelmas 1390 to Michaelmas 1391, "Hanse imports from Bergen amounted to £3,779" or "74% of all alien imports" into Boston to confirm the dominance of the Norway trade.[48] Imports of stockfish, wax, iron, pitch and timber products direct from Lübeck and Danzig to Boston were on a smaller scale. Hanseatic merchants had a virtual monopoly of the substantial quantities of wax shipped to Boston. It was in demand in England for candles in churches and palaces and merchant houses as well as for the sealing of documents.

Cloth and salt were exported by the Bergenfahrer from Boston to Bergen and the Low Countries at first, then by the Danzigers to the Baltic in the late 14th century, with increasing quantities of cloth leaving its harbour. Bostonians were also taking cloth to Danzig by 1400 and visiting the Scania herring fairs on the coast of southern Sweden. Some Coventry cloth merchants had access to Baltic markets through the Wash ports too. Dollinger asserts that until the end of the 14th century the amount of English cloth exported by Hanseatic merchants from Boston "greatly exceeded" that from all the other English ports together, including London, and "this export trade flourished up to the mid-fifteenth century".[49] The Germans became far less involved in Boston in the course of the 15th century partly as the result of Anglo-Hanseatic hostilities. By 1430 Hull and Lynn were each exporting as much cloth as the Lincolnshire harbour and the Cologne merchants much more from London.

How many Germans lived and worked in Boston in the 13th and 14th centuries? Some Bergenfahrer resident in Norway employed agents to transact business in the town. However, a significant group of Hanseatic traders were permanently based in Boston, enrolling in local guilds and becoming benefactors of the friaries. The Franciscan friary was located near the German kontor and closely associated with it. German names can be identified amongst the brethren who traced the foundation of their Boston house in 1268 to their secular compatriots. Friars were itinerant with international horizons not unlike the Hanseatic merchants themselves. It is no surprise that the latter who died in Boston chose to be buried in the Franciscan precinct there. In 1813 a sepulchral stone was excavated on the site with an engraved figure of a man whose feet rest on a dog and an inscription around the edges. He was Wisselus Smalenburg, a merchant from Münster in western Germany, who died in 1340. This fine memorial marble slab was imported from Tournai in Flanders and can now be seen in St Botolph's Church. Krüger says that Smalenburg was so well integrated in the Wash port that, after his death, "his mortal remains were not taken back to his home country but a monument of the highest artistic standards was ordered from the area of the River Maas and transported to Boston".[50] The cost of such an exercise must have been "immense" and suggests that our merchant felt more at home in England than Germany. Hanseatic traders were sometimes domiciled for many years in Boston or Lynn which places became their preferred abode rather than their home towns. Dollinger claims that the increase in Anglo-Hanseatic trade in the first half of the 14th century was reflected in "the large number" of Germans "who settled permanently in the country".[51]

The rapid growth of Boston had been interwoven with the remarkable rise of the English wool export trade in the 13th century. The cultivation of the highest quality wool was found in the eastern counties. A royal fifteenth or tax charged on the value of England's imports and exports in 1203-04 shows that Boston alone "handled 29 per cent" of its overseas trade, followed by London, Hull and Lynn.[52] In 1287-88 over 9,000 wool sacks were shipped from the Lincolnshire harbour (far more than any other east coast port). Italian and German merchants were the chief foreign exporters. Hanseatic traders from western Germany were still exporting large amounts of English wool to Flanders around 1340, and over 60 per cent came from Boston, but the traffic "fell away almost to nothing in the second half of the century".[53] Although cloth was certainly replacing wool as England's leading export commodity at this time, the decline in wool exports from the Lincolnshire port, at least by the English, was not as dramatic as Dollinger portrays. Reviewing a scholarly work on Boston's overseas trade in the reign of Richard II, Nightingale concludes its role in the national economy in the late 14th century should not be underestimated:

Tomb slab of Wissel Smalenburg (died 1340) in St Botolph's Parish Church in Boston.
From: Wheedon, J., The Monumental Brasses in St Botolph's Parish Church (Boston, 1973).

> Steven Rigby's meticulous work provides a corrective to this notion and shows that Boston still had a significant merchant class capable of finding 22 local men to join a consortium that exported 5,781 sacks of wool from the port in 1377-8. The five sets of particulars for the new subsidy of tonnage and poundage provide valuable details of previously unrecorded imports and exports of denizen merchants, and they show the transforming effect of the cloth industry on the regional economy. In 1383-4 merchants were importing quantities of dyes, alum, and oil for the latter, from the Low Countries, as well as timber and iron from the Baltic, and they exported cloth and wool in return. The Hansards were particularly important as they shipped 60 per cent of the cloth from Boston that they took from England. [54]

Boston enjoyed short periods of boom in wool exports into the 15th century, but the trade declined sharply thereafter. German merchants had a large slice of the cloth export trade from the Lincolnshire haven by 1380.

IX

The medieval trade of the Wash ports with the Hanseatic towns of the North Sea and Baltic was slowly but surely usurped by London. The Steelyard there "overtook that of Boston in economic importance" at the end of the 14th century "though until then it may have occupied second place".[55] The growth of London as England's commercial centre in the course of the 14th century at the expense of the provincial ports is indicated by the fur trade dominated by Hanseatic merchants. The use of luxury fur (worn in summer and winter) in medieval Europe was primarily for high quality garment trimming. Although the Germans continued to import furs into England's east coast harbours in the late 14th century, the quantities they brought to London were now far bigger, and the international fairs of the eastern counties lost the business. Even London's skinners had once frequented St Botolph's Fair! In 1480 Hanseatic trade through the English capital was greater than all the nation's provincial ports together (Sandwich and Dover were more or less its outports). London already accounted for approximately 36 per cent of England's overseas trade at the commencement of the 14th century, but this had mounted to "an extraordinary" 61 per cent at the end of the 15th century.[56] Nevertheless, Lynn and Boston remained two of England's largest and richest towns in the 14th and 15th centuries, hosting significant numbers of German merchants.

The Poll Tax of 1377 provides a good indicator of the total populations of England's major provincial east coast ports. Edward III's Parliament granted this capitation tax of four pence for all lay persons over fourteen. Of the total number of recorded taxpayers, Lynn had 3,217, Boston 2,871, Newcastle 2,647, Great Yarmouth 1,941, Hull 1,557 and Ipswich 1,507. Clarke and Carter offer a useful discussion on estimating Lynn's population in 1377. If the children are calculated at forty per cent of the total population, and the clergy at two per cent, a figure (excluding other possible exemptions or avoidance) of 5,546 results. It is normally assumed that by 1377 England's population had declined to around 60 per cent of its level before the Black Death (1348-49), which could mean "that at its peak before the plague the population of Lynn was in the region of 9,000".[57] If Lynn and Boston had total populations of about 9,000 and 7,000 respectively about 1340, Lübeck numbered approximately 18,000 inhabitants at this time The city had suffered from the Great Pestilence in 1350, and again in 1356, but quickly recovered mainly by migration from the West. In Hamburg and Bremen an even greater percentage of their home populations perished during the plague than at Lübeck.

Though Lynn retained its status as a leading English market town and port into the 16th century, Boston was hampered by the silting of its river. In the

1334 subsidy (tax on moveable property) the Lincolnshire town was the fifth wealthiest in the country. Boston's mercantile prosperity and piety is visible in the rebuilding of St Botolph's Church in the course of the 14th century. The spacious nave with its guild chapels is reminiscent of a friary church and designed to impress. However, the famous 'Stump' or magnificent western tower was not finished until circa 1520, when the local maritime economy had become depressed. Boston lost more than 50 per cent of its population between 1377 and 1524, or a fall from approximately 5,000 to 2,000 inhabitants. As a consequence the town's ranking in England's urban league fell from tenth to fifty-first.

The late medieval guildhalls built in the Wash ports testify to their place in England's premier urban league and the assertiveness of their respective merchant rulers. St Mary's Hall in Boston was erected in the 1390s as recent dendrochronological examination of the roof (of Baltic oak) tells; Lynn's Holy Trinity Hall was largely rebuilt in 1421-23 following a fire in January 1421 witnessed by Margery Kempe. St George's Guildhall in King Street was equally as grand and definitely completed by 1428. Public building on this scale represented a large investment by the merchant guilds. Of two storeys in brick on long narrow plots, with undercrofts on the ground floor and halls above, these guildhalls have high gables overlooking the street. St Mary's Guildhall in Boston and Lynn's two similar edifices bear comparison with the brick town halls of the Hanseatic cities of northern Germany. The latter may have influenced the design of these dominant public buildings in the Wash ports (if on a more modest scale) whose merchant class had strong trading links with Hanseatic Europe. Spaces within these impressive English buildings were likewise used flexibly to foster commerce and civic authority. Undercrofts, for example, were not only for the storage of goods but probably for their sale too. Their location was also highly significant. All three guildhalls were built in the town centres adjacent to the market places and the grand houses of the merchant rulers. They were the local hubs of economic and political power and material expressions of high social status. These buildings stand as striking examples of medieval secular architecture which still impact on their respective townscapes in the 21st century.

Medieval Boston does not seem to have sought a royal grant of self-government (it was under the control of four different lords), but St Mary's Guildhall probably reflected the desire of townspeople for an architecturally superior meeting place. St Mary's Guild received a royal charter of incorporation in 1392. Its membership composed of merchants and landowners neatly combining secular and religious activities. Women could also become members. At Lynn the famous religious mystic and business woman, Margery Kempe, belonged to the Guild of the Holy Trinity. Its Guildhall faced the Priory Church established by the Norwich bishops across the Saturday Market Place and symbolised the rise of the merchant class. Of the social orders in the medieval town, the merchant oligarchy was classified as the potentiores, below them were the tradesmen or mediocres, and the labouring thousands were the inferiores. The latter two classes rebelled against their merchant rulers in 1411 and 1416 demanding fairer taxation and power sharing. As a result the potentiores gave the mediocres a role in local government, and the Norwich bishop approved Lynn's new constitution in 1420, after several years of bitter civil strife.

X

Trade between the Wash ports and the Hanseatic cities involved small armies of labourers loading and unloading ships as well as numerous sailors. How were cargoes carried? Furs, including the huge quantities of squirrel pelts or 'greyworks' sent from East to West, were put into barrels. Fish, beer, flour, wax, tar, pitch, salt, ash, steel, iron, resin and woad were also transported in barrels. So, too, was wine, but the tun cask was bigger (an English Act of 1423 assessed the wine tun as not less than 252 gallons) and needed several men plus tackle to load and unload. Dunnage was wedged between and under barrels to keep them steady once on board. Wool sacks (wrapped in canvas) of roughly twenty-six stones could be lifted by four labourers for stacking in the hold (or being removed from it). Rough sea voyages could damage the wool sacks and drenched wool had to be dried by fires on arrival in Flanders or Holland. A vessel transporting only wool would have been too light in the water and unstable in bad weather without ballast. The latter could be iron, copper, lead, millstones or building materials. Cloth (and often furs) was wrapped in canvas in bundles trussed with cord by skilled port workers. Grain was measured by the 'last' (equivalent to probably twelve barrels) and usually carried in sacks or bagged as was (sometimes) salt. Discharging loose bulk grain or salt would have been both labour intensive and wasteful, with the cargo at sea liable to shift, and the resulting instability endangering the ship. Timber boards or sawn wood up to two inches thick, and of any length or width, were usually gathered into bundles before being hoisted in and out of holds. Ship masts were lashed to the deck and could be floated to vessels for loading and simply pushed overboard when unloading. German cogges departing Lübeck or Hamburg by 1400 were mostly big enough to carry 400 or more barrels of beer or herring. Convenience, economy and stability at sea dictated to ship owners and crews how cargoes should be handled and stored. Cats on board tackled the rats gnawing into sacks! All merchants had individual marks or seals on barrels and bundles to identify their goods because cargo space was shared.

To enable the crew to load and unload cargoes in harbours without port facilities, the masts of German and English ships must have doubled as the centre posts of derricks. In Lynn the public quays acquired cranes funded by the town council or the Holy Trinity Guild. The Common Staith to the west of the Tuesday Market Place was the town's main public quay by the 14th century, owned by this Great Guild, with the biggest crane. It was repaired in 1385-86 (barrels, millstones and bells were amongst the loads hoisted). A description from a survey in 1577 reveals a "wooden crane covered with lead and two wheels inside" powered by port labourers as was the great crane in Danzig.[58] Such cranes were found in both English and Hanseatic ports in the 14th century modelled on the tread wheel cranes used for cathedral building. These harbour treadmill cranes were efficient and saved labour, but big investment was required to construct stone quay walls apart from the crane itself. The Common Staith was only accessible through secure gates from the Tuesday Market Place.

St Mary's Guildhall in Boston was built in brick in the 1390s with roof timbers from the Baltic imported no doubt on Hanseatic ships. It became the Town Hall in 1545; today it is the Guildhall Museum.

Hanseatic ships arriving at Lynn in the 14th and 15th centuries were almost certainly directed to the Common Staith or Purfleet quay and their cargoes sold. Alien merchants had long used their vessels as warehouses or storage in their commercial operations in the absence of port facilities. Presumably local traders had boarded the ship to negotiate a deal with the skipper or merchant. However, an entry in Lynn's Red Register (a municipal record) in 1368 apparently ruled that cargoes be landed on the quay before

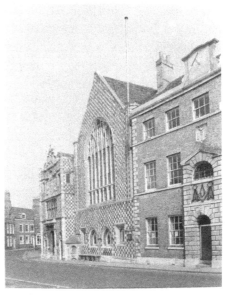

The Guildhall of the Holy Trinity in the Saturday Market Place was rebuilt in the early 1420s after the destruction of part of the building by fire in 1421.

business started, as directed by a royal statute. Similar regulations were imposed on foreign merchants in other English east coast havens. English "harassment" of Hanseatic merchants included Hull's decision to stop Prussians selling goods from their ships in 1408 "insisting that these must first be unloaded and warehoused".[59] London had followed Hull's example. Imports were normally customed on board ship before the cargo was unloaded and exports examined by the royal officials on land. In 1412 Hamburg ordered all ships using the Elbe to land their goods for sale to stop merchants bypassing the port!

Quaysides (furnished with public privies) were bustling places in Hanseatic Europe where home and foreign merchants exchanged information which gave opportunities to link with local and international trade networks. The languages spoken by East Anglian and north German merchants in the 14th century were closely enough related to facilitate mutual understanding. Translators were anyway available by the waterside in Lynn or Hamburg. English and German merchants were not slow to learn foreign languages when it was to their advantage.

Disputes between merchants were also resolved on Lynn's quays in what was in effect outdoor arbitration. In 1372 two traders settled their differences on the quay of the Holy Trinity Guild with the town's mayor almost certainly the arbitrator. In June 1408 a plea of debt against an alien trader was considered according to law merchant on the quay of a Lynn alderman. The principal purpose of law merchant was to expedite justice and protect foreign merchants from unfair treatment by national or local legal systems. It had been developed and administered by the merchants themselves, but urban rulers usually played a key role. Lynn's mayor in 1408 was, unsurprisingly, a merchant. A Danzig ship had been arrested by the port bailiffs "at the suit of John Patryk", a Lynn 'clothman', who claimed that an alien merchant, Nicholas Warpull, owed him money. The mayor assembled Lynn burgesses and foreign mariners who had petitioned him "to examine" John Patryk. Mayor Brygges motivation was "that alien merchants coming to Lynn should receive justice and be treated fairly". Under oath a dyer and a goldsmith supported Patryk and the skipper of the Danzig ship paid him the debt owed with his expenses. The ship was released as a result on 1 July 1408. Lynn's mayor had brought this dispute to a successful conclusion without seeking the involvement of Warpull's home town. It is probable that Nicholas Warpull was the 'Nicholas Wapull' who was a Prussian accused in October 1408 of stealing four anchors from a ship belonging to three Lynn merchants at Marstrand in Norway in 1405.[60]

The rapid and fair settlement of disputes between home and foreign merchants was important in maintaining mutual trust in international commerce, but Parliament was becoming more unfriendly to alien traders. In 1425 they were ordered to sell all imports and purchase their quota of English goods within forty days "on pain of forfeiture".[61] English kings continued to endorse the commercial privileges Hanseatic merchants had long enjoyed in England. They were not subject to the Act of Parliament of 1439 which obliged alien traders to lodge with English hosts. The latter were charged with the responsibility of keeping a record of their transactions to ensure the foreigners spent money on English goods to export. Lynn and Boston were two of the seventeen national ports whose mayors were instructed by the King's government to oversee the implementation of the Act. Both foreign merchants and their assigned hosts could be heavily fined if they refused to comply with the law, but enforcement was always difficult, and it was only in operation for eight years.

Notes

1. Carus Wilson, E.M., 'The Medieval Trade of the Wash Ports', *Medieval Archaeology* (1962-63), 195.
2. Williams, N. J., *The Maritime Trade of the East Anglian Ports 1550-90* (Oxford 1988), 54.
3. Owen, D. ed., *The Making of King's Lynn: A Documentary Survey* (London 1984), 42.
4. Simon, U., *Simon von Staveren: Ältermann der Deutschen oder 'king's merchant'?* (Hamburg 2012), 29.
5. Owen, *The Making of King's Lynn*, 295.
6. Friedland, K., *Die Hanse* (Stuttgart 1991), 126.
7. Owen, *The Making of King's Lynn*, 46.
8. Parker, V., *The Making of King's Lynn* (Chichester 1971), 67.
9. Friedland & Richards, *Essays*, 97.
10. Owen, *The Making of King's Lynn*, 46.
11. Ibid., 304.
12. Grassmann, *Lübeckische Geschichte*, 175.
13. Hillen, H., *History of the Borough of King's Lynn* (EP Publishing 1978), 749.
14. Harrison, *The Close Rolls 1256-1377*, 621.
15. Parker, *The Making of King's Lynn*, 180.
16. Carus Wilson, 'The Medieval Trade of the Wash Ports', 185.
17. Friedland & Richards, *Essays*, 98.
18. Owen, *The Making of King's Lynn*, 53.
19. Carus Wilson, *The Medieval Trade of the Wash Ports*, 191.
20. Owen, *The Making of King's Lynn*, 53.
21. Pullat, *Tallinn*, 66.
22. Fudge, *Cargoes, Embargoes and Emissaries*, 43.
23. Hybel, N. 'The Grain Trade in Northern Europe before 1350', *Economic History Review* LV (2002), 237.
24. Ibid., 244.
25. Sharp, B., *Famine and Scarcity in Late Medieval and Early Modern England* (Cambridge 2016), 135.
26. Harrison, *The Close Rolls 1256-1377*, 636.
27. Ibid., 639.
28. Sharp, *Famine and Scarcity in Late Medieval and Early Modern England*, 59.

29. Gras, N.S.B., *The Evolution of the English Corn Market* (Harvard 1926), 172.

30. Harrison, R., *The Patent Rolls 1327-1377* (King's Lynn 1993), 145.

31. Gras, *The Evolution of the English Corn Market*, 62.

32. Hillen, *History of the Borough of King's Lynn*, 99.

33. Parker, *The Making of King's Lynn*, 10.

34. Lloyd, T.H., *The English Wool Trade in the Middle Ages* (Cambridge 1977), 68.

35. Parker, *The Making of King's Lynn*, 10.

36. Gras, *The Evolution of the English Corn Market*, 173.

37. Lloyd, *England and the German Hanse*, 96.

38. Owen, *The Making of King's Lynn*, 49.

39. Lloyd, T.H., *Alien Merchants in England in the High Medieval Ages* (Brighton 1982), 48.

40. Ibid., 49.

41. Gras, N.S.D., *The Early English Customs System* (Harvard 1918), 374.

42. Lloyd, *England and the German Hanse*, 58.

43. Harrison, R., *The Chancery Rolls 1377-1399* (King's Lynn 1999), 43.

44. Rigby, S.H., *Boston 1086-1225: A Medieval Boom Town* (Society for Lincolnshire History and Archaeology 2017), 67.

45. Carus Wilson, 'The Medieval Trade of the Wash Ports', 189.

46. Thompson, P., *The History of the Antiquaries of Boston* (Boston 1856), 326.

47. Lloyd, *England and the German Hanse*, 82.

48. Ibid..

49. Dollinger, *The German Hansa*, 243.

50. Friedland & Richards, *Essays*, 81.

51. Dollinger, *The German Hansa*, 56.

52. Palliser, D.M. ed., *The Cambridge Urban History of Britain 600-1540* (Cambridge 2000), 476.

53. Dollinger, *The German Hansa*, 244.

54. Nightingale, P., Review of the Overseas Trade of Boston in the reign of Richard II, by S.H. Rigby, *Economic History Review* LIX (2006), 839.

55. Lloyd, *England and the German Hanse*, 75.

56. Palliser, *The Urban History of Britain*, 478.

57. Clarke, H. & Carter, A., *Excavations in King's Lynn 1963-70* (London 1977), 429.

58. NRO. 'With Ships and Goods and Merchandise', 3.

59. Lloyd, *England and the German Hanse*, 121.

60. NRO, 'With Ships and Goods and Merchandise', 4, 5, 13.

61. Lloyd, *England and the German Hanse*, 110.

Lynn's Prussia Connection

I

The cogge and its further development as a bulk carrier was a critical factor in Hanseatic command of north European international trade in the 13th and 14th centuries. German ships arrived in Lynn and Boston from the East at regular intervals. English vessels were sailing to Norway, the Low Countries and France well before 1300, but did they access the Baltic too? At Kampen in the Netherlands the Museum holds a document showing that in 1251 the Danish King allowed its ships to sail around Jutland to the Baltic. The annual herring fairs in Scania (southern Sweden) highlighted in chapter one were almost certainly visited by English ships by 1300 using the same passage. A Lynn citizen called Ricardus Almania (possibly a German immigrant) received permission from Edward I in 1284 to sail to Norway and 'Estland' to buy corn for sale in

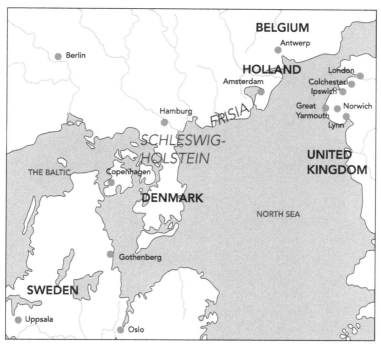

This 'upside down' map of northern Europe highlights how Lynn's geographical position encouraged trade between the Wash and the Baltic.
From: Williamson, T., England's Landscape: East Anglia (English Heritage 2006).

85

England. There are also "indications" that the grain trade from the Baltic into the North Sea involved shippers from England and Holland as well as the Hanseatic towns from "the late 1270s".[1] The English were certainly sailing into the western Baltic to trade by the early 14th century. In 1312 Peter Elmham of Lynn and eleven other merchants had their goods "arrested" at Stralsund in "Estland" in retaliation for the burning of one of that city's ships at Berwick, where it was deemed to be supporting the King's Scottish foe.[2] Lynn men were soon being drawn even further to the East. Thomas Bubbe shipped a cargo of rye from Prussia to the Wash port in 1371, though he had to seek buyers in Norway, and he was "probably only one of many such".[3]

St Nicholas Chapel in Lynn as it appeared in the late 17th century.
Drawn by Henry Bell (1647-1711).

To match Hanseatic advances in ship technology and carrying capacity for trade with the East, the English had been building new types of sea faring vessels. It is possible that native shipwrights in east coast ports observed and adapted the design of German built cogges. The investment by merchants in new and bigger cargo ships was encouraged by the growth of the national cloth industry and the drive for export markets in Europe. Lynn was well placed to benefit from the Baltic trade and Carus Wilson in *Medieval Merchant Venturers* uses a local ship carved on a bench end in St Nicholas Chapel in the early 15th century to exemplify English marine progress:

At the same time a striking advance was being made in English shipbuilding, rendering ocean trade practicable to an unprecedented degree. The single masted vessel with its one square sail, familiar from the days of the Vikings to the fourteenth century, had by the fifteenth century developed into a two or three masted vessel more adaptable to ocean gales, with high pointed bows to resist the buffetings of a strong head sea. Such an English ship was then carved on a pew end in the new church at Lynn, a church described in 1419 as 'that most beautiful chapel of St Nicholas newly built and constructed by the arms of the benevolent'. The ship has two masts; the main is square rigged as of old, but the mizzen has the new three-cornered lateen sail, recently borrowed from the Mediterranean; this greatly facilitated the working of the ship by making it possible to sail nearer the wind. The castles built up at stem and stern are now an integral part of the ship itself, the 'forecastle' being noticeably the higher of the two.[4]

This Lynn ship is clinker built like a cogge, with high deck erections or castles at stem and stern integral parts to resist piratical attacks, but this vessel seems to be arranged for war. Its mainmast has a top castle (with gads or spears) and a conventional square sail which is furled on a yard. There is a forward projecting foremast and a mizzenmast carrying the new type of lateen sail, also furled, as identified by Carus Wilson. As ships increased in size there was a need for improved propulsion hence the adoption of more than the one mast of the 14th century cogge. The sky is decorated with a crescent moon and sun, stars and clouds. In the wavy sea are two fish and a crab. Another bench end from St Nicholas depicts a smaller ship with a single mast; it has a yard and large square sail with a high forecastle. Both carvings can be interpreted as symbols of the commercial success and

Bench ends once in St Nicholas Chapel at Lynn showing two early 15th century ships.

high ranking of the Wash port in England. Had both vessels been made in Lynn? Ship building was already well established in the town as the launch of a royal galley and fitting out of the King's *Grande Cogge* in 1337 tells.

An example of ship graffiti located in the south porch of St Nicholas Chapel

The Kieler Hansekogge which visited the Wash Ports in August 2004 is seen in the river Witham heading towards Boston dock. The author on board.

in 2014 reflects the style and type of ship graffiti inscription found in other Norfolk churches. The vessel appears to be single masted with its sail furled and in full hull profile. It shows striking similarities with the Lynn ships carved on the bench ends described above (once in St Nicholas Chapel) and an early 15th century date seems probable. The graffiti survey also revealed at least one incised merchant mark in the south porch. Porches were the venue for business deals where contracts were signed or agreed verbally and merchant marks may have indicated a desire for a spiritual blessing. Churches dedicated to St Nicholas as the patron saint of merchants and mariners had a special status in Europe's port towns. The new Chapel itself was doubtless built to match St Margaret's Priory Church which was more closely associated with Lynn's unpopular overlord, the Norwich bishop. St Nicholas carried a high spire no doubt to rival that on St Margaret's which likewise provided sailors with a majestic seamark. Lübeck's merchant rulers determined that their parish church or Marienkirche boasted two spires on its twin towers higher than those on the city's cathedral.

There is another picture of a 'Lenn' ship in the historiated initial 'H' of the name Henry in letters patent granted by Henry IV in 1441 to confirm all the town's royal charters since 1204. The image of the vessel is somewhat stylistic as normal in medieval manuscripts, but it has enough realistic detail to indicate that it was clinker built, with cross beams protruding through the hull. The drawing appears to represent a hulk rather than a cogge as its form is similar to the hulk shown on the reverse side of the gold Angelle coin issued by Henry VII in 1489. There is only one mast. The hulk originated in the Low Countries and was usually clinker built like the cogge but broader beamed. It became progressively larger in the 15th century and therefore could carry more cargo than the cogge. It can be said that the cogge and the hulk merged into one composite design with the new vessel having features of both. The rounded form of the hulk was kept but added to it were a broad flat bottom and a strong keel in addition to stern and stem posts.

The Lenn Ship in the historiated initial 'H' of the name Henry in letters patent granted by Henry VI to the town in 1441.

Europe's changing commercial circumstances impacted the shipbuilding industry. The fall in population and consequently in volume of sea traffic in bulk commodities following the Black Death (1348-50) obliged merchants to seek cheaper transport costs as prices fell. However, it took time to introduce the new larger cargo ship or hulk mainly because the investment required was considerable, and older vessels could not just be discarded for economic reasons. In turn, the hulk was the technological predecessor of the caravel, but the latter was skeleton built with three masts and larger than the hulk. In ships constructed using the clinker method the frames or ribs were fitted inside the hull and secured to the overlapping planks. The clinker built ship lacked rigidity the larger the vessel but the carvel method gave ships greater strength because of the internal heavy ribs. It might be useful to quote Dollinger's summary of Hanseatic ship development:

Finally from about 1450 onwards an even larger vessel made its appearance, the caravel (*Krawel*), first built in Mediterranean and Atlantic ports. It was characterised by three masts instead of one, and by a smooth hull, with planks laid edge to edge and no longer overlapping. The caravel allied speed to a greater carrying capacity, at times exceeding 400 tons. It was sheer chance that ensured the success of this new type of ship. In 1462 an exceptionally large French caravel, the *Saint-Pierre de La Rochelle*, was abandoned in the port of Danzig by its captain. Fitted out by the town as a privateer against the English, it created a sensation everywhere by its enormous size, even though it was not a very efficient fighting ship. Other caravels were then built; but up to the seventeenth century the hulk remained the chief type of large Hanseatic ship.[5]

The French caravel mentioned by Dollinger reappears in the next chapter which covers the Anglo-Hanseatic Sea War. It was about 43 metres long with room for 400 soldiers and sailors. The first caravel known to be built in England was the *Edward* in the 1460s at Dunwich in Suffolk.

It is difficult to compare the two Lynn medieval ships discussed above because both are artistic depictions, albeit with realistic elements. The clinker construction and the cross beams of the Lenn ship and the particularly detailed rigging of the St Nicholas ship are authentic enough. The Lenn ship may have been similar to the Newport ship discovered in 2002 on the west bank of the river Usk; the latter was single masted with a clinker built hull fastened by about 13,000 iron nails, and 25 metres in length and 8 metres in width. It was built around 1450 in northern Spain probably over eight or nine months. In 2015 the excavation of three medieval shipwrecks commenced in the river Ijssel near Kampen in the Netherlands. The largest is a 15th century oak built cogge about 20 metres long which was raised in 2016 and currently undergoing conservation. On board divers found the first galley (brick dome oven and glazed tiles) ever discovered on a medieval ship. In 2000 and 2002 two medieval cogges were uncovered by dredgers operating in the construction of a dock at Antwerp. A publication (2012) of the German National Shipping Museum at Bremerhaven concerns the Ebersdorf ship model. The vessel is flat bottomed and clinker built with the characteristic features of the cogges built in the late 14th century. It was probably common practice in Hanseatic shipyards for shipwrights to make a model of the vessel about to be constructed. Historical research and archaeological excavations since the 1940s have been helping to bridge gaps in our knowledge about European medieval ships. Scholars will no doubt continue to debate developments in ship design and the timescale of the implementation of new types of vessel.

II

Lynn's medieval merchants rarely mention ships in their wills and no list of shipowners or vessels belonging to the town is likely to materialise. The extent of its coastal and overseas trade before 1500 strongly suggests a local fleet to equal those in England's other major provincial ports. In 1318 Edward II sent John Griffoun to Lynn to freight for the King "two or three great ships" to transport

Danzig as it appeared circa 1628 from an engraving.

corn and other foodstuffs to Berwick castle.[6] It was seen in chapter one how ship ownership in the Hanseatic towns was normally shared to spread the risks involved in profitable but hazardous seaborne commerce. Lynn's merchants were equally prudent. Owen refers to "the lastage" (on which assessments for royal taxation were based) to show part shares in ships were included amongst a citizen's moveable property. How many merchants were part owners of particular vessels is unknown, but two Lynn men in 1318 took corn and provisions to Norway "with their ship" called the *Kateryn*.[7] An interesting example of shared ownership is the *Maryknyght*. In 1416 it was taken by French pirates near Dunwich and the skipper sought the help of Lynn's mayor for the return of a ship "part of which belongs to merchants of Lynn and part to merchants of Danzig".[8] There were certainly a number of individual owners such as Adam Le Clerk whose vessel *Le Plente* was captured off the Norfolk coast in 1318 by men said to be from the Hanseatic towns. The vessel itself was valued at £100 but the ship and cargo together assessed at £300 (equivalent to £150,000 today).

The Wash ports were the home of considerable cohorts of native mariners who were employed to sail the ships belonging to the merchant class. At Lynn there was a guild of a religious and no doubt charitable character for shipmen or sailors by 1368. The names of Lynn mariners appear in *William Asshebourne's Book* because their vessel had been captured or "pirated" by the King's foreign foes. Of special interest is the entry relating to Robert Furneys, a sailor on *La Margarete* of Lynn, who died in Lisbon in 1416. His widow Agnes had sought the help of the mayor "in recovering her husband's goods".[9] This suggests that the mariners on English cargo ships traded in a modest way on their own account as did their Hanseatic counterparts. On the feast of Corpus Christi in 1461 or 1462 Lynn sailors and skinners were singled out for financial "reward" for their assistance with the procession on the day. Not all mariners on Lynn ships would

The Great Crane at Gdansk today; it was restored after 1945 but follows the design of the 1440s.

have been local men and several nationalities were probably represented on most voyages (Zeelanders, Scandinavians, Germans).

The quality of life at sea in medieval merchant ships left much to be desired. The crew may have had no more than canvas shelters on deck, but the shipmaster and important passengers lived in the stern castle or below the quarter deck. Salted meat and fish with beer were the staple foodstuffs for all on board. Travelling merchants were also provided with water, wine, and lamps. They were often given permission by their hometowns to carry swords for self-defence. A priest was usually on board to implore God's protection when storms or pirates appeared on the horizon and reassure the passengers. Sea sickness was common and sanitary arrangements appalling with buckets on deck or barrels suspended over the ship's side. The environment on board must have been difficult to tolerate. Sometimes the crew and passengers slept ashore and stocked up with fresh water (medieval ships kept as close to the coast as possible). Sailors were armed with daggers and some had crossbows to defend the ship against sea robbers. Thomas Melchbourne, a leading Lynn merchant identified in chapter two, hired a military catapult from the town around 1330 for one of his ships. On occasions a large cross bow would be mounted on a ship's structure and the heavy bolt might even have punched through the hull of 'the enemy'. The sea voyage between the Wash ports and the eastern Baltic was long and dangerous so ships sailed in convoy. German convoys often had a commander appointed by the Hanseatic city whose merchants were involved in the venture. Urban militias (a kind of home guard) from German towns might also be posted on cogges to support crews in war time. The latter were sometimes bonded by family connections with fathers, sons, uncles and cousins from a particular place.

The disruption of the trade routes between East and West by piracy and sea warfare had prompted the Hanseatic cities to sail their ships in convoy. In 1392 the Prussian towns decided that no fewer than ten ships in convoy should sail through the Sound between Denmark and Sweden and around Jutland. Sea wars between the Hanseatic towns and Denmark as well as Holland in the 15th century made the convoy system a logical response to deter the enemy. Hanseatic vessels from the Baltic ports making the annual voyage to south-west France for salt and wine sailed as one big fleet. However, all convoys or

St Mary's Church in Gdansk drawn by Paul Kreisel circa 1925. Building began in 1343 but work was not complete until 1502.

It is the largest of the brick churches built in the Hanseatic cities on the Baltic and reflects civic wealth and pride. St Mary's is said to provide space for over 23,000 people.

fleets were difficult to assemble and manage, nor were they immune from attack by pirates. Skippers who deserted a convoy or missed the date of its departure could be subject to fines or other sanctions. Dollinger says that the convoy system was not only favoured by German merchants as a security measure, but also ensured that they all had "equal opportunity" both as "buyers and sellers".[10] Smaller ships were nevertheless exempt and concessions were negotiated by Wismar and the Prussian ports to avoid the most strict regulations.

A Hanseatic maritime code evolved from the disparate body of regulations or edicts relating to ships, voyages, cargoes and crews, which had sprung from the periodic assemblies of the member towns. One important influence on its development was the Rôles d'Oléron (drawn up about 1300 at Oléron) for use by French wine merchants from Bordeaux and La Rochelle trading with Bruges. It concerned the procedures to be followed in the event of collisions or disputes involving the crew of a vessel. The document was translated into Flemish in the 14th century as the 'Customary of Damme'. It was also written up in Low German and combined with similar guidelines originating in Lübeck and Hamburg. This became known as the 'Waterrecht' or Sea Law of the Hanseatic towns and, by 1500, as the Sea Law of Gotland because Visby was the seat of the highest naval court in the Baltic. In 1614 a Hanseatic maritime code was printed and distributed after approval by a Hanseatic assembly (Lübeck, Hamburg and Danzig were the architects). However, it could not be enforced in full, and there were always variations in practice according to time and place. The towns that remained members of the community tended to administer their own sea law rather than to follow a common path.

III

What kind of country was Prussia in the 14th and 15th centuries when Lynn merchants and sailors were visiting this distant Baltic land? The Teutonic Knights had annexed Danzig and its region into their new state in 1309. In the 1340s they asserted their overlordship through the building of a castle and city walls. However, the Grand Master in his Marienburg fortress (not far to the south of Danzig) gave Prussia internal security, and its towns were allowed to join the Hanseatic community to promote economic development. The Teutonic Order played a key role in the growth of the Prussian towns of Danzig, Stettin, Thorn, Elbing and Königsberg. It owned landed estates from which timber and cereals were marketed through Hanseatic trading networks. From Königsberg in the 1390s the Knights exported furs and wax to Flanders for cloth. The monopoly of minting coins emphasised their political supremacy in Prussia and Livonia. The Grand Master also secured a monopoly of the export of amber used for beads, rosaries, crosses, boxes and candlesticks, but this trade was lost to Danzig by 1454. Danzig took an active part in Hanseatic assemblies from 1361 and in the meetings of the Prussian member towns where its leadership seems confirmed by the claim that "it had to pay the greater part of the costs of all the diplomatic and military undertakings of the Hanseatic League".[11] Funds were raised by the Pfundzoll imposed on maritime trade and shipping through Danzig for the military operations of the German Hanse, though the Teutonic Knights earned local hostility by top slicing this income (they had originally levied the tax). It had been used to finance the war against Denmark which concluded with the Treaty of Stralsund in 1370.

The wars between the Teutonic Knights and Poland with Lithuania in the early 15th century (1414, 1422 and 1431-35) sapped their strength and authority. They were also challenged by the formation of the Prussian Union in 1440; it comprised the gentry and clergy as well as nineteen towns. An uprising in Danzig in February 1454 drove out the Teutonic Knights whose castle was torn down as a symbol of oppression. The city seceded from Prussia and placed itself under the Polish King Kasimir who granted the Danzigers virtual autonomy in 1457. Their red banner with its two crosses was now topped by the golden crown of the Polish King. Population movement from West to East in northern Europe had continued to boost the growth of Danzig and other Hanseatic towns.

Immigrants might be more numerous than natives in the merchant class making these German urban centres open and free societies. By 1400 at least 25 per cent of Danzig's population had come from west of the Elbe and newcomers could quickly rise to prominence in the city. It became the principal Hanseatic haven in the eastern Baltic and supplied grain and forest products to western Europe, with its ships circumnavigating Denmark into the North Sea. Such long-distance carriage of low value bulk cargoes might be possible several times a year for ships sailing between the Prussian city and Lynn. Danzig's vast hinterland served by the Vistula guaranteed its success. Down river came the tar, pitch, flax, hemp and timber much in demand from ship builders in western Europe. Cereals were regularly exported from Danzig to England and

Bales being wrapped for shipment. English and German harbours needed a small army of labourers to operate effectively.
Detail: Josi Amann, 'Allegorie des Handels' (1585).

Flanders too, particularly when there was a poor harvest in the West. Iron from Sweden with copper and lead from central Europe were used as ballast in Prussian ships. English merchants, in turn, found buoyant new markets for their cloth in Prussia and eastern Europe.

Lynn sailors arriving in Danzig in the late 14th century would have been impressed with its great crane, slightly leaning over the Motlawa river. It is first mentioned in 1367. The structure burnt down in 1442 before being rebuilt partly in brick by 1444 (to the design seen today), but much restored due to severe damage in the Second World War. The great crane balanced between two brick towers was used to erect masts on ships as well as for loading and unloading vessels, the power coming from men walking inside two huge wooden wheels. It also served a defence function as one of the harbour gates of the medieval city. Today the great crane is an important part of the Polish Maritime Museum and a strong symbol of the city's historic ranking amongst European ports. Its defences with their gates lined the left bank of the Motlawa but the granaries were built across the river. Here was Granary Island whose many warehouses and yards were often full of goods for export to England and western Europe (cereals, timber, pitch, linen, wax, furs and amber collected from the Baltic shores). Civic officers undertook quality control of imports and exports. The Motlawa was also dug deeper to maintain navigability and its quays remade to facilitate loading and unloading as ships grew in size.

Danzig was an important ship building centre where new methods allowed bigger vessels to be constructed. In 1412 a Hanseatic assembly decreed against the building of ships too large to access some of the more shallow Baltic harbours. At Lübeck the new and great caravels could not navigate upriver from the mouth of the Trave to its quays. Teams of labourers or horses had to pull loaded barges along the route (today the Trave is wider and deeper than it was in the Middle Ages). The Dutch and English purchased ships in Danzig and shared ownership of vessels with German merchants, though Hanseatic assemblies feared more foreign competition. In 1426 a Hanseatic assembly "forbade the sale of ships to foreigners" and this decree was "periodically renewed".[12] Danzig did not comply until 1441, and only fell into line during war time. Building and repairing medieval ships (they needed constant maintenance) was a profitable business. The monopolistic tendencies shown by the Hanseatic towns encouraged both the Dutch and English to invest more in their own marine industries.

IV

Danzigers had become the most numerous Hanseatic merchants in Lynn by the 1370s and 1380s, replacing Germans mainly from Lübeck, and demonstrating that the commercial interests of the Wash port were moving eastwards. Lübeck's overall seaborne trade shrank to some extent between 1368 and 1379, the city probably badly affected by the return of the bubonic plague. Lynn merchants had established footholds in Prussian seaports by the late 14th century, alongside their English counterparts, including Robert Botkesham and Edmund Beleyeter. Botkesham (died 1411) imported timber and pitch from the Baltic and mainly exported cloth to Danzig, Bremen and Dordrecht. Beleyeter (died 1417) imported timber, iron, wax and herring from the Baltic and exported cloth to Danzig and Wismar. English merchants not only exported cloth but sold and distributed it in the Baltic too, particularly from Danzig, so arousing local resentment. The Englanders from the West appeared to be taking charge of Prussia's textile trade! And, moreover, they rented houses and shops in Danzig rather than lodging with German hosts as they were supposed to do. For their part the English were very unhappy that they were denied the same commercial privileges or tax concessions enjoyed by Hanseatic traders in Lynn or Boston. Unsurprisingly, Prussia rapidly emerged as the principal flashpoint of Anglo-Hanseatic economic rivalry.

As Lynn was becoming more dependent on eastern Baltic markets than other English ports, perhaps with the exception of Hull, its foreign commerce was damaged more by Anglo-Prussian conflict. Jenks has emphasised how much

the town's trade from the 1380s was
"pressing inexorably eastwards".[13]
Not only did the Norfolk men
employ their own ships in voyages to
Danzig and beyond, but chartered
vessels from Wismar, Bremen,
Hamburg and Danzig to carry their
exports and imports. They needed
foreign bottoms to help transport all
their cloth, wine, salt, fish, wax, tin
and pewter. Lynn merchants often
formed business partnerships with
fellow townsmen, or even traders
from Hull, as did Robert Brunham,
who exported cloth and corn from
the 1390s (he was probably the son
of John Brunham whose glittering
career in trade and politics he
emulated). But the intermittent
arrests of ships and harassment of
English merchants from the 1380s,
especially in Danzig, seriously

*St George's Guildhall in King Street built in the
1420s by merchants engaged in Anglo-Hanseatic
commerce.
A drawing by Henry Baines (1860).*

hampered Lynn's overseas commerce. Lists of "English losses" in trade with
Prussia (1370-88, 1388-1436 and 1474-91) show that its merchants "usually"
accounted for "about a third" of all damages claimed.[14] Lynn men in the eastern
Baltic catalogued numerous complaints about Prussian embezzlement, robbery
and arrest of their ships.

Trouble for English merchants in Prussia could spring from events in far-
away western Europe. In May 1385 an English royal fleet had attacked and
robbed six Prussian ships in the Zwin or inlet connecting Bruges to the sea
because the Germans were allegedly supporting the King's Flemish enemy. In
July 1385 a meeting of Prussian towns retaliated by ordering the seizure of
English merchandise in Danzig and Ebling and banned all trade with England.
The English Parliament in October 1385 responded by directing the arrest of all
Prussian property from London north to the Wash ports, where most was likely
to be located, and by June 1386 enough had been found to cover English losses
in Prussia. Two Wismar ships were mistakenly seized at Lynn by the mayor and
bailiffs who were ordered "to dearrest" them by the King's council which knew
from "credible persons" that the ships and their masters were "of Wissemere
and not of Sprucia".[15] This serious international dispute involved England and
Prussia but not the Hanseatic towns to the west of Danzig; Lübeck, Wismar and

Stralsund did not come to Prussia's aid. Some English merchants forced out of Danzig went west to Stralsund whose fleet consisted of 300 vessels and where there were a dozen ship building yards.

To take direct action against merchants and their ships to satisfy grievances of whatever kind was not only testimony to the failure of Anglo-Prussian diplomacy; it halted trade, destroyed businesses and sometimes cost lives. Peace was in the interests of both sides. In April 1386 two envoys sent by the Teutonic Order had arrived in London to talk to the King's council, but no compromise was possible on the Zwin incident. Then Richard II decided to send an embassy to Prussia to negotiate a general Anglo-Prussian settlement with the Grand Master of the Teutonic Order. Lynn, London, Colchester, Ipswich, Yarmouth, Norwich, Boston and Hull merchant representatives were called to London in the summer of 1386 to provide information on their losses in Prussia. It was clearly essential that the royal ambassadors to Grand Master Conrad Rothenstein at Marienburg were as fully briefed as possible. Lynn was at the forefront of these preparations. The claim for damages submitted by nineteen of its merchants was about £2,000 (following English arrests in Prussia) which was "the largest of any town" despite being "whittled away" to nearly half.[16] No fewer than ten royal letters were sent to Lynn in 1388 in connection with this Anglo-Prussian affair. It took the King's officials a considerable time to collect the evidence of so many English merchants. In March 1388 York, Beverley, Nottingham, Coventry, Winchester and New Sarum men had also been added to the list of informants.

Two ambassadors to Prussia were appointed: Walter Sibille of London and Thomas Graa of York were merchants assisted by a royal clerk called Nicholas Stocket. They were joined by John Bebys of London who was to act as their "informer".[17] In June 1388 they set sail for Prussia from Lynn on a ship requisitioned into the King's service by the mayor. The considerable cost of the embassy was met from the funds accumulated in Lynn from its recent arrest of Prussian vessels following the King's writ in retaliation for attacks on English ships in Prussia. John Brunham (c1330-1413), five times mayor and six times Member of Parliament for his hometown as well as alderman of the Holy Trinity Guild (1393-1402), had been commissioned by the King's council to transfer these funds from Lynn to London. He duly delivered £340 to the mayor of the capital. The King prohibited English cloth and other exports to Prussia whilst his embassy was on its mission. Lynn, York, Yarmouth (Norwich's outport), Newcastle, Hull, Boston, Colchester, Ipswich, Sandwich, Southampton and Bristol were the ports mainly affected by the ban. From the first the King's council had made it clear to the merchants from these towns that they would eventually have to pay for the embassy to Prussia. They were to be individually assessed on their goods and valuables released by the Prussians once an Anglo-Prussian agreement had been signed.

The English embassy presented its credentials to the Grand Master of the Teutonic Order at Marienburg, on 28 July 1388, and began negotiations with his representatives who consulted the Prussian towns. The Anglo-Prussian Treaty of Marienburg was sealed on 21 August 1388. The urgent need for both Prussian and English merchants to secure satisfactory outcomes to their claims for damages in the courts of their host nations was recognised. Hanseatic privileges in England were reaffirmed by the English whose freedom to live and trade in Prussia was confirmed by the Germans. The treaty was too general and unspecific to give the English the same commercial liberties enjoyed by the Hanseatic merchants in England; there was to be no English kontor in Danzig independent of the local authorities similar to the London Steelyard. Nevertheless, the King's ambassadors had concluded an important international treaty with Conrad Rothenstein, the Grand Master at Marienburg, and England's position in Prussia seemed all the stronger as a result. It is hardly surprising that the English regarded the Teutonic Order as the head of the German Hanse rather than Lübeck!

V

After the signing of the Treaty of Marienburg in 1388 steps were immediately taken by Richard II to ensure that Prussian merchants, whose ships and goods had been arrested in England, had their possessions and money returned. The mayors of London and other towns trading with Prussia had been the custodians of such property. The King reminded his subjects in October 1388 that peaceful commercial operations between England and Prussia required both sides to enact the provisions of the treaty. Moreover, all the English towns with trading connections to Prussia were directed to send at least one representative to London, there to establish exactly what must be done "for ending the matter".[18] The mayors of London, York, Norwich, Boston, Hull, Colchester and Lynn all received the royal letter. York, Beverley, Norwich, Boston, Hull and Colchester were also told to recompense Lynn for bearing the costs of the recent embassy to Prussia. They were obliged to send an official to Lynn to pay John Brunham the amounts for which their merchants had been assessed in proportion to their claims against the Prussians. About twenty Lynn merchants were also assessed to help fund the King's embassy to Prussia. Roger Paxman, John Atte Lathe, Walter Urry, Thomas Waterden, Edmund Beleyeter, John Kempe, John Brandon, Henry Betley and John Lok amongst others reads like a roll call of the town's potentiores. Paxman was mayor in 1381 and 1388 and assessed for a greater contribution than any of his colleagues. York merchants in February and Beverley men in April 1389 had still failed to send their fair share to Lynn and faced the King's "wrath" and large fines as a consequence. To return to

Prussian merchants their goods and money was even more urgent unless "a second dispute" arose between the King and Prussia.[19] By November 1389 even Lynn's potentiores had not returned to Prussian merchants in the town all their confiscated property, although they were in contact with Danzig to resolve such issues. Prussian goods were probably being kept in the undercroft of the Holy Trinity Guildhall on the Saturday Market Place (cloth, iron and coined money kept in chests for trading purposes are mentioned).

In the summer and autumn of 1389, a Prussian delegation travelled to London to check English compliance with the 1388 treaty and assist German merchants to prosecute claims for damages in England's courts. One of the Hanseatic ambassadors visited Lynn, 100 miles due north of the capital, to consult with its merchant rulers. By 1388 a group of Prussian traders was "established" in the town who must have greeted him.[20] The ambassador received gifts of wine and even oats for his horses. However, this Prussian lord returned to London shortly before the feast in his honour at the Trinity Guildhall, having left mayor Paxman and Bishop Spencer waiting. Expenses relating to the diplomatic visit were not inconsiderable, including the time of the Norwich bishop's cook and other servants, though the guests soon consumed the fine repast! Hillen's colourful account of this strange episode when the Prussian diplomat suddenly decided not to prolong his Lynn visit is noteworthy:

> How terrible the disappointment! But the Bishop and Mayor exchanged significant glances; the sympathising guests who were present vigorously attacked the tempting viands, and the feast was consummated, without perambulating the highways and hedges. Truly was it a season of exceptional jollification after all, for 40s. is charged for a pipe of Gascon wine, 11s. 8d. for a series of mysterious culinary operations, and 18s. 4d. for ten quarters of oats—not for the guests, but for his lordship's hungry horses.[21]

This event indicates that Lynn's merchant class did not spend all its time in the Trinity Guildhall conducting business but indulged in banqueting and merrymaking too. At feasts organised by the mayor or alderman of the Great Guild at Christmas and on key anniversaries, music and dancing would have delighted the assemblies, as in the town halls of the Hanseatic cities. When Edward III (1327-77) visited Lynn, his own minstrels entertained both his hosts and distinguished guests in the Guildhall. Sometimes the town paid minstrels from aristocratic houses to enliven special occasions. The mayor also employed his own small band called the waits who played on the streets as well as at civic events. They are first mentioned in 1362 when a fee was paid to the "wayte", Johannen de Boys, and town records for 1388 refer to payments to other waits.

They would surely have been present at the feast prepared in June 1388 in honour of the Prussian ambassador who left Lynn in a hurry.

Once commercial intercourse between England and Prussia resumed, it was the islanders from the West who proved themselves the energetic entrepreneurs, as they again dominated the import of cloth and its distribution in that Baltic land. Some brought their families from London and England's east coast ports to Prussian towns where they rented houses and shops. Single English traders sometimes married German women. All this activity did not directly impact on Lübeck and the Hanseatic towns in the western Baltic, but it engendered Prussian hostility. The English were taking full advantage of the vague provisions of the 1388 Treaty of Marienburg which could be interpreted to grant them similar rights in Prussia exercised by the Germans in England. Lynn merchants led the English pack in this penetration of the Baltic despite the troubles they had recently endured there. The commercial rewards were clearly too enticing for the Norfolk men to hold back from voyaging to Prussia, but their daring deserves respect:

> Undeterred, many of these men continued to trade there and figure prominently in the surviving customs particulars of the 1390s, which prove that the town was staking its prosperity on the Baltic and Norway markets. Between 1 April 1390 and Michaelmas 1391 forty-three of Lynn's own ships entered the port with cargoes from foreign parts; eight brought wine from Gascony, five salt (probably from the Bay) and two lampreys; this leaves two from Norway with stockfish (£653), four from Skania with herrings (£1,355) and twenty-two with general Baltic goods (£1503). But the town's own ships by no means sufficed to carry all the goods imported by its merchants and they had to charter an even larger number of foreign vessels for their exclusive, or nearly exclusive, use.[22]

For Prussian merchants the Norfolk town remained an attractive destination too. Ships from "Dantzig" were far more frequently seen in the Wash port (1392-5) than those from other Hanseatic towns.[23] Between 13 and 16 August 1398, ten vessels from Prussia and the Wendish towns moored in Lynn's river and sailed again in convoy on 1 September "probably" for the Baltic.[24] It can be seen how the Wash ports experienced short periods of heightened riverside activity between the arrival and departure of Hanseatic fleets.

Political events in England during the 1390s had nevertheless alarmed all the Hanseatic towns, particularly attempts to impose new taxes on German merchants, and this prompted the Prussians to curb English penetration of their country. Lynn's overseas trade was badly affected by the mass arrest of English ships in Danzig between February and August 1396. In 1398 the Grand Master officially quashed the 1388 Treaty bowing to the pressure of the Prussian towns. All English merchants were ordered to leave Prussia within a year, but this was not enforced. Henry IV came to the English throne in 1399; his military exploits in Prussia in 1390 had won the admiration of his German hosts. By confirming German commercial privileges in the kingdom on his accession, he allayed the fears of most Hanseatic towns, but many Prussians had lost patience with the English:

> The only group clamouring for retaliation was the one which would have welcomed any opportunity for a quarrel, the Prussians, and the measure of retaliation upon which they decided was the one which they would have taken in any case: the curtailment of English trade in Danzig. In February, 1398, Prussia officially terminated the treaty with England; in 1396 the diet of Prussian towns had decided to restrict the English rights of residence, and in 1402, when the conflict passed into an acute stage, the rules against the English settling with 'wife and children' and trading with foreigners, or in the interior of Prussia, were singled out for immediate enforcement. The Prussian towns also tried for years to organise a boycott of English cloth. At first these attempts failed through the indifference of the other parts of the Hanse, but in the end the other towns were won over. It was English piracies that decided the attitude of the non-Prussian towns. The prevailing tension provided a good incentive for mutual attacks on the high seas, and the English did not confine their exploits to Prussian shipping alone.[25]

English piracy was undermining Anglo-Hanseatic relations, but Lynn merchants were not slow to accuse German traders of acts of violence and robbery. In 1397 John Brandon and Thomas Cok complained that they had been "spoiled of their goods and merchandise" in Prussia by men from Lübeck, Wismar, Rostock and Stralsund. Their men and servants had also been imprisoned in Stralsund until the merchants had paid fines for their release. Brandon and Cok identified Mercnard Stenehorst and Bertram Fanhalter amongst other "malefactors" from those towns, and "several persons to whose hands their goods have come are in different parts of England".[26] The latter were apparently in Boston, Lynn and Yarmouth. The commissions of the peace in Lincolnshire and Norfolk were to investigate and arrest the guilty parties. Brandon had also apparently secured royal permission to exact reprisals. In June 1404 the magistrates at Stralsund wrote to Henry IV demanding compensation for Brandon's outrages and the seizure (in November and December 1397) of significant quantities of wine, herring and timber from its ships. The mayor of the Baltic port had already retaliated by imprisoning English merchants in that city where they may have been residents.

John Brandon was a feisty and formidable merchant who had made Lynn his home and acquired property in the town. His trade with Calais, Norway and Prussia included cloth, corn, malt, hides, dyestuffs, soap, pitch, timber and fish. Brandon's political clout is reflected in the fact that he represented Lynn in two Parliaments and benefited from royal office as a collector of customs. With Bart Sistern and John Snailwell he was in that trio of trustees of the charter granted by Henry IV in 1406 to the Guild of St George, which later built the magnificent Hall seen in King Street today. In 1400 Brandon had gone to sea on the King's command with six ships to fight the Scots though Hanseatic vessels did not escape his attention. He emerged as an English champion of retaliatory action against the German Hanse as diplomacy again gave way to violence. Brandon seized a German ship at Boston and launched assaults on Hanseatic bottoms in the North Sea deploying four vessels. No fewer than ten ships from Cley and Cromer in north Norfolk were also licensed by the Crown as privateers to hunt Prussian vessels to compensate for English losses in the Baltic. Lynn men apprehended a ship belonging to the Teutonic Knights which they claimed the Scots had taken, but this act soon "led to reprisals against Lynn merchants in Prussia".[27]

Between 1402 and 1404 the English were responsible for "a minimum" of fifty-eight or fifty-nine attacks on Hanseatic vessels involving ships from northern ports such as Hull as well as East Anglian harbours.[28] German ships were doubly vulnerable if they were suspected of carrying the merchandise of England's Scottish and French enemies. The spark was the refusal of the Grand Master of the Teutonic Order to stop his subjects trading with Scotland when requested by Henry IV. The financial losses incurred by Hanseatic merchants in this short "undeclared sea war" undertaken by the English were substantial. For the Prussians the English attacks on their merchant ships from Scotland to the Channel was blatant piracy and John Brandon of Lynn the chief culprit. An 'official fleet' assembled in 1402 under Admiral Lord Grey assaulted German ships in a Scottish port but there was no royal navy. The King was more dependent on the merchants and ship owners from England's east coast towns to fight his foreign foes. Brandon and his like saw themselves as the vanguard of a robust naval policy to protect the commonweal. There were moreover the freebooters without any royal commission who attacked French or German vessels on the high seas. Yet Henry IV opposed violent and indiscriminate assaults by his subjects on Hanseatic ships. He initiated the diplomatic exchanges in 1403 which brought about an Anglo-Prussian truce and the resumption of trade in 1404. The king ordered that Hanseatic merchandise taken by the English should be restored to their owners and compensation paid for the goods and vessels which had been destroyed. This was naturally to be a bilateral agreement with the Prussians whereby Englanders who had suffered similar losses in the Baltic would also be compensated.

A Hanseatic assembly at Lübeck in 1405 showed solidarity with Prussia in its quest to exact damages for commercial losses following English attacks on its ships, and some cities even demanded a halt to trade with England, but a boycott could not be enforced because the Hanseatic towns had diverse interests. London was an important market for the wine and industrial goods of Cologne and the Rhineland towns which imported English cloth. The Dutch towns associated with the German Hanse were strong trading partners of the English too; nor did all Prussians wish to cut profitable economic ties with England. The King's promise to take firm action against English mariners for attacks on Hanseatic vessels helped to maintain diplomatic exchanges. An English embassy was sent to Prussia in May 1405 and arrived at Marienburg on 8 August. A provisional peace treaty was agreed with the Hanseatic towns whereby the embargo on trade was lifted and compensation claims were to be settled within a year, even if challenging to implement, and success was limited. On 15 December the English ambassadors addressed Hanseatic delegates at Dortrecht in the Netherlands and the truce was further extended. An important step forward came in 1406 when the Germans were granted exemption from the tunnage and poundage taxes on foreign traders to England which had been reinstated in 1401. These taxes on general goods and wine passing through the ports had been introduced in 1347 as an emergency measure to raise funds for Edward III's war in France. The subsidy was reintroduced for short periods in 1371 and again in 1382 as it became a permanent part of the King's revenue rather than a temporary wartime tax.

VI

William Asshebourne's Book can be found in the Borough Archive at Lynn's Town Hall. It is a small volume, of parchment in a hide cover. It was the private memorandum book kept by the council's chief clerk for around a decade after 1408 when Asshebourne left the service of the Norwich bishops for that of the town. The book is peppered with important references to Lynn's domestic and international politics and thus of immense value. Asshebourne played a key role in the Town Hall and dealt with correspondence (packed in barrels with other fragile items) coming and going by ship. He was obviously competent in Latin and Low German which was then closer to English and understood by many in East Anglia. Asshebourne would have read letters written in Latin or Low German to Lynn's council in what was described as "the mother tongue" of English. Subsequent town clerks required such skills to translate letters from the Hanseatic towns and Denmark. It should however be noted that literacy amongst the potentiores was high and many were conversant with Low German and even Latin.

Asshebourne's tenure coincided with that dramatic period in Lynn's history when it was in the forefront of English commercial activity in the Baltic. He copied into his book a letter sent by Lynn merchants living in Danzig to "your worships" containing the ordinances "recently" drawn up by the English Company.[29] A significant segment of "the English nation" resident in Danzig in the early 15th century, the traders, apprentices, servants, women and children, was from the Wash port. Henry IV's letters patent in 1404 empowered English merchants in Prussia, Scandinavia and "the Hanse regions" to form their own machinery of government and justice. Those living in Danzig had drawn up (or revised) ordinances or regulations to govern their community as a result. In the letter to their hometown Lynn merchants requested it endorsed them under its seal without which there would be "worse government" than previously "among the young men"[30] Similar letters must have been dispatched to England by London, Hull and Yarmouth traders amongst others. The bad behaviour of some members of the English communities in Prussia and Scandinavia was clearly a big issue, the focus being on apprentices and servants guilty of fighting, gambling and womanising. Procedure for making a complaint against a fellow trader and settling grievances was inevitably another. A general court was to be held every two weeks. The English Company in Danzig was to be overseen by a committee of twelve headsmen holding office under its seal for one year. Henry IV championed good governance in English mercantile communities in northern Europe in recognition of the crucial importance of international trade for his kingdom. This royal agenda was naturally shared by Lynn's potentiores who petitioned the Crown for the endorsement and revision of the letters patent of 1404. The latter were confirmed by Henry IV's grandson, Henry VI, in 1428.

Although the Danzigers knew that trade with western Europe was fully

Henry IV in his royal robes receiving a book in 1408. He spent nine days in Lynn in 1404 and probably discussed Anglo-Prussian affairs with its merchant rulers.
The Royal and Ecclesiastical Antiquities of England (London 1842).

consistent with their commercial interests, some feared foreign colonisation. An official English Company was only grudgingly allowed at best; it seemed like a step towards the establishment of a kontor with the economic and political clout of the Hanseatic Steelyard in London. In the Treaty of Marienburg (1388) the English in Danzig had requested recognition of their corporate organisation but the Prussians had blocked it. They were never allowed to occupy an autonomous commercial and residential headquarters in the city. A meeting hall called the 'English House' was accepted but English traders complained in 1404 that the Danzig authorities forbade them organising a governing assembly. Indeed, Anglo-Prussian relations had broken down to the extent that English merchants in Danzig were threatened with expulsion (in 1402 and 1404), although those married to German women could remain longer. In 1404 the Prussians also curtailed their freedom to trade, including access to the interior and dealing with other foreign merchants. The English were denied doing business in the trading hall which other nationalities used. Dutch and Flemish men were likewise unpopular in Danzig and their activities subject to strict regulation. Despite this portrayal of xenophobia and commercial rivalry in Prussia, both home and foreign merchants did business together and formed close friendships. Some English merchants in Danzig appear to have lived in the private houses of their German counterparts. This could not only be a convenient business arrangement but probably encouraged by the city council keen that foreign merchants were closely observed.

VII

Henry IV tried hard to improve Anglo-Hanseatic relations which had largely been undone by the consequences of his war with the Scots and French. Prussia was central because England's overseas commerce was more interwoven with that far away country than other Hanseatic regions. Trade also generated the wealth which English medieval kings taxed to support their military campaigns against Scotland and France. Henry IV had initiated diplomatic exchanges between England and Prussia which demonstrated that both countries desired peace. Prussia's overlord, the Grand Master sitting in his Marienburg fortress, was jogged by regional political problems to curry favour with Henry IV. Pagan tribes on his eastern border were in a state of unrest and the kingdom of Poland was asserting its power in eastern Europe. Henry IV was himself a member of the Teutonic Order and saw an opportunity to conclude a treaty with Prussia alone; Lübeck would be excluded and the Hanseatic community divided. Diplomatic activity between England and Prussia intensified with further progress possible by 1407. The conference venue was the The Hague rather than Dordrecht in the Netherlands which had been proposed earlier. England would address Prussian claims for compensation for damages springing from the recent naval conflict, and promised to deal with them first, before those from other Hanseatic towns.

A Lynn merchant called John Brown looms large as a representative of both his home town and the King in Anglo-Hanseatic diplomacy. Trade with the Baltic cities made the town's merchants the experts in this branch of English foreign affairs as Jenks observes:

> Every single English embassy which negotiated with the Hanse in the 15th century included a Lynn merchant. Indeed, in 1408, Henry IV ordered Lynn to send a delegation post haste to the council in London, since Prussian delegates had arrived and, as the King said, 'The men of Lynn understand commerce in Prussia better than any other merchants of the realm'.[31]

Following English piratical attacks on Hanseatic ships, Brown travelled to Prussia in June 1404, with an apologetic royal letter to the Grand Master requesting time for relations to mend. In 1405 he took Henry IV's letter to Prussia granting his merchants in northern and eastern Europe the power to elect a governor and he may have "already been nominated governor".[32] In August 1406 Brown was appointed by 'the Mayor and Commons of Lynn' to negotiate with King Henry of Denmark about the privileges of English merchants visiting his territories, with the request that "all merchants of Lynn who go regularly to the various parts of King Henry's realms, and to Prussia and the Hansa, to assist him as best they can".[33] In May 1407 Lynn's council appointed him as its representative in an embassy to Prussia and the Hanseatic cities "with full authority to negotiate and make agreement on the town's behalf".[34] Brown's first stop appears to have been The Hague at a conference with Hanseatic delegates about the compensation claimed by both sides for damages arising from the arrest of ships and confiscation of goods. In March 1408 Lynn's Baltic traders agreed to pay Brown's travel costs on the embassy "to Prussia and the Hansa" by a levy "of fourpence on every poundsworth of merchandise despatched by Lynn merchants from the port to Prussia" totalling over £103.[35] In January 1409 he was again promoting good relations with foreign merchants by acting on behalf of envoys of the German Hanse in meetings with the King's council. Surprisingly, Brown was supported by John Brandon, the Lynn merchant who had once been its enthusiastic opponent. No doubt because of his frequent absences abroad, Brown took little part in local government at home, though he engaged in trade in a modest way. He died circa 1422, almost certainly at his house in Norfolk Street.

English merchants pressed for a settlement to facilitate international trade despite Anglo-Prussian differences. Probably in 1408 they petitioned the King (who was exchanging letters with the Teutonic Knights) to remember that corn "is now scarce in England" and the Prussians possessed ample supplies but had not "so far allowed export to England".[36] In March 1409 Henry IV again took the initiative and invited the Grand Master to send envoys to negotiate a new treaty to settle all outstanding issues between England and Prussia. A draft treaty was agreed by English and Prussian delegates in London in December 1409. Paying compensation for damages and losses claimed by merchants on both sides was the crux of the matter. It seems likely that the King's summons to Lynn's mayor to Westminster "for consultation" over a treaty "with the Grand Master of Prussia" occurred at this time.[37] Henry IV guaranteed payments to Prussian and other Hanseatic merchants who had been demanding compensation for English seizures of their property since the 1380s. The King authorised these payments from his exchequer amounting to around £11,000. He and the Grand Master determined that there would be six instalments between 1409 and 1412. Henry IV was said to feel 'a child of Prussia' because of his affiliation to the Teutonic Knights, but their disastrous defeat by the combined Polish and Lithuanian army at Tannenberg in July 1410 made him hesitant. His compensation payments continued albeit more slowly. No more than 50 per cent of the total had been handed over to the German merchants when Henry IV died in 1413. His grandson, Henry VI, was to pay some of the remaining debts in 1437. The money was always to be refunded by English merchants engaged in Anglo-Hanseatic commerce, although this proved unsurprisingly hard work, and threats of imprisonment were required to force payments to the King's exchequer.

In 1410 the Prussians ratified the treaty Henry IV and the Grand Master had overseen; it confirmed the rights and privileges of Prussian merchants in England and clarified English liberties in Prussia. The English could not only trade directly with home and foreign merchants in Prussia itself but conduct business there overland or by sea with Poland and Russia. The residence of English people in Prussia was also accepted, even if the treaty was less precise on this key issue. For Henry IV and his merchants the 1388 treaty had been surpassed and there seems little doubt that the English "got the better bargain".[38] For the Hanseatic towns outside Prussia the treaty had indeed conceded too much to the English and their consternation was evident. The German Hanse had been divided to England's advantage which had been the King's diplomatic goal. When Henry IV died in 1413 his son, Henry V, endorsed the royal charters in its favour for a fine of forty marks, which must have been welcomed even in Lübeck.

During the peace negotiations described above Lynn took the opportunity to seek bilateral agreements with Hanseatic towns with which it had dealings. That the Norfolk port was negotiating independently rather than having to rely on royal embassies testifies to its prominence. Asshebourne is again a good primary source. In August 1409 Lynn's mayor despatched a letter to the authorities of Wismar and Rostock requesting a meeting in his town or another place to discuss "the differences" between them. The Germans had not responded to an earlier letter, but were urged to reply via Scania "where there are many Lynn merchants who will convey it safely".[39] About the same time John Brandon and John Brown composed a letter sent by the town's mayor to Simon Clawston, town clerk and proctor of Stralsund, "announcing their own coming".[40] *Asshebourne's Book* also includes the copy of a royal letter to Hamburg in 1409 declaring that, following negotiations with the Grand Master of the Teutonic Order, "English merchants would again be encouraged to go to Lübeck, Prussia, and Livonia".[41] This suggests that their ships were sailing as far as Riga and Reval (Tallinn). Russian furs and other forest products would have attracted them to the latter towns in exchange for English cloth.

VIII

The Anglo-Prussian Treaty of 1410 did not stop English traders and ships encountering hostility in Prussia. In August 1412 no fewer than nine Lynn merchants had been "gravely injured" by the arrest of their ship at Kolberg (now Kolobrzeg in Poland), a port with salt pits and famous for its market in salted herring.[42] Overall, however, this period saw Anglo-Hanseatic trade buoyant as English and German merchants made the most of their opportunities. *Asshebourne's Book* contains an entry indicating how the traders in Lynn's extensive hinterland had a strong interest in keeping the wheels of Baltic commerce turning. In 1416 John Porter of Chelsworth in Suffolk was in the town when he was assessed for national taxation on his moveable property. Amongst his possessions were two barrels of potash (ashes for dyeing), fifteen barrels of osmund (iron), four pieces of wax weighing 100 pounds, 200 Prussian canvasses, 150 wainscots (oak boards or panels) and five saddles of Bremen work. Chelsworth is near Lavenham (about sixty miles from Lynn) in what was the Suffolk cloth manufacturing belt. In all probability John Porter had brought Suffolk cloth to the Wash port for export to Prussia in exchange for Baltic goods. Gottfried and other writers have shown that increasing quantities of cloth were reaching Lynn from Bury and Suffolk's industrial towns in the course of the 15th century.

Events in the daily lives of Lynn people in Danzig in 1416 crop up in *Asshebourne's Book* too. Armed with a letter of attorney, John Maumpas, merchant and burgess of Lynn, appointed Richard Bringer and Thomas Burgh, two English merchants "frequenting" Danzig, to recover a debt of over £43 from his kinsman, John Maumpas, "who also frequented Danzig".[43] Robert Usher was a Lynn mariner employed in the Baltic by various traders from his hometown and involved in a case of mistaken identity over the abduction of a woman in Nottingham. John Brown, John Brandon, John Wesenham, John Waterden and Robert Sarum all confirmed his presence in Prussia at the time of the crime. Such merchants took their apprentices from Lynn to Danzig for what might be described as 'on the job training' in a foreign country. These young men were sometimes presented by their masters before Town Hall congregations to receive the borough freedom. In 1434 Thomas Spicer successfully claimed the borough freedom for his apprentice, Robert Paschelee. Evidence of English artisans working in the Baltic comes from a licence granted in 1373 to a York bowyer to send six apprentices to Prussia for four years to fashion bows for export. Bow staves were regularly imported into Lynn from Danzig

A medieval window in King Street where Lynn merchants were building houses on claimed land on its western side in the 14th and 15th centuries.

and there may have been similar arrangements involving Norfolk craftsmen on working tours in Prussia.

A not inconsiderable number of English people were passengers on merchant ships sailing to and from the Hanseatic cities on the Baltic by 1400. Sailors, apprentices, servants and families were temporary residents in Danzig and other east German towns. Some may have settled there permanently. A valuable insight into Anglo-Prussian connections in the 15th century comes from The *Book of Margery Kempe*, believed to be the first autobiography written in English. Margery (c1373–1440) was the daughter of John Brunham (whose elevated position in Lynn has already been noted) and the wife of another merchant called John Kempe. Her book might be described as a celebrity memoir of one of medieval England's most charismatic women. After fourteen pregnancies she rebelled against bourgeois convention following a series of visions or "revelations" which transformed her life into that of a Christian mystic with a nationwide reputation. Margery became notorious for weeping and screaming in public places as she experienced divine communication. Margery cried for mankind and Christ's passion. One of her sons was an overseas trader who had apparently once lapsed into a promiscuous existence. In 2015 Professor Sobecki of Groningen University found a letter in a Gdansk archive which substantiates Margery's account of his presence in the city. Margery undertook three extremely challenging pilgrimages to Jerusalem and Santiago as well as to the Baltic shrines.

A late medieval house being demolished in King Street in 1827.
The premises ran down to the river.

It seems certain that Margery's (eldest?) son in Danzig was John Kempe who had married a German woman. In the summer of 1431 both husband and wife travelled overland to England to visit Margery and conduct business at Lynn. He carried a letter from the Danzig council requesting the English authorities assist him in recovering a security of fifteen Prussian marks he had paid to a Danzig merchant on behalf of Robert Prinart of Boston. The latter cannot be identified but John Kempe may have journeyed to Boston to find him for reimbursement. His mother, Margery, was well known in the Lincolnshire port as a holy and blessed woman. Sobecki presents a sound case that Margery had dictated part of her life story to John who wrote in Low German. This could, however, have occurred on a previous visit he had apparently made to Lynn in 1430; he had already responded to his mother's scolding for his past immoral behaviour by going on pilgrimage and returned a reformed character. Unfortunately, John fell ill in Lynn and died in August 1431. Margery's German daughter-in-law stayed in Norfolk for eighteen months before deciding to return to Danzig. Although Margery was about sixty years of age with a deep fear of the sea, she escorted her daughter-in-law to Prussia, sailing from Ipswich. Margery remained in Danzig for five or six weeks before being accompanied on a pilgrimage to Wilsnack via Stralsund. She endured a very difficult and hazardous journey back to England through Aachen and Calais. Shortly before her death Margery's life story partly dictated to her son was rewritten more professionally by her confessor, Robert Spryngold, the parish priest at St Margaret's. The manuscript we have today in the British Library was written by a monk at Norwich Cathedral Priory. This was Richard Salthouse whose *Book of Margery Kempe* was discovered in 1934.

In the early 15th century Danzig was an expanding port town of approximately 15,000 inhabitants attracting immigrants from western Europe. It was also a manufacturing city with a profusion of craft guilds which played a significant role in local society but "the merchants were the group of people who brought most glory to Gdánsk and made it famous internationally" whilst "acquiring the greatest influence in the city".[44] The English settled mainly in the district called the 'Long Gardens' near Grobla Angielska (the 'English Dam'). They would have been familiar with the Artushof or Merchants' Exchange, built in the 14th century, and remodelled in 1552. Urban markets and fairs were naturally frequented by foreign traders in Prussia. In the late 14th century Danzig had several weekly markets specialising in fish, vegetables, bread and clothes. Since before 1300 its annual fair had taken place on the feast of St Dominic (5 August) when foreign merchants could engage in free trade. English, Dutch, Spanish and French dealers mingled with Russians and Germans at this annual 'Dominikmart' where they could stock up for autumn shipments to the West. Danzig could, however, be a turbulent city. In 1363 conflict between Germans and Poles had erupted at the Dominican Fair, with the latter targeting the Teutonic Knights in their rallying cry, but "the Poles were beaten and many perished".[45] At this time the Poles numbered not more than 10 per cent of Danzig's inhabitants, although its Slavonic population increased in the 15th century through immigration from the countryside. In June 1416 townspeople attacked and demolished the Town Hall as the symbol of the power of the despised German patrician families who sought the protection of the Teutonic Knights. The status quo ante in Danzig was restored through the intervention of the German Order in 1417.

IX

When Henry V died in 1422 the charters granted by English Kings to the Hanseatic towns once again came up for renewal. Unfortunately, disputes between German and English merchants continued to harm relations, nor had the provisions of the 1410 treaty been fulfilled. In 1415 Henry V had fobbed off two envoys from Danzig sent to London by the Grand Master to seek payment of 10,000 marks that he had promised to pay the Prussians. Trouble was guaranteed when merchants at the London Steelyard refused to pay the tax on imports and exports called tunnage and poundage. After Agincourt Henry V had been granted the subsidy for life and it was continued from 1422 to benefit the new King, but this time English merchants were exempted. For the Hanseatic merchants this imposition constituted a breach of their commercial liberties conferred by royal charters. Some were temporality imprisoned for contumacy. This sparked anger at the Lübeck Assembly in July 1423 with demands that English merchants in Hanseatic towns be imprisoned too. Almost all were in Danzig and Stralsund. In 1422 Danzig's authorities had already imprisoned twelve Englanders until they paid a poll tax. In 1424 they tried to impose restrictions on English freedom to trade in Prussia by forbidding movement outside the ports. Dollinger says that the English 'factory' had been closed in 1420, though its merchants remained organised with an elected alderman. Lynn men were clearly amongst the English traders visiting or resident in Danzig at this time and said "to have numbered fifty-five".[46] The Prussian towns refused to implement the most severe measures recommended by Lübeck against the English because international trade was too important to lose but their maltreatment in Prussia had repercussions back home. On 12 October 1424 over thirty Lynn merchants meeting at the Town Hall raised £20 to support the campaign in Parliament and the country against the renewal of the Hanseatic privileges.

The London Steelyard warned Lübeck that German commercial liberties in England could be lost unless decisive action was taken. The Hanseatic capital was certainly in contact with Lynn because a letter (contents unknown) from there was read to the above congregation at the Town Hall on 12 October 1424. Present were merchants like Thomas Brigge and Andrew Swanton who had represented the town in the Parliament of December 1420. Such Norfolk men were naturally acquainted with Anglo-Hanseatic politics and knew how to influence the King's government. In 1413 Lynn's two representatives in Parliament had been asked to petition against "certain dubious practices" of Prussian and Southampton merchants and took with them a copy of Henry IV's charter to the German Hanse!

War between Lübeck with the Wendish towns of the German Hanse and Denmark (1426-35) again threatened English trade with the Baltic. To sail around Jutland exposed both English and German ships to great danger before Lübeck blockaded the Sound, that narrow strait between Denmark and Sweden. In 1428 some English ships ran the blockade to bring salt and cloth to Danzig where English merchants retained a degree of commercial liberty. That Anglo-Prussian differences persisted is clear from a congregation of the mayor and merchants at Lynn, in February 1428, when they heard "the contents of a letter sent from the merchants of Prussia with various complaints", presumably against men from the Norfolk port. A town merchant called John Saluz was chosen to travel to London "to pursue these matters" with the King's government.[47] In December 1428 the Grand Master of the Teutonic Order allowed the English in Danzig to elect an alderman as Henry VI (1422-61) ratified their right to establish a company with self-governing powers. On his accession the King was an infant whose aristocratic guardians constituted a council to direct the nation's affairs. The compensation payments to Prussian traders promised by Henry IV in 1409 had still not been paid in 1429 when Prussian envoys were in London.

The English government came to the conclusion that Hanseatic trade was too important to lose. Henry VI's council demanded the harassment of German merchants cease and finally confirmed their long held commercial privileges in 1430. Hanseatic merchants clad in red velvet had been riders in the coronation procession when the boy King was crowned at Westminster in November 1429. An embassy sent by the King to Denmark and the German towns to repair relations included John Saluz who reported its "deeds" to the mayor and his fellow merchants at Lynn in December 1431. Such manoeuvres did not end the unrest between the Norfolk town and Prussia. In the summer of 1432 merchandise taken from a Prussian ship in Lynn had been "conveyed" to three private quays, including that belonging to John Saluz! A congregation at the Town Hall agreed that those "who had this merchandise in custody should swear not to pass it off as part of their own goods".[48] During the war between Denmark and the Wendish towns led by Lübeck, English and Dutch merchants suffered losses due to piracy, and attacks on their ships by both protagonists. Henry VI's council had ordered the arrest of Hanseatic vessels in 1432 as a result. The English singled out the Bergenfahrer (men from the Wendish towns involved in the Norway trade) as the main culprits. The Germans feared that the English would take advantage of their conflict with Denmark to win a greater share of the lucrative fish market at Bergen. Boston was far more dependent on the Bergenfahrer than Lynn and therefore bound to be adversely affected. The Danes had indeed taken Bergen in 1427 in what had been a major setback for Lübeck and the Wendish towns.

A Hanseatic assembly was called in 1434 to resolve German disputes with Spain, Denmark, Flanders, Holland and England, indicating that the community was facing formidable international challenges, with the latter nation paid special attention. In 1434 German traders in England were subjected to higher import duties to force them to pay compensation for English losses in the Baltic. The Hanseatic assembly announced a trade boycott of England until rapid progress was made on settling the differences dividing them. The Grand Master of the Teutonic Order sent a letter to Henry VI emphasising that English merchants must leave his country in six months if Hanseatic privileges in England were not protected. Significantly, he sent copies of this letter to London and Lynn, suggesting they joined forces with York to apply pressure on the English government to reach an agreement. The young Henry VI was in Lynn in the spring of 1434 on route to the Shrine of Our Lady at Walsingham and his advisers probably conferred with local merchants on Prussian affairs. When English and German envoys met at the Carmelite Friary in Bruges in May 1435, Lynn's mayor, Thomas Burgh, a merchant who knew the Baltic well, headed the "officially accredited" small English team.[49] English grievances and claims for damages against "the Duche Hanse" were to be tabled. That Lynn was again top of the list of complainants is inferred by Burgh's leading role. He was accompanied by two assistants or proctors, the merchant Walter Curson and the town clerk John Bampton, who carried letters from the town detailing the grievances of local merchants trading with the "Duche Hanse" and Prussia, with the request for compensation to cover their losses. Travel expenses were paid by Lynn's Baltic traders through a levy on their overseas transactions. In March 1436 Curson acted again as proctor for Lynn's merchants at Calais and read out letters from the Hanseatic towns to the assembled burgesses at the Trinity Guildhall on his return. He spent most of his time involved in municipal

Henry VI (1421-1471).
Artist or workshop unknown. Oil on oak panel circa 1520-40.

In 1434 he visited Lynn where Anglo-Hanseatic trade and politics were always high on the agenda of its merchant rulers.

affairs but was the son of a merchant who had traded with Prussia. He lived on Damgate (Norfolk Street) close to the Tuesday Market Place where he leased two shops.

The Bruges conference in 1435 did not improve Anglo-Hanseatic relations. In 1436 the Crown issued licences to merchants and shipowners "to resist the King's enemies at sea" which encouraged men from the east coast ports to take the opportunity to raid German shipping. Vessels from London, Lynn, Hull and Ipswich went into action. The search for a peace formula came closer when a Hanseatic delegation arrived in England in October 1436, led by Danzig's mayor, Henry Vorrath. Long meetings with the English negotiators followed before the Treaty of London was signed in the capital in March 1437. Although the existing trading rights of the Germans in England and the English in Hanseatic territories were confirmed, the agreement was both general and ambiguous, particularly on the matter of taxation (it was written in Latin). Did it or did it not give the English immunity to new taxation in the Hanseatic towns? Vorrath had no intention to extend English liberties in Prussia and Lloyd concludes that the treaty did not bring them the advantages sometimes supposed:

The Hanseatic privileges in England were confirmed and they made certain legal gains. English rights in Hanseatic territories were confirmed but, except for the dubious matter of taxation, were not increased. For the first time the principle of reciprocity was acknowledged by the Hanse as a whole, but since the English were concerned chiefly about trade in Prussia and the eastern Baltic this was not a significant advance. All in all this was hardly the great victory of English diplomacy and determination which it is generally claimed to have been. [50]

The English, nevertheless, interpreted the 1437 treaty as giving them reciprocity or economic concessions similar to those granted to the Germans in England. The latter were to be exempt from tunnage and poundage on their imports and exports which had so irked the Hanseatic towns. The Treaty of London was accepted by the German Hanse as a whole, but the Prussians demonstrated their discontent once Vorrath had returned home in March 1438. He received a frosty reception. The Prussians were dismayed with the terms of the peace settlement made on their behalf and insisted that the English had not been granted new trading privileges in the East; they refused to ratify it. In 1438 the Danzigers even warned the Hanseatic towns that England was trying to turn Prussia into an English colony rather like Gascony in south-west France.

Post the Treaty of London the English sailed back to the Baltic believing that the tax concessions to the Germans in England justified their own exemption from local tolls there. Prussian unhappiness was exacerbated by what appeared to be the delaying tactics of English customs officials who favoured native over foreign merchants leaving the ports. The English could therefore take first advantage of the high demand for their cloth in the Baltic following the disruption of the trade. Lynn, Boston and Hull customs officers were implicated. There were reports from Prussia that English traders were being maltreated and their property confiscated whilst trade was interrupted by hostilities between Holland and the German Hanse (1438 - 41). The Dutch had seized twenty-three Hanseatic salt ships returning from France in retaliation for their losses during the war between Denmark and the Wendish towns. The Hollanders had to pay a large indemnity to end the conflict. Thereafter, Dutch and English ships voyaged to the Baltic in increasing numbers, with Lynn's Prussia commerce successfully restarted despite the fact that Danzig bitterly resented the Treaty of London. The Prussians never ratified it, although Lübeck and Cologne urged acceptance, no doubt worried about English cancellation of the Hanseatic franchises.

To offer "some observations" on trade between Danzig and Lynn, Walter Stark highlighted the notebook of a Danzig merchant called Johann Pisz for the years 1421-56. [51] Of more than 200 names of merchants from places across northern Europe, there are about twenty English ones. The English merchants imported salt or 'baien solt' from the Atlantic coast, cloth from East Anglia and Beverley, as well as 'lynen cloth' and canvas. Wax was the main commodity exported by English traders in the earlier period; their second most important export was seal fat, with the brittle Swedish iron (known as Osmund) third. Pisz's book records no transactions in timber and wood products such as ashes and pitch, probably because he did not deal in them. He was acquainted with Richard Schottun, a Lynn merchant in Danzig whose host was Claus Rogge, a leading citizen. The Englander exported wax, iron and timber whose quality led to a dispute between Lynn men and the city authorities in 1439. Schottun was a familiar figure in Danzig. In 1428 he went into partnership with another Lynn man and two other English merchants to buy a ship there, the hulk "Krystoffer". They had to pay the money in good English nobles, in Bruges, by Whitsuntide in 1429. Payment was delayed because of the financial problems of one of the purchasers of the vessel who owed a Danzig merchant a large sum. Schottun was also in debt by the end of 1429 and promised not to leave the city until the money was paid. Stark provides an excellent example of how a Lynn merchant had significant commercial dealings in Danzig at a difficult time in Anglo-Hanseatic relations. Schottun sold cloth, canvas and salt, and "bought timber, wax, iron and a ship", having business partners "amongst the citizens of Danzig", and lived "in the house of a member of the city council" and, moreover, "he had credit — in German: sinen loven"! There is also evidence that Lynn merchants in Danzig issued promissory notes or written promises to pay a sum of money on some future day.

X

Kowaleski tells us that there were significant numbers of European immigrants in England's port towns by 1500, including "the numerous foreign shipmen who made Boston or Lynn their home".[52] So were the English communities in Danzig and Bergen and Bruges in the 15th century mirrored (if on a smaller scale) in the Wash ports by European settlers or residents? For Lynn there is sufficient evidence to answer in the affirmative.

Attempts were occasionally made by the Lynn authorities to jog foreign tradesmen into citizenship, or enrolment as borough freemen, to facilitate both supervision and taxation. In a list of about forty-five immigrants living in the town and district liable to pay a subsidy granted to the Crown in 1440, for sea defences, at least six were identified as "Duchemen" and one "Duchewoman".[53] They appear to be German speakers like Thomas Bower who was a shoemaker living in Chequer Ward (King Street). He can also be found in annual leet court rolls (about neighbourhood policing) when his wife, Marion, assaulted two other German speaking residents. That there was a sizable number of

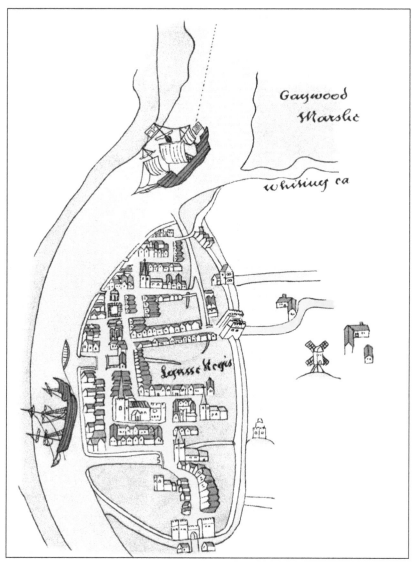

This hand coloured first known map of Lynn (1588) shows the town with its river and defences.

Part of an original map of Castle Rising Chase now in the Norfolk Record Office.

German shoemakers in Lynn in the 1420s and 1430s is confirmed by a court case recorded in the Hall Books (council proceedings). In August 1424 a dealer in Cordovan leather and three shoemakers in the town appeared at the Trinity Guildhall before the mayor accused of false denunciation of German speaking shoemakers. The native craftsmen admitted to having accused them of theft and even high treason initiating a lawsuit in London. The mayor ordered their spokesman, John Draper, to ride at his own expense to London to have the lawsuit quashed, paying the German artisans the cost of the case and accepting a surety of £20 each. Despite what was a high financial penalty or legal safeguard, the Lynn shoemakers paid the money in two days! This is an example of trade rivalry and envy, probably mixed with xenophobia. The German shoemakers may have been former mariners who had settled in Lynn and transferred skills like sail repair. Artisans with German origins were earning a living in other European ports with strong Hanseatic connections particularly cordwainers and coopers.

All together at least eighty immigrants can be identified in Lynn in the 1430s and 1440s, with the majority from the Low Countries (Brabanters, Zeelanders, Hollanders and Flemings). All were men save for Margaret Selander. There are only a few clues carried by surnames with regard to occupational status but John and William Berebrewer are of special interest. They settled in South Lynn, possibly running a brewery on the Millfleet. Kerling argues that these Zeelanders and Hollanders introduced beer to England and their presence in Lynn combined with the importation of hops supports her case. It seems the town's brewing industry largely developed as a result of immigration from the Low Counties. Beer imports into the Wash port from the 1420s consequently fell because of the rise in local production. Hollanders continued to export beer to England but only to Lynn "did they not come" because "the competition of the ale brewed in that town was too great".[54] There were few immigrant women involved in brewing but Alice Hosedowyn from Brabant is recorded as an independent brewer in 1483.

Notes

1. Hybel, *The Grain Trade*, 224.
2. Harrison, *The Close Rolls, 1256-1377*, 456.
3. Owen, *The Making of King's Lynn*, 47.
4. Carus Wilson, E.M., *Medieval Merchant Venturers* (London 1967), 105.
5. Dollinger, *The German Hansa*, 142.
6. Harrison, R., *The Chancery Rolls, The Patent Rolls 1258-1327* (King's Lynn 1992), 55.
7. Ibid., 55.
8. Owen, *The Making of King's Lynn*, 285.
9. Owen, D. ed., *William Asshebourne's Book* (Norfolk Record Society 1981), 98.
10. Dollinger, *The German Hansa*, 147.
11. Biernat, C. & Cieslak, E., *History of Gdansk* (Gdansk 1988), 48.
12. Dollinger, *The German Hansa*, 144.
13. Friedland & Richards, *Essays*, 100.
14. Ibid.
15. Harrison, *The Chancery Rolls 1377-1399*, 82.
16. Lloyd, *England and the German Hanse*, 91.
17. Ibid., 65.
18. Harrison, *The Chancery Rolls, 1377-1399*, 131.
19. Ibid., 143.

20. Owen, *The Making of King's Lynn*, 46.

21. Hillen, *The History of the Borough of King's Lynn*, 174.

22. Lloyd, *England and the German Hanse*, 91.

23. Gras, *The Early English Customs System*, 526.

24. S. Jenks, *England, die Hanse und Preussen: Handel und Diplomatie 1377-1474* (Köln 1992), vol.1, 417.

25. Postan, M. & Power, E., eds., *Studies in English Trade in the Fifteenth Century* (London 1966), 109.

26. Harrison, *The Chancery Rolls 1377-1399*, 223.

27. Lloyd, *England and the German Hanse*, 112.

28. Ibid., 113.

29. Owen, *William Asshebourne's Book*, 71.

30. NRO, 'With Ships and Goods and Merchandise', 6.

31. Friedland & Richards, *Essays*, 101.

32. Lloyd, *England and the German Hanse*, 115.

33. Owen, *The Making of King's Lynn*, 281.

34. NRO, 'With Ships and Goods and Merchandise', 9.

35. Owen, *William Asshebourne's Book*, 80.

36. Ibid., 76.

37. Ibid., 84.

38. Lloyd, *England and the German Hanse*, 122.

39. Owen, *William Asshebourne's Book*, 80.

40. Ibid., 84.

41. Ibid., 75.

42. Ibid., 70.

43. Ibid., 94.

44. Biernat & Cieslak, *History of Gdansk*, 47.

45. Ibid., 64.

46. Lloyd, *England and the German Hanse*, 129.

47. NRO, 'With Ships and Goods and Merchandise', 9.

48. Ibid., 5.

49. Lloyd, *England and the German Hanse*, 144.

50. Ibid., 155.

51. Friedland & Richards, *Essays*, 64-66.

52. Palliser, *The Cambridge Urban History of Britain*, 493.

53. Owen, *The Making of King's Lynn*, 457-59.

54. N. Kerling, *Commercial Relations of Holland and Zealand with England from the late Thirteenth Century to the close of the Middle Ages* (Leiden 1954), 114.

Trade, War, Treaties

I

To help assess the national significance of Lynn and other east coast ports in overseas trade during the 15th century we can refer to an article by Bonney. With the help of computer programming, she derived figures from the Enrolled Customs Accounts for the medieval centuries representing "simply the volume of exports of wool and cloth which were accounted for in the head ports of England".[1] Her work is not concerned with the relative values of wool and cloth or the revenue gathered by the Crown at England's chief or head ports. The latter also oversaw minor ports on the neighbouring coastline (for example Lynn's customs district ran from Wisbech to Blakeney in North Norfolk). The royal clerks at the Exchequer were responsible for extracting the Enrolled Customs Accounts from the more detailed Particular Accounts received from their colleagues in the head ports. Lynn, Boston, Yarmouth, Ipswich, Hull and Newcastle were the principal provincial east coast ports. It is noteworthy that wool exports were greater than cloth in volume until the mid-15th century but, thereafter, cloth became the dominant English export commodity. The total volume of cloth and wool exports in the 15th century did not, however, overtake that reached in the early 14th century when Europe's population was still increasing. A catastrophic end to population and therefore economic expansion arrived with the Black Death of 1348-49 when probably a third of England's inhabitants died.

The general trend of English overseas trade in the 15th century was the loss of business by the provincial east coast ports to London which took a growing share of both wool and cloth exports. The former ports did not experience a marked fall in the volume of wool and cloth exports relative to England's total until the late 15th century, although wool had become "very insignificant" by the 1520s. Cloth exports from these North Sea havens never "consistently" overtook the declining wool exports in terms of volume. London accounted for 51 per cent of English wool exported in the 1440s and 1450s and no less than 71 per cent in the 1540s; the figures for cloth exports show the capital exporting 46 per cent of the national total in 1400-19 but 81 per cent in the 1540s. Bristol and Southampton in the west and south respectively lost market share of the overseas trade in cloth to London (Exeter increased its share a little) as well as the east coast ports. What about the role of foreign merchants and Hanseatic

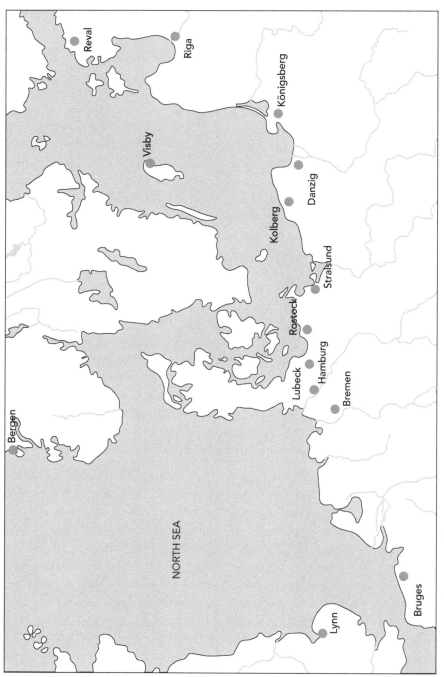

Reval

Riga

Königsberg

Visby

Danzig

Kolberg

Stralsund

Rostock

Hamburg

Lubeck

Bremen

Bergen

NORTH SEA

Lynn

Bruges

Northern Europe demonstrating Lynn's geographical relationship to the chief Hanseatic towns as well as Bruges and Bergen.

ones especially? Referring to a chart indicating exports of English cloth by alien merchants, Bonney concludes:

> An analysis of the groups exporting cloth shows that the trade was in the hands of alien merchants in the periods 1300-19 and 1320-39, but thereafter English merchants always handled over 50 per cent of the trade except in the period 1400-19. However, the share of the foreign merchants remained consistently high after 1400. It is not clear from this chart that Hanseatic merchants enjoyed an almost complete monopoly of cloth shipments along the east coast, although they were the dominant alien merchant group. The period 1380-99 marked the high point of their activity in the east, and even then it only amounted to 12.8 per cent of the total. But the shift of their activities from the east to the south, and in particular to London, can be seen, as their share grew from 10.6 per cent in 1400-19 to 23.8 per cent in 1480-99. By 1540-7, their presence on the east coast was negligible.[2]

Dollinger tells us that in the 15th century cloth comprised "nearly 90 per cent" of Hanseatic exports from England and, in the last quarter of the 14th century, "the quantity of cloth they dispatched was tripled". The German share of the total amount of English cloth (usually undyed) exported "varied between 20 and 30 per cent".[3] Hanseatic trade was also being channelled through London at the expense of the provincial ports. Yet Bonney reminds us that the provincial ports have their own peculiar histories in overseas commerce and rash generalisations should be avoided. The Wash ports whose trading links with the north German towns had been as important as London's should receive special attention.

II

England's interpretation of the 1437 Treaty of London as giving its merchants reciprocity, or similar privileges in Danzig to those possessed by Hanseatic traders in London and Lynn, was highlighted in chapter three. The Grand Master of the Teutonic Order representing the Prussian towns refused to ratify it. The latter feared England's further commercial penetration of the Baltic and denied its merchants had new rights conferred by the treaty. There were reports from Prussia that the English were being maltreated; that their assembly hall had been closed and houses confiscated. The king and Parliament became more impatient with the Hanseatic towns whose taxation immunities in England they threatened to suspend. Anglo-Prussian trade was nevertheless buoyant in the years after 1437. Lynn's exports trebled as English and German merchants shipped cloth to the Baltic region where demand was high. Overall, the Prussia trade of the Wash port "throve" in the decade after 1437 with turnover averaging about £5,000 a year.[4] Danzig was the main destination in the East for Lynn ships and merchants; Danzig's Englandfahrer in turn specialised in commercial intercourse with Lynn and Hull. Boston, Lynn and Hull accounted for 23 per cent of the total of Hanseatic cloth exports from England in 1436-37, but this export surge from the three ports was not sustained through the 1440s, and together they "handled" about 12 per cent of all Hanseatic cloth exports in the decade 1437-47.[5] Despite losing ships to German and Dutch privateers in the approaches to the Baltic during the war between the Hollanders and Wendish towns, English merchants kept trading with the East, and brought grain to England when food prices

The 15th century Hall of the Holy Trinity Guild where Lynn merchants met in their groups or hanses.

were high. Prussian ships had been prohibited from accessing the West around Denmark by Lübeck's blockade against the Hollanders which greatly reduced available shipping space. Between 1438 and 1441 Englanders purchased many ships or shares in ships at Danzig "and complained" in July 1440 when the city tried to stop the sales.[6]

In 1446 Henry VI and his retinue stayed at the Augustinian Friary at Lynn (where his host was Prior John Capgrave) and may have discussed Anglo-Hanseatic affairs with local merchants. The King applied a brake to Anglo-Hanseatic trade in 1447. He issued an ultimatum to the Germans that their privileges in England would be abolished unless English merchants in Prussia acquired similar benefits. For the English this was the crux of the 1437 treaty. No response was forthcoming. As a consequence, Hanseatic tax immunities in England were rescinded in September 1447. Worse was to follow for the German towns in April 1449 when Parliament revived the tax on foreigners engaged in maritime trade called tunnage and poundage. They regarded this charge as contrary to the liberties granted to them by successive English Kings. The resumption of war with France had encouraged Henry VI to despatch an embassy to Lübeck in early 1449 to negotiate an Anglo-Hanseatic settlement. It was still there in April when the English Parliament imposed tunnage and poundage! Progress seemed impossible but diplomats on both sides agreed to meet at Deventer in The Netherlands in May 1451.

Hopes for an Anglo-Hanseatic reconciliation were finally dashed in May 1449 when English privateers captured a great fleet of 110 Hanseatic and Netherlandish vessels in the Channel. It was sailing north from the Bay of Bourgneuf near Nantes transporting wine and salt back to the Baltic which voyage would normally take several weeks (the convoy included sixteen Lübeck and fourteen Danzig ships). The English commander was the Dartmouth shipowner and merchant, Robert Wenyngton, who possessed a royal licence to sail the seas to challenge "the king's enemies". The English ships were fired upon with guns (rarely used at sea) and crossbows and suffered casualties. But their aggressive

The north gate of the Augustinian Friary at Lynn where English medieval kings sometimes lodged.

Thomas Capgrave (1393-1464), friar and historian, lived here.

manoeuvring forced the surrender of the much bigger Hanseatic fleet which was escorted to the Isle of Wight. The Dutch and Flemish vessels were released before the German ships were robbed of their cargoes. The latter seem to have ended up in the warehouses of some of England's most powerful men, including members of the King's government, with premises on the river Thames opposite the London Steelyard! Wenyngton's bold but stupid act of international piracy was almost certainly unplanned, though complicity with important men must have followed, and the national interest sacrificed to private greed. It all smacked of weak or failing central government and the consequence has been summed up by Fudge:

> It would be difficult to find a more important or representative reflection of the Anglo-Hanseatic controversy in the mid-fifteenth century than the seizure of the Bay fleet in 1449. It was a pivotal incident in the course of relations between the Hanse and England, in that it broadened the dimensions of the existing conflict, and remained a source of bitter enmity for two decades. The long-term repercussions were both political and economic. In particular, responses from within the Hanseatic membership came to reflect a number of the fundamental contradictions that would characterise internal Hanseatic politics throughout the second half of the century.[7]

The repercussions springing from Wenyngton's seizure of the Hanseatic fleet in 1449 were serious for England's east coast ports, and for Boston and Lynn in particular, whose overseas trade was largely dependent on Lübeck and Danzig respectively. The Lübeckers stopped trading with England for five years which diminished economic activity at the Lincolnshire haven and, when they returned in 1455, Boston's commerce failed to fully recover. Over 60 per cent of the German merchants in the town were Bergenfahrer mostly from Lübeck.

Lübeck's (perhaps understandable) anglophobia ensured an impasse in Anglo-Hanseatic politics. The large manufacturing city of Cologne was nevertheless impatient to return to normal trading relations with England which was its principal market. At the Hanseatic assemblies at Lübeck and Bremen in 1447 and 1450 respectively the Rhineland city moved a resolution to replace Lübeck as the capital of the German Hanse! The member towns refused to support Cologne. Yet there was growing unrest that Lübeck's refusal to talk to the English was not in the general interest of the community. The leadership of the city on the Trave depended on its ability to work for the commonweal.

III

The Hanseatic towns could not forget their differences in order to confront the English following the attack on their fleet returning from France in May 1449. Cologne and Danzig failed to support Lübeck's insistence that retaliation should be immediate, unless compensation was quickly paid, clearly because they benefited far more from Anglo-German trade. English merchants in Prussia had been arrested and their goods confiscated, but an Anglo-Hanseatic meeting at Bruges in November 1449 avoided a war. Baltic naval stores (timber, pitch, tar, hemp) were as ever too important for England to lose. A truce was agreed to permit Anglo-German intercity seaborne commerce to continue. In December Hanseatic trading rights in the island kingdom were restored by the King though Lübeck and Danzig were excluded. The latter city still offered English ships safe conduct to the eastern Baltic which showed its desire for peace. Another step forward had arrived in October 1449 when the Hanseatic towns were freed from tunnage and poundage, but Lübeck and Danzig had again been excluded. Henry VI finally included the Prussians in this important tax exemption in 1454 to leave Lübeck as the outsider. The English had unsuccessfully pressed the Prussians to ratify the 1437 treaty before making the concession.

In July 1450 Henry VI had sent two ships to Prussia on a diplomatic mission to the Grand Master of the Teutonic Order, led by Dr Thomas Kent, clerk of the King's Council, which included Lynn's Henry Bermingham. Another passenger was the London merchant John Stocker whose cargo of cloth was on board. Only one ship reached Danzig because the other was seized by Lübeck vessels as it entered the Baltic. The English captives (including Kent and Stocker) were taken to Lübeck and put under arrest. In September 1450 the English responded by arresting Hanseatic crews and ships in Lynn, London, Colchester and Ipswich, although they were released by November, save those from Lübeck. Thomas Kent and others were released from prison on parole; they would seek a settlement of Lübeck's grievances in England and return to the city. That Kent in particular turned renegade and failed to return to Lübeck confirmed him in the eyes of the Germans as their arch enemy. Lübeck's precipitant action isolated it still further from Cologne and Danzig which wanted an Anglo-German settlement.

An Anglo-Hanseatic meeting in Utrecht in May 1451 led to an agreement whereby both sides determined to keep trading as Hanseatic privileges in England were restored to the Prussians. Although the historic commercial advantages acquired by the German Hanse were to end in September 1452, they were regularly extended. Only Lübeck of the Hanseatic towns was now excluded from its English franchises. The anticipated early ratification of the agreement in a treaty emboldened both German and English merchants to step up business. The presence of a Lynn man in the English delegation at Utrecht once again illustrated the Prussian interests of the Wash port. This was again Henry Bermingham whose house was by the waterside in King Street alongside the premises of other merchants. Lübeck's entrenched position that the English must pay compensation for its losses incurred in the attack on the Hanseatic fleet in 1449, if peace talks were to be successful between England and the German Hanse as a whole, was a hurdle yet to be overcome. Another conference at Utrecht in 1452 was to be arranged to make progress towards a final Anglo-Hanseatic agreement.

In 1452 the city on the Trave surprised nobody when it concluded a pact with the Danish King to stop English ships sailing around Jutland into the Baltic. In 1453 merchants from Wismar, Stralsund and Braunschweig had been granted safe conduct to sail to England only to be mistakenly arrested in Lynn as Lübeckers. The latter were regarded as the guilty ones holding the persons and property of the English embassy to Prussia and threatening England's trade route to the East. The Grand Master in Prussia was also dismayed at Lübeck's action. In 1454 the city finally lifted its ban on English cloth carried overland or by sea and, in January 1456, released its remaining English prisoners taken in 1450. Without any prospect of a second Utrecht conference, Henry VI agreed an eight-year truce with all the Hanseatic towns, including Lübeck, whose merchants were also freed from paying tunnage and poundage.

Trade between the Wash ports and Prussia had been on-going in a modest way since 1449, despite Lübeck's attempt to obstruct it, before the situation changed in 1454. Danzig seceded from Prussia and placed itself under the Polish king who granted the city exclusive control over its shipping and commerce in 1457. Although the Danzigers wanted Anglo-Hanseatic trade to flourish which was in the interests of both sides, they curbed the commercial freedom the English had exploited under the Grand Master of the Teutonic Order. Lynn merchants were particularly affected, and Jenks underlines the impact of Danzig's new economic policy on the Wash port:

> While this did not affect the volume of trade with Lynn, it did shift its terms. Although Danzig was more than willing to grant Lynn shippers and merchants safe conducts for trade, it was now free to deny any Englishmen the right of abode, and this destroyed the English cloth distribution system, which depended on resident factors. As a result, Prussian merchants for the first time in the 15th century consistently handled over half the traffic with Lynn.[8]

Nonetheless, English merchants continued to reside in Danzig, including Lynn men like John Thoresby who bought a ship there in 1457. He was a member of the Thoresby family who were strongly represented amongst its Baltic traders. English merchants were probably reaching Riga in Latvia and perhaps Ravel (Tallinn) in Estonia as well as Danzig. In June 1458 Hanseatic merchants at Riga told colleagues in Lübeck and Bruges that Russians were now buying less cloth from Flanders because cheaper English cloth was available, though Danzigers had, for some time, taken it to Livonia.

In 1454 vessels from Hull and Lynn had been given safe conduct to Danzig where their merchants exchanged cloth, grain, pewter and hides for the usual Baltic goods. One Lynn man doing business in Danzig in 1455 was John Joxall who was

College Lane leads from the riverside to the Trinity Guildhall with Thoresby College on the left.

The latter was founded (completed 1511) by Thomas Thoresby for the priests attached to the Great Guild.

readily given credit by a German merchant resident there. The use of credit in that city was probably more advanced than in Lübeck or Hamburg because of its significant trade with England and Flanders. Danzig ships now carried most of the timber (including wainscot or fine oak board and clapholt for barrel staves) and forest products (wax and pitch especially) discharged at Lynn and Hull. Despite the Anglo-German desire for peaceful and profitable commercial intercourse, Hanseatic traders from Hamburg and Danzig complained to the King that English pirates were still a menace in the North Sea. Their ships had not dared to depart from Ipswich in 1456.

Slow progress in mending Anglo-Hanseatic relations after the adverse impact on trade caused by the attack on the Hanseatic fleet in 1449 was reversed in 1458. England's so-called 'King Maker' and governor of Calais, the Earl of Warwick, instigated an assault by a dozen English privateers on another Hanseatic fleet transporting salt from La Rochelle to the Baltic. No fewer than seventeen Lübeck ships were seized. Once again the Lübeckers did not win the enthusiastic support they expected from the other Hanseatic towns for counter attacks on English vessels in the Baltic. Danzig, less hurt by losses than Lübeck by Warwick's plunder of German ships, warned English merchants to venture into the Baltic only in convoys, but temporarily imprisoned seven Lynn traders. Trade between England's east coast ports and the Baltic was now confined to Danzig. By 1463 there were signs of a trade revival, although one Lynn ship homeward bound from the Baltic was taken by Lübeckers. Hanseatic ships from Danzig were still arriving in Lynn and Hull with bulk cargoes for return loads of cloth. Lynn men appear to have imported Baltic goods from Hamburg and Holland too. Some Danzig vessels landed timber and forest products at the Norfolk port before sailing to the Bay of Biscay for salt which was carried to the Baltic. Hildebrand van der Wald of Danzig imported Baltic goods at Lynn in November 1459, almost certainly leaving in ballast for France, then appearing in his home port in 1460 "laden with salt".[9]

IV

Another key turning point in Anglo-Hanseatic affairs had arrived when Edward IV ascended the throne in 1461. The Germans hoped he would confirm their historic trading rights in England though many English merchants were opposed and complained of harassment in Prussia. For reasons of political expediency Edward IV needed to placate the London merchants in particular, but Hanseatic liberties were extended until September 1465. The condition was that the Crown must know which towns were members of the German Hanse and how English traders fared in its regions.

In *The Hanse in Medieval and Early Modern Europe* Jenks has carefully examined an important but challenging source relevant to Anglo-Hanseatic trade in this period. It comprises the certificates issued by the London Steelyard following the order by Edward IV that no merchant bringing goods into England could claim Hanseatic privileges without proof of identity. It was "reacting" to mounting concern in England that "non-Hansards" were claiming the privileges given only to the German Hanse.[10] The Steelyard admitted to Lübeck in 1465 that it was impossible to know all the Hanseatic traders or skippers and sailors who imported freight. It depended upon information supplied by the individual Hanseatic towns to confirm whether or not a merchant was a member of "our Guildhall and Society". The skippers of Hanseatic vessels arriving in England were also charged with sending to London the names of the merchants and the nature of their cargoes. A further safeguard against fraud was the King's Book despatched by the Exchequer to the English customs officials at the ports, to enter the names of merchants and their goods, along with the arrival and departure times of the ships in question. Whenever a Hanseatic merchant shipped a cargo in a non-Hanseatic bottom it was the responsibility of the 'Hansard' himself to notify the London Steelyard.

English suspicions about German traders claiming to be 'Hansards' and consequently entitled to reduced taxation at the ports were not new in the 1460s, but there was now a political will to tackle the issue, especially as Edward IV remained under pressure from English merchants to cancel Hanseatic privileges. In 1463 individual merchants declaring eligibility for Hanseatic privileges had been investigated in Southampton, Boston, Hull and Lynn. The London Steelyard made its enquiries and reassured the English authorities that they were indeed members of 'The Guildhall of the Germans' in the City. The sole exception was Clays Edemak who was probably a sailor trading in a very modest way. Of interest are the eight Hanseatic merchants held to account by the customs officials in Lynn: Michael Strangge, Clays Plate, Reginald Godebek, Hans Wyse, Paul Symond, Henrich Owstaff, Hans Yonge and the said "non-Hansard", Clays Edemak. Only Wyse and Plate in this group reappear in the customs accounts at Lynn two years later as discussed below.

What can the Steelyard certificates tell us about the home ports of Hanseatic merchants and mariners listed between 1461 and 1474? Jenks provides an interesting summary of his research. The largest groups of traders were from Cologne (103), Danzig (75), Lübeck (17) and Hamburg (13). London, Sandwich, Ipswich, Lynn, Hull, Boston and Yarmouth were their English destinations. Cologne men more or less dominated Hanseatic commerce through London and the Danzigers specialised in seaborne trade with Lynn and Hull. Lübeck and Stralsund ships sometimes called at Boston to exchange Bergen stockfish for cloth, though such traffic was only a fraction of 14th century totals. Hamburg merchants occasionally used Lynn, but more often Ipswich, where Cologne traders also frequented the quays. The Norfolk port was in addition the destination for a few Cologne and Lübeck ships. On 22 November 1465 the London Steelyard informed "the customers at Lynn" that twenty-four merchants using the port could be certified as members of their Teutonic Hall.[11] A second certificate was issued on 23 November with two more names. This qualified the individuals concerned to benefit from the trading rights conferred on Hanseatic merchants by successive English Kings. They can be found in the accounts of the collector of national customs at "Lenn" from 19 November 1464 to 19 November 1465 and printed in Owen.[12] Paul Roole, Paul Nyman, Paul Stolte, Roloffe Rouge and Henry Shroder were identified as shipowners who carried the goods of fellow Hanseatic merchants as well as their own cargo. Peter Monke imported herring in a cogge belonging to Cornellii Gylesson (in February 1465) who was not a certified merchant. Hans Hoyman was described as "de Hans" but is not amongst the names sent to Lynn by the London Steelyard. Wessell Bruske may be another example but this is likely to be a misspelling of Wessell Bussch who is listed.

The Hanseatic cogges sailed together for mutual support against pirates and storms as was normal. Nyman, Stolte and Rouge arrived in Lynn's river on 27 May 1465 and the two former skippers departed the port on 29 June, accompanied by Roole, who had apparently arrived on 21 May. Rouge's vessel followed them back to the Baltic on 2 July. Nyman, Stolte and Shroeder returned to the Wash haven from the East on 10 September and their ships departed together on 8 October 1465. The cogges belonging to Brant Ote and Tydman Burger were also trading through Lynn over 1464-65 carrying the goods of Hanseatic merchants. In all probability the two men were Germans from Baltic or North Sea ports, but their names are absent from the list sent by the London Steelyard to Lynn in November 1465. It is clear that there was a sizeable group of German or Hanseatic merchants who were familiar faces in the Wash port in the 1460s importing Baltic staples and other cargo in exchange for woollen cloth.

V

Lynn and Bremen had long cultivated friendly commercial relations which continued into the 1460s. However, the Norfolk town sent a letter to the councillors of the north German port in 1462, following a report that seven of its merchants had been imprisoned there, apparently in retaliation for the theft of goods by Newcastle men. Lynn's mayor and burgesses were "astonished" by such unwarranted action "since we and all merchants and natives of our town of

Lenn have always shown all good and continuing friendships with your citizens, natives and inhabitants; no citizens nor natives of your city when they came to the town of Lenn aforesaid suffering in goods nor in person there".[13] Lynn's mayor requested the release of the imprisoned merchants as the Bremen authorities would wish to see their merchants treated in similar circumstances. The councils in the major port towns involved in Anglo-Hanseatic commerce represented the interests of their home merchants abroad. This was an urban network which sought justice in serious disputes between merchants from cities around the Baltic and North Sea. The fact that most local councillors were themselves merchants offered expert and efficient conciliation on behalf of the individual merchant who needed help. Intercity communication was by correspondence, so it took time to solve problems and establish the facts in any one case. It was imperative that damaging disputes between traders from different countries were satisfactorily settled for international commerce to thrive but was particularly difficult during periods of Anglo-Hanseatic tension. Bilateral negotiations could, however, proceed unhindered even then. Following the Treaty of Marienburg (1388), which temporarily brought Anglo-Prussian hostilities to an end, some German ships remained under arrest at Lynn. Danzig's councillors approached the town's mayor in June 1389 to assist a Prussian merchant to retrieve his property from one of the detained vessels. Lynn's usually amicable relationship with Bremen had broken down in 1462 when its council imprisoned innocent merchants from the Norfolk haven.

Lynn's trade with the Hanseatic towns of the North Sea and Baltic above all remained important:

> Although comparatively small, the Hanse trade at Lynn in the 1460s was clearly well established and engaged the interest of the same ships and merchants year after year, some ships coming two or three times each year. It was essentially an Anglo-Baltic trade, chiefly occupying Danzig and Hamburg ships, and some of it probably followed the Hamburg-Lübeck route. Among the merchants involved can be identified men from Hamburg, Danzig and Cologne, though it is impossible to establish the exact proportions of each.[14]

Town merchants were exporting more cloth in the 1450s and 1460s than Hanseatic men who were responsible for about a quarter of the total leaving their harbour. Cloth exports from East Anglian ports and Hull were, however, considerably lower in the 1450s and 1460s than in the 1440s. The war between the Prussian towns allied with Poland and the Teutonic Order (1456-66) further depressed England's seaborne commerce with the Baltic. Easterlings sailed to Lynn and Hull less to buy cloth than to sell Baltic goods for distribution in their

King's Lynn about 1700

Tuesday
Market Place

By the 15th century the Common Staith with its great crane (in red) was Lynn's principal public quay.

hinterlands via the Great Ouse and Humber rivers respectively. The lion's share of Hanseatic trade in these two principal English east coast ports was now firmly in the hands of the Danzigers.

Hanseatic ships arrived at Lynn in the 1460s with the Baltic staples which had long been important for England's economy, including various timber products, iron, canvas, flax, wax, furs and fish. The variety of imported goods continued to increase. The 1464-65 national customs accounts for Lynn reveal linen, soap, garlic, purses, gloves, globes, pillows, counters, tankards, trenchers (wooden plates) and chests which often contained fragile items on the journey from East to West. The same source for 1466-67 adds further to the list of "interesting commodities" imported. Paving tile, glass, mead, cruses (pots or bottles), scythes, straw hats and wrapping paper were recorded. The total number of shipments for the twelve months was 120, of which seventy-one belonged to native and forty-nine (twelve Hanseatic) to alien merchants. Evidence of London looming ever larger in England's overseas and coastal trades is also highlighted: "In one case we meet with a London citizen, John Blaunche, importing wine into Lynn, an instance indicative of the growing tendency of London to do the foreign trading for other English ports".[15] The English population may have been smaller in the 1460s than before the Black Death but it was wealthier overall, thus creating the demand for more consumer goods. The development of the cloth industry in several regions from the 14th century was a key factor in boosting the incomes of a significant segment of English society. The holds of German cogges departing Lynn in the 1460s were full of varieties of woollen cloth, with occasional bundles of coverlets or bedcovers made in the town itself, and sometimes quantities of cereals, beer, rabbit and lamb skins.

How long did sea voyages following Hanseatic trade routes take? A cogge sailed well when the wind was dead astern and in most conditions one man could easily steer. The author can confirm this from his experience at the helm of the replica Kieler Hansekogge in the Wash in August 2004. Such vessels had an average speed of five knots. Hamburg to Bruges and back took about seven weeks but the return journey from Hamburg to Bergen might take twelve weeks. Lynn's overseas commerce depended greatly on the long voyage to Danzig and back. A cogge could complete the round trip at least two or three times in a calendar year and Fudge cites the "Danzig shipper" Paul Roole.[16] He had been visiting Lynn for twenty-five years. Roole moored in its harbour in December 1467 and sailed for his home port with cloth at the end of February 1468; he was back in the Wash port unloading wood, iron and canvas in May. At Whitsuntide 1468 Roole was entering the Baltic on the return voyage to the East and appears again in Lynn in August with a cargo of boards, oars, tar and iron. He had completed two return journeys between Lynn and Danzig in about seven months. Roole seems not to have strictly followed the decree issued by a Hanseatic assembly in 1403 that navigation was to be prohibited between 11 November and 22 February each year. To reduce the number of shipwrecks was the main motivation but if vessels were laid up in ports for three months every year their owners could lose a considerable amount of money. Hanseatic vessels in the 15th century frequently arrived in London and England's east coast harbours during the winter to show that the ban had limited effect. Yet foreign ships were usually banned from wintering in German ports whose authorities were no doubt reluctant to offer shelter to their competitors.

Anglo-Hanseatic trade was maintained despite the political crisis created by English attacks on the Hanseatic fleets returning from France to the Baltic in

1449 and 1458. Edward IV pressed for a peace conference in England to settle all the disputes between the German Hanse and his kingdom. The closure of the Antwerp market to English cloth in October 1464 followed a quarrel between England and Burgundy which encouraged the English King to seek Anglo-German reconciliation. Cloth exports were extremely important for England's prosperity and might otherwise be shut out of Europe altogether. Lübeck remained the adopted leader of the Hanseatic towns and rejected the royal proposal to meet in London, though such Anglophobia was undermining its authority. Hamburg was eventually chosen as the conference venue in September 1465. Walter Coney and Henry Bermingham were the two Lynn merchants included in the English diplomatic team chosen by Edward IV. It offered the Germans a five-year extension of their franchises from 1466 if another conference to deal with the outstanding issues was held in England in two years. They refused to discuss Lübeck's claims for compensation for the damage inflicted by the English on its seaborne commerce. The Hamburg encounter ended in stalemate but Cologne amongst other Hanseatic towns had shown more flexibility than Lübeck in trying to reach an agreement with England. The secretary of the London Steelyard (Hermann Wanmate) travelled around the Hanseatic towns urging them to accept the English invitation to reconvene in London. Yet a breakdown in Anglo-Danish relations ensured that the 1460s ended with the German Hanse and England going to war rather than a peace conference.

VI

In the 14th and 15th centuries Lynn merchants came into contact with their German counterparts through trade with Norway and Iceland as well as the Baltic. The Hanseatic kontor in Bergen was established by1360 but this increased German fears that the English would work to replace them as the dominant foreign group. As a result, Anglo-Hanseatic relations in Bergen became even more strained. A Norwegian history gives an overview of the English presence in that great fish market and their interaction with the German kontor:

When the Kontor was abandoned on account of the Hansa League's conflict with Denmark and Norway (1368-69) Englishmen settled in Bergen and founded their own warehouses there. When the men of the Kontor returned, they tried to drive them out by force. Nevertheless, the English still had, in the reign of Erik of Pommern, early in the fifteenth century, a gård of their own in Vågsbotn. During Erik's later quarrel with the Hansa the Kontor was again abandoned, this time for six whole years (1427-33). Again, the English tried to fill the vacuum. On the occasion of the Mecklenburg pirates' attack on the town in 1432 no fewer than 17 English ships were lying in Vågen.[17]

A 19th century drawing of St Botolph's Parish Church mostly rebuilt in the 14th century. The lantern tower was erected between 1440 and 1510 when Boston was past its zenith as an English port.
From: Thompson, P., The History and Antiquities of Boston (Boston 1856).

Bergen in the 19th century showing the harbour around which German and English medieval merchants lived.

The English had apparently been absent from Bergen for about twenty years but between April and November 1390 Lynn men brought home stockfish "worth £1,094" in one Lynn and three Hanseatic ships.[18] In the years thereafter the English foothold in Norway remained precarious. Lynn merchants later complained that the Germans had "destroyed" their property in Bergen a year or so before the Vitalien Brothers arrived in its harbour in April 1393. These pirates had sailed from the Baltic with eighteen ships and this was probably the occasion of the attack described below rather than 1394. Nash quotes Hakluyt (1553-1616):

> Item, pitifully complaining the marchants of Lenne doe avouch, verifie and affirme, that about the feast of S. George the martyr, in the yeere of our Lord 1394, sundry malefactors and robbers of Wismer and Rostok, and others of the Hans, with a great multitude of ships, arrived at the towne of Norbern in Norway, and tooke the said town by strong assault, and also wickedly and unjustly took al the marchants of Lenne there residing with their goods and cattels, and burnt their houses and mansions in the said place, and put their persons unto great ransoms: even as by the letters of safeconduct delivered unto the said marchants it may more evidently appear to the great damage and impoverishment of the marchants of Lenne: namely, Imprimis they burnt there 21 houses belonging unto the said marchants, to the value of 440 nobles. Item, they tooke from Edmund Belyetere, Thomas Hunt, John Brandon, and from other marchants of Lenne, to the value of 1815 pounds.[19]

The English came to believe that the Germans deployed the Vitalien Brothers as allies against the 'non-Hansards' in Norway whenever necessary. This was vigorously denied by the Bergenfahrer and the two were not always allies. The Vitalien Brothers had requested the German colony remain neutral when they plundered Bergen in 1393, but the latter helped to defend the town against the pirates. Tyskebrugge was also attacked as a result! Rostock and Wismar on the Baltic coast to the east of Lübeck were supposedly the two Hanseatic ports which had some control over the Vitalien Brothers who used them as bases. These Baltic Germans were nevertheless amongst the Bergenfarhrer or Hanseatic merchants in Bergen assaulted by the pirates!

Lynn traders had returned to Bergen by 1402 when they complained to Henry IV about their treatment there. Several Boston based Bergenfahrer were summoned before the King's council to be told that they must pay compensation if English subjects in Bergen were harmed. In 1406 at least 100 north Norfolk fishermen off southern Norway took refuge in a local harbour when threatened by a superior Hanseatic naval force. It was alleged they were attacked by about 500 armed men from the Bergen kontor and thrown, with arms and legs bound, into the sea to drown. In 1407 the Boston Bergenfahrer were ordered to appear before the King but convinced him that they had no part in the outrage. Lloyds says the Germans were "probably" from Hamburg.[20] The King's intervention on behalf of Norfolk merchants and mariners in Norway reminds us how much feeding his nation depended on foreign fish imports.

In August 1406 Henry IV had led his family to Lynn with a large retinue of splendidly attired lords and ladies. The royal occasion was the departure of his daughter, Princess Philippa, who sailed to Helsingborg to marry King Eric of Denmark and Norway. Two of her escorts by royal appointment under Admiral Nicholas Blackburn were the Lynn merchants Thomas Brigge and the ubiquitous John Brandon. Philippa's embarkment was witnessed by a young local boy named John Capgrave (1393-1464) who became a prominent Augustinian friar and historian. He tells us that Queen Philippa's husband, Eric, suffered "infirmities" and "all the causes of the Kingdom were laid before her" and by "her prudent counsel she brought everything to a prosperous issue".[21] She may have secured the commercial privileges in Bergen in 1408 for the English akin to those granted by Norwegian kings to the Germans. Lynn merchants with Norwegian interests formed a strong group or hanse at congregations in the Trinity Guildhall in their hometown. Their own guild was dedicated to St William named after the youth, William Jurnepin of Norwich, who was supposedly crucified by Jews. Thomas Crosse and John Foullere were two such merchants who took apprentices to Bergen to live and work in wooden buildings similar to those across the harbour belonging to the Germans. The two men (both died in Norway) were members of the company of English merchants there who had been trading with Bergen long before the Hanseatic Kontor was established.

The Germans operated the Bergen to Boston route to import fish into England but Lynn merchants were also heavily engaged in the trade. William Lok was involved in both the Baltic and Norway with his business partners John Weasenham and Robert Botkesham. In February 1409 they freighted a Bremen ship to sail to Bergen with instructions for the skipper to proceed to Wismar to load beer and return to Bergen. Certain Hanseatic merchants in Bergen "prevented" the master from sailing to Wismar where he would have received a hostile reception.[22] The vessel returned to Lynn where Lok suffered severe financial loss as a result. Lynn men had clearly provoked the Bergenfahrer by trying to break into the trade between Germany and Norway. Yet English and German merchants could share commercial projects in Norway. This is confirmed by the decision of the Bergen Kontor in 1412 when it banned Anglo-Hanseatic dealing as a threat to its interests. Such an attitude made peaceful and permanent co-existence between the two communities almost impossible. In 1411 Henry IV imposed a ban on Hanseatic merchants from Norway coming to Lynn following the petition of three local men, John Copernot, Nicholas Alderman and Thomas Grym, who reported violent clashes in Bergen. In 1413 Bergenfahrer were arrested in Boston at the instigation of several citizens who claimed that they had been attacked in Bergen where one of their number was slain "and a Lynn merchant".[23] In response the Bergenfahrer imposed a trade embargo on the Lincolnshire port which must have depressed its economy. Protracted negotiations for an Anglo-Hanseatic peace settlement mediated by the King of Denmark and Norway followed. John Copenot and Nicholas Alderman were to represent Lynn merchants but storms at sea stopped them appearing before King Eric at Bergen in 1415. In 1417 he asked the Germans and the English whether they wished him to impose an agreement if they could not reconcile their differences in Norway. Nothing happened. There was a resurgence of Anglo-German disputes in Bergen in 1424 and the King's council raised the grievances of three Lynn men with the ministers of King Eric.

Bergen was sacked three times in 1428 and 1429 by German pirates and the trade of the port badly disrupted. Whether they were aided by the Hanseatic kontor determined to unseat the English there is uncertain. Boston's overseas commerce depended more on Norway than England's other east coast ports and was consequently severely affected. On 21 May 1428 those Lynn merchants who had been forced to flee Bergen (Norbern) told their story to a congregation in the Town Hall of the Wash port. What could be done? The confirmation of English privileges in Bergen in 1429 by the King of Denmark and Norway may have sparked another major incident in 1430. Nine English ships were seized in Bergen, presumably by the Germans, and the owners demanded £20,000 compensation in 1436. In response the Hanseatic towns accused the English of an attack "on Danzig ships in Bergen in 1432" and "for an attack there in 1434" claiming appropriate compensation for both.[24]

VII

The difficulty of accessing Bergen in the early 15th century drove the English to the inhospitable and thinly populated Iceland whose waters offered their fishermen plentiful cod. Iceland was settled from around 870 AD by Scandinavians and united with Norway in 1262 when the two monarchies of Denmark and Norway become one, though the former country was the dominant partner. Bergen became the capital of the North Atlantic island where Norwegians sold its fish to the Germans who took cargoes to the Wash ports. It was a North Atlantic staple where fish from Iceland and Norwegian waters had to be brought to facilitate the king's collection of taxes. Ships from the Norfolk ports may not have sailed to Iceland before 1412 when Icelandic sources first mention English fishermen. The voyage of around three weeks usually began in March in ships of 100 tons or less sailing in convoy and returning to Norfolk in August. Not only did the English exchange grain, butter, beer, clothes and shoes for the stockfish (wind dried cod) of the Icelandic fisherfolk, but established stations

on the south and south-western coasts to fish on their own account, salting
the catch and packing it in barrels. These sites consisted of one or two wooden
buildings for storage which also operated as shops to deal with the Icelanders.
Trade was simple barter. The Icelanders favoured English men who traded with
them at these stations but bitterly resented outsiders who did nothing except fish
in their waters. Fishing in such northerly and hazardous seas exposed all ships to
danger and in 1419 no fewer than twenty-five English vessels were driven onto
the coast in three hours. It might be noted however that the Icelanders went
fishing in open rowing boats using hand lines!

Lynn appears to have been in the vanguard of English voyages to Iceland in
the early 15th century, though Hull and Bristol were involved too. The King of
Norway and Denmark posted a governor on the island to deter foreign fishermen
rather than to help the native inhabitants. Alien merchants were required to
trade through Bergen. In 1415 King Eric wrote to the Lynn authorities to protest
against the "repeated incursions" to trade and fish by their townsmen into his
Iceland territories.[25] He requested such voyages should be proclaimed contrary
to the laws of his realm. The Scandinavian King also lobbied his brother-in-law,
England's Henry V, who issued a proclamation in November 1415 to the mayors
of Lynn, Yarmouth, Hull and Newcastle, amongst other coastal towns, to refrain
from fishing in Danish, Norwegian and Icelandic waters for twelve months.
The unhappy merchants of these port towns petitioned their king against the
proclamation in 1416. It seems to have had little or no impact anyway. In 1420
a new Danish governor called Palsson arrived in Iceland determined to impose
regulations on foreign fishermen who sailed there or expel them from local waters.
In *Medieval Merchant Venturers* Carus Wilson tells us that he and his companion
Van Dammin not only failed to curb English activities in Iceland, but in 1425
were captured and "carried off to England".[26] Icelanders were probably pleased to
see the back of Danish overlords like Palsson. However, once in England he was
allowed to prepare an indictment against English merchants, claiming they had
fortified a trading station on the Westman islands, and had "even exterminated"
the inhabitants of some rural settlements.[27] That they were trying to make
Iceland an English colony was the accusation which followed. Englanders had,
moreover, kidnapped and enslaved Icelandic children according to Palsson, and
Lynn men were apparently seen as the main culprits. Some young Icelanders
were certainly brought to the Norfolk port in the 1420s. Karlsson states that
there is evidence that the English did kidnap Icelandic children, although it
was also said that Icelanders sold or gave away their children to foreigners no
doubt because of extreme poverty. In the Trinity Guildhall at Lynn in 1427 local
merchants promised to return the small group of boys and girls in question to
Iceland. Some Icelanders in Hull and Lynn in the 15th century were men and
teenage boys who had travelled to England as servants or sailors.

Henry VI's government had endorsed the warning of the Danish King and forbade English ships to sail to Iceland. To regain access to Bergen was no doubt why Lynn merchants had already complied with the demand of King Eric in 1426 not to voyage there. This example was not followed by men from other English harbours such as Hull and Bristol. In 1432 an Anglo-Danish Treaty affirmed that the English must not fish in Danish territorial waters but should trade through Bergen. Its terms could, however, be circumvented by purchasing licences from the Danes to fish off Iceland. English interlopers risked confiscation of their ships by sailing there without such official permission. In Icelandic history the 15th century is known as 'The English Century' and Anglo-Danish conflict over fishing off Iceland at this time is seen as the start of no fewer than ten 'Cod Wars' up to 1972.

VIII

English ventures to harvest the rich fisheries around Iceland continued into the later 15th century. It ensured Danish hostility and exposed their ships to attack when circumnavigating Jutland into the Baltic. Edward IV agreed to stop his subjects sailing to Iceland to allow a peace treaty between the two nations to be signed at Hamburg in October 1465. Lynn's major stake in both Baltic and Iceland trades was again reflected by two of its merchants acting as royal envoys at Hamburg. They were Walter Coney and Henry Bermingham who had also been involved in the talks there in September with Hanseatic delegates. As both Danish and English kings profited from the granting of licences to merchants for access to the Iceland fisheries, the political will to enforce any ban was weak.

Traders from England's ports continued to fish off Iceland without obtaining permission or the necessary licences. They were even accused of pillaging Icelandic villages and probably murdered the native-born Danish governor in the autumn of 1467. The consequence was inevitable. In June 1468 a small English fleet carrying cloth to Prussia was intercepted in the Sound between present day Sweden and Denmark by eight ships. Two or three of the latter were crewed by Danzigers acting as mercenaries for the Danes. The attack was orchestrated by the Danish king who blamed men from Lynn in particular for the atrocities in Iceland, though only two of the seven English ships hijacked (waiting to pay Danish tolls) came from the Norfolk port. He insisted that his action was not anti-English in general; Lynn must suffer because its merchants had transgressed and now had to endure these losses. Of the ten vessels in the English fleet, three had escaped to reach Danzig, and returned safely to their home harbours.

This relatively minor international incident played into the hands of anti-

Hanseatic factions in England where Edward IV was too weak to stop the march to an unnecessary and damaging Sea War (1469-73). Jogged into action by the London merchants who were jealous of the economic privileges enjoyed by the Germans in their city, and influenced by certain members of his government, the King decided the Hanseatic towns must be punished for their supposed complicity in the Danish assault on the English fleet. His Privy Council demanded £20,000 in compensation from the Germans as a result of the arrest of the English ships. That expatriates from Danzig, Lübeck and Stralsund had been under Danish command was conveniently forgotten. The London Steelyard was closed in July and its occupants imprisoned at Ludgate at the beginning of December 1468. An inventory of Hanseatic goods seized throughout England in 1468 shows that about two-thirds were taken from the Steelyard. German ships arriving in England's east coast ports ignorant of what had happened in London were subject to arrest. At Lynn, the crews of two Prussian ships were detained and the cargoes confiscated, along with a vessel from Lübeck. German cogges and crews in Hull and Newcastle met the same fate. Cologne merchants in England were soon freed and their property returned because of their wish to keep peace with the English. They were left in sole

The monumental brass of Walter Coney once in St Margaret's Priory Church (the matrix remains).

He represented Lynn in Parliament and was prominent in Anglo-Hanseatic commerce and politics until his death in 1479.

From: W Taylor. The Antiquities of King' Lynn (Lynn 1844).

charge of the London Steelyard but set up their own trading post in the capital. A Hanseatic assembly in Lübeck protested the innocence of its member towns and offered negotiations, though the Germans in England were not released from prison until April 1469 when recalled home. From the Hanseatic towns came repeated denials of English allegations of their participation in the Danish attack on ships from Lynn and other east coast ports in 1468. Lübeck

Walter Coney's house built around 1440 overlooked the Saturday Market Place.
It is believed he entertained Edward IV there when the king fled to the Low Countries via Lynn in 1470.
From: W Taylor. The Antiquities of King' Lynn (Lynn 1844).

demanded full compensation for all Hanseatic losses arising from the English reprisals following an international incident now elevated from minor to major significance.

We cannot delve into the Wars of the Roses between the Houses of Lancaster and York but the enmity between Edward IV and the Earl of Warwick impacted on Anglo-Hanseatic politics. The King and his retinue had been forced to flee England for Holland via Lynn in three ships early in September 1470 as Louis IX of France invaded the country supported by Warwick and Lancastrian forces. Edward IV then returned to England in March 1471 with his own invasion army, landing on the Humber, before the Yorkists defeated Warwick and the Lancastrians at the battles of Barnet and Tewkesbury. Although having secured logistical support from Burgundy for his 2,000 strong expeditionary force, the King had needed fourteen Hanseatic ships to bolster his fleet to England and paid hard cash for the service. He had almost certainly assured the Germans that their commercial privileges in England would be restored. Once back in power, however, the monarch only favoured Cologne whose merchants had distanced themselves from Lübeck. This inflamed Anglo-Hanseatic politics still further.

Edward IV had extended Hanseatic economic liberties in England for only short periods in the 1460s, to placate anti-Hanseatic factions, promising a

more permanent settlement if the Germans would agree to reciprocity or parity for English Baltic traders. Lübeck again represented several important Hanseatic cities in demanding that the English should first pay them compensation arising from the attacks on their Atlantic fleets in 1449 and 1458.

Without any apparent prospect of a negotiated agreement, the Danish action in 1468 led to an Anglo-Hanseatic naval war in the Channel and North Sea, with merchant vessels temporarily converted to battle ships, patrolling the ocean for victims. The Bruges kontor took the initiative and paid for two Danzig vessels to assault English ships in January and February 1470. Hamburg, Bremen, Danzig and (to a lesser extent) Lübeck were the most enthusiastic sponsors of the privateers whose owners and crews were naturally hoping to profit from plundering enemy ships. Other Hanseatic towns were mere onlookers rather than participants in this Sea War. Neither the Germans nor English commissioned more than twenty privateers or warships apiece. Danzig had fitted out and sent the *Great Caravel* into the North Sea but Dollinger informs us that the vessel "impressed the enemy more by her size than by her success".[28] In 1472 the giant vessel came under the command of the famous Danzig privateer, Paul Beneke, who had already taken enemy ships in the Channel. The German naval force funded mainly by Danzig targeted French and Flemish vessels as well as English ones. Ship artillery had become common by this period and may have been used (the culverin was a long and narrow 15th century cannon).

The boycott of English goods agreed by the Hanseatic towns was not strictly implemented and Cologne was expelled from the community for refusing to support the war. During this period more fish than usual was imported into Lynn and Boston by the Hollanders and Zeelanders who probably took corn from the Wash ports. English merchants became more dependent on trade with the Low Countries because the Baltic was closed in the war years. English cloth was consequently distributed in eastern Europe via Nüremberg and other south German towns rather than Lübeck or Danzig. The Sea War deprived the provincial ports north of London of most of their overseas commerce because Hanseatic merchants had accounted for so much of it. In the east coast harbours of Ipswich, Lynn, Boston and Hull they had been "the only foreigners of any significance" in the cloth export trade which sustained the national economy.[29]

Despite the English losing some ships in the summer of 1470 and 1471, they took four Lübeck privateers in July 1472 at the mouth of the Scheldt (between Belgium and Holland). At the same time French warships disabled or captured Hanseatic vessels in retaliation for attacks by German privateers on their compatriots. The Germans faced bad weather and shortages of supplies as well as manpower as the English began to strengthen their fleet. All this persuaded Lübeck to conclude what was a damaging and distant naval conflict. Edward IV was also anxious to negotiate an Anglo-German settlement so that he could marshal his resources for war against France. Peace talks

Edward IV (1442–1483).
The King reigned 1461-70 and 1471-83.
Artist or workshop unknown. Oil on oak panel, after 1510.

began at Utrecht in The Netherlands in July 1473, but delays did not allow an agreement until February 1474. The English delegation was led by the King's secretary, William Hatclyff, and the German party by Lübeck's mayor, Hinrich Castorp (1419-88). Hamburg and Danzig had pursued the war against England with greater zeal than Lübeck because the former cities had lost most in the English confiscation of Hanseatic property in 1468. That not all the Hanseatic towns had enforced the embargo on English goods had "frustrated" Danzig in particular.[30]

Danzig and Hamburg were well represented at Utrecht amongst the two-dozen strong Hanseatic delegation. Bürgermeister Castorp had thirty-two years' experience of international diplomacy and his hard bargaining greatly impressed the English. The latter had no problem with the restoration of the historic Hanseatic commercial privileges in their kingdom. The king's diplomats had succeeded in greatly reducing the German claim for damages arising from the confiscation of their goods in 1449, 1458 and 1468. It had at first been set at £200,000! The £10,000 that the Hanseatic diplomats agreed to accept was to be transferred through tax exemption on all Hanseatic cargoes arriving in English

Lynn's South Gate was rebuilt in brick in the 1440s and given an ashlar front in 1520. It testified to the wealth and status of the medieval town.

ports. This process was completed by 1488. Edward IV was, however, unable to defend Cologne. Its conduct had unsurprisingly been condemned as treacherous by Lübeck because the Rhineland city's Anglophile policy had undermined the community. The German delegation at Utrecht refused to allow Cologne to be a party to the agreement; it was nevertheless re-admitted to the community at the Bremen assembly in 1476 (but not to the London Steelyard until 1478).

The German insistence on the return of their trading posts in London and

Boston and a new riverside business headquarters at Lynn was conceded by the English without much hesitation. Jenks observes:

> After both sides had exhausted themselves in the war and the peace negotiations had begun, the Hanseatic delegates made it very plain that they regarded London, Lynn and Boston as the principal cause of all the strife which had sundered England and the Hanse since 1468. Hence, they said, it was only right that these towns should cede the properties in question as compensation for all the ignominious injuries, harms and rebukes the Hanse had suffered at their hands. No other measure proposed by the English, the Hanse's delegates said, was better suited to assuage Hanseatic feelings and create a true and lasting peace.[31]

Edward IV granted the freehold titles of the existing kontors at London and Boston and to a new house in Lynn to the Hanseatic towns in the Treaty of Utrecht (February 1474). For the Germans the repossession or ceding of these three English properties (together with English consent to exclude Cologne from the settlement) was the key to their willingness to accept £10,000 rather than £200,000 in damages. Edward IV did not play up England's regular demand for reciprocity, that English merchants should receive the same privileges in Hanseatic towns as the latter enjoyed in England. Yet it is "incorrect" to conclude that "the English abandoned their claim to reciprocal rights" in the treaty and were consequently absent from the Baltic post 1474.[32] The trading rights of the English in the Hanseatic towns and Prussia were protected by the treaty which upheld the principle of reciprocity too. Edward IV ratified it in July 1474 and again confirmed the Hanseatic franchises in England. The German delegation had reassembled at Bruges in May 1474 to ratify the treaty which was locked in a wooden chest in the Carmelite friary there for safe keeping. It took time for all the Hanseatic towns to endorse it and both sides did not exchange ratifications until September 1475. Danzig waited until 1476. It seems to have supported the treaty in general but insisted that the English had not acquired any new commercial liberties in Prussia.

Dollinger has no doubt that the Treaty of Utrecht was a victory for the German Hanse: "This marked a resounding and almost unhoped for triumph for the Hansa". He concludes:

> The Peace of Utrecht was one of the great events in the history of the Hansa. It came at a critical moment, when the community was threatened with dissolution by the disintegration of its economic system, by the irresistible rise of its rivals, by attacks made in almost all countries on its privileges and by the increasing separatist tendencies of the towns. Consequently the victory had far-reaching effects. The Hansa recovered

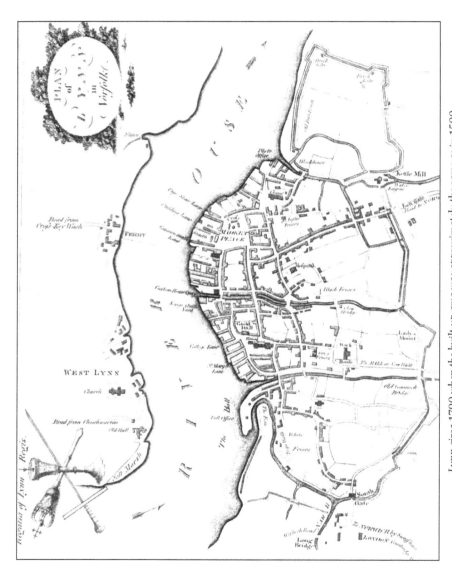

Lynn circa 1790 when the built-up area was approximately the same as in 1500.
The riverside streets were lined with merchant mansions whose warehouses ran back to private quays on the Great Ouse.

her international status and strengthened her commercial position in England for the next hundred years while at the same time preventing English expansion in the Baltic. The submission of Cologne had proved her strength and solidarity and would serve to discourage further tendencies towards secession among her members. The main causes of weakness were still there, but their harmful effects were not to become apparent for some time.[33]

The Treaty of Utrecht cannot, however, be regarded as a diplomatic defeat for Edward IV whose priority was to fight France and seek normalisation of relations with the Germans. In June 1475 the King invaded France with the biggest English army deployed against the French in the 15th century. Lübeck and the Hanseatic towns could nevertheless be pleased with the terms of the peace settlement agreed at Utrecht in February 1474. They retained their traditional commercial advantages in England and exemption from the customs duty of poundage (an ad valorem levy of twelve pence in the pound) on all exports and imports. Postan tells us that the Hanseatic share of English foreign trade "soon passed" the highest point it had reached previously as their annual cloth exports rose "to well above 13,500 between 1479 and 1482". [34] What seems surprising is that Lynn and Boston rated so highly in the peace talks when London was capturing most of England's overseas trade. The Wash ports apparently possessed both commercial and political significance for the Germans.

The international clout of the Hanseatic towns had indeed been demonstrated or rather reasserted at Utrecht. The treaty temporarily protected and prolonged their commercial foothold in England. Henry VII (1485-1509) confirmed its provisions in 1486. English traders to Prussia received no more than "a vague assurance" that their liberties in Danzig would continue as heretofore.[35] Colvin says that the Danzigers at Utrecht were justified in their boast that: "We have made an end of the English".[36] The London Steelyard benefited from the expanding commerce of the City, but business at the other German trading posts on England's east coast "dwindled" as the next chapter tells.[37] Lynn can be said to be the notable exception. Its trade with Danzig had been important through the 15th century and its merchants returned to the eastern Baltic very soon after 1474.

Notes

1. Bonney, M., 'The English medieval wool and cloth trade: new approaches for the local historian', in *The Local Historian* (February 1992), 38.
2. Ibid., 38.
3. Dollinger, *The German Hansa*, 245.
4. Friedland & Richards,.*Essays*, 102.

5. Lloyd, *England and the German Hanse*, 219.

6. Ibid., 223.

7. Fudge, *Cargoes, Embargoes and Emissaries*, 18.

8. Friedland and Richards, *Essays*, 102.

9. Fudge, *Cargoes, Embargoes and Emissaries*, 42.

10. Jenks, S., 'The London Steelyard's Certifications of Membership 1463-1474 and the European Distribution Revolution', in Wubs-Mrozewicz, J. & Jenks, S. eds., *The Hanse in Medieval and Early Modern Europe* (Leiden 2013), 61.

11. Owen, *The Making of King's Lynn*, 335.

12. Ibid., 366-78.

13. NRO, 'With Ships and Goods and Merchandise', 8.

14. Lloyd, *England and the German Hanse*, 227.

15. Gras, *The Early English Customs System*, 607.

16. Fudge, *Cargoes, Embargoes and Emissaries*, 41.

17. Secretan, *The Hanseatic Settlement in Bergen*, 24.

18. Lloyd, *England and the German Hanse*, 137.

19. Nash, *The Hansa: Its History and Romance*, 90.

20. Lloyd, *England and the German Hanse*, 138.

21. Hillen, *History of the Borough of King's Lynn*, 141.

22. Lloyd, *England and the German Hanse*, 138.

23. Ibid., 138.

24. Ibid., 139.

25. Owen, *William Asshebourne's Book*, 92.

26. Carus Wilson, *Medieval Merchant Venturers*, 113.

27. Karlsson, G., *A Brief History of Iceland* (Reykjavik 2000), 28.

28. Dollinger, *The German Hansa*, 308.

29. Fudge, Cargoes, *Embargoes and Emissaries*, 171.

30. Ibid., 74.

31. Friedland & Richards, *Essays*, 103.

32. Lloyd, *England and the German Hanse*, 376.

33. Dollinger, *The German Hansa*, 310.

34. Postan, M., *Medieval Trade and Finance* (Cambridge 1973), 286.

35. Jörn, 'With money and blood', 561.

36. Colvin, I.D., *The Germans in England 1066-1598* (London 1915), 127.

37. Dollinger, *The German Hansa*, 316.

Lynn and Anglo-Hanseatic Trade

Medieval merchants involved in long distance commerce overseas and overland required trading posts or stations to stay and store their goods. The Hanseatic kontor at Lynn is an example. It provided lodging, offices, warehousing and shops or stalls. Many such commercial complexes for foreign merchants existed in Europe in the Middle Ages, although these buildings are not often studied compared to church architecture. Of those hundreds that have survived, most have been remodelled or partly demolished. Lynn's German trading post has undergone a great deal of internal alteration, but three of its four ranges enclosing a courtyard still stand, and medieval brickwork has been found in the street range rebuilt after 1751.

The term kontor was only widely used to describe German trading posts in the 16th century. It springs from comptoir or counting house and emphasises how Hanseatic establishments across Europe were usually business headquarters. The Lynn and Boston kontors were sometimes called 'steelyards' after the London Steelyard. Another name for such mercantile compounds is factory used by merchants or factors in a foreign land. Hanseatic kontors were usually gated enclosures with rooms for lodging, offices, shops, dining and meetings, though most space was allocated to storage. They not only gave some protection to the residents and their wares but maintained group discipline abroad where urban populations might be hostile. Provincial east coast kontors listed by the London Steelyard in 1554 included Lynn, Boston, Hull, York, Newcastle, Scarborough, Norwich, Yarmouth, Ipswich, Colchester and Sandwich. However, they were almost certainly unused with no resident German merchants in 1554, save Lynn, where Hanseatic activity was by then modest.

Hanseatic merchants had been resident in Lynn from the 1270s, and probably before, but no kontor had been set up as in nearby Boston. Or had there been one? Brodt says that in 1286 the community established "a kontor in the thriving harbour which became one of the leading East Anglian ports through which corn, wool and cloth were traded along the English coasts and to the continent".[1] Harrod tells us that the Letters Patent (1428) during the reign of Henry VI for "erecting a steelyard" at Lynn demonstrates that "the Hanse merchants were then assembling there in considerable numbers".[2] He acknowledges its location is not "indicated" nor "is it noticed elsewhere". Lloyd's position is that there does not seem to have been "a recognised kontor" at Lynn since the early 14th century, and there is "no evidence" Hanseatic merchants held property in the town in 1468, but "the possibility cannot be dismissed"[3]. No confirmation has come to light in local sources that the Hanseatic towns possessed a trading post in Lynn before 1474. They had presumably been content with renting waterside houses and warehouses whilst good relations prevailed with local merchants. Even in Bruges the Germans had no fully fledged kontor until 1478. Their insistence that the Treaty of Utrecht included the grant of a Lynn kontor shows that the Norfolk port remained significant for them. In September 1473 their delegation at Utrecht had wanted a property in Chequer Street, today's King Street, where merchant complexes ran down to the river and deeper water than south of the Purfleet. Bigger ships could access the quays as a result. However, no commercial premises could be found for sale in King Street, as the German diplomats were told in February 1474. Several of Lynn's merchant rulers possessed extensive properties there which they did not wish to vacate.

The layout of Lynn's second medieval town from the north showing the Tuesday Market Place with King Street (right) and High Street (left). The Alexandra Dock (1869) is in the foreground.

Local influence in determining the location of the Lynn kontor was probably decisive as discussed by Jenks. In November 1473 a letter from Edward IV about the provisional contents of the Treaty of Utrecht had been read before the mayor and congregation in the Town Hall. They appointed a commission to negotiate with the King. William Wales, Thomas Leighton, Walter Coney and Thomas Thoresby were members of Lynn's governing body. All had traded with Prussia and well versed in Anglo-Hanseatic affairs. Leighton and Thoresby knew Danzig. Coney had been in the delegation which met representatives of the Hanseatic towns in Hamburg in 1465 (the matrix of his lost brass can be found in St Margaret's Priory Church). The four men appear to have travelled to London in late 1473 to discuss the German preference for a kontor in King Street with the King's council. Once the prospect of a trading post there had dissolved, they turned attention to a property in the vicinity of the Saturday Market Place, where Coney and Thoresby lived. It was opposite St Margaret's Priory Church and well known to Thoresby and Coney who had witnessed its penultimate conveyance in 1468. Two more Lynn merchants now loom large. Thomas Barker and Thomas Wright had been joint owners of this merchant complex since 1468, with two London citizens, but the Lynn duo now relinquished all claims to it. This soon led to its sale by the two Londoners to Edward IV who transferred the title deeds to the London Steelyard on 29 April 1475, where they remained for 125 years before going to Lübeck. Jenks concludes that on balance "it would seem that Lynn wanted the Hanse" and "in particular its old trading partners from Danzig to re-establish a presence in Lynn".[4]

The German community at London's Steelyard were probably content, not only to repossess the Boston kontor, but also to secure a new trading post in the Norfolk port across the Wash. Hermann Wanmate and Arnd Brekerfeld (alderman of the London Steelyard) were appointed by Lübeck to take possession of both Boston and Lynn kontors in June 1475. The former had been the Steelyard's secretary and his excellent knowledge of England earned him a special role as an intermediary in both Utrecht and London in 1473-74. He had avoided arrest in the dark days of late 1468 by seeking sanctuary in Westminster Abbey! Purcell gives us the contemporary overview of what Wanmate found when he arrived in Lynn to organise the move into the new kontor:

An entry in the Patents Register for the 15th year of the reign of Edward IV (1475) confirms the grant 'to the merchants from Germany of the league of the Teutonic Hansa who own the building Guildhall of the Teutons in the City of London and to their successors, of the parcel of land and the dwellings with mooring place and garden and the houses, cellars, lofts and accessories in the town of Bishop's Lenn, which formerly belonged to Philip Wyth, citizen of the same town Lenn, opposite the St. Margaret's church, between the highway to the east, the pond in the aforesaid town Lenn to the west, the dwelling which once belonged to John Lakynghithe and later John Thoresby, to the north and the dwelling which formerly belonged to Robert att Lathe, to the south which parcel of land recently fell to the King after the deaths of John Tate and Thomas Bledlowe, city councillors of London.'[5]

This account describes an extensive property by the Great Ouse constituting several houses, cellars, lofts, garden and a quay, with Thomas Thoresby's house next door, and "the dwelling" which formerly belonged to Robert Lathe, being today's Hampton Court, on the other side of St Margaret's Lane. These original buildings were described in 1476 as "very old" and consisting of seven houses with ten rooms and eight chimneys as well as a kitchen, hall and courtyard.[6] The "Haupthaus" or hall house had eight rooms in addition to "en schone halle" (on the first floor?) and a kitchen and a stable on the ground floor.[7] There appears to have been stalls for trading on the property but it is unknown whether there were permanent shops. In 1476 the Germans considered it sufficient for the moment to repair 'the bridge', although it is again unclear what this was, unless a first-floor structure connecting individual buildings. It was not long before the new Teutonic owners decided to redevelop the whole complex.

Lübeck called upon Danzig to take responsibility for the Lynn kontor because its merchants frequented the Wash port more than those of any other

The Tuesday Market Place circa 1700 with the Custom House (left) and the medieval Market Cross (centre).

Hanseatic city, but the Prussians did not ratify the Treaty of Utrecht until 1476. In the interim the Danzigers must have made arrangements for their English friends in the town to manage it. Henry Baxter, Henry Patenmaker and Thomas Wright were the trio in question "who had stuck to them loyally since the dark days of 1468".[8] Wright had already been instrumental in the unfolding of the process which resulted in the King granting these ancient premises to the German Hanse. He resumed his involvement in the cloth trade to Danzig after 1475 and was twice town mayor before his death in 1495. John Patenmaker was a German immigrant in Lynn before 1450 and Henry may have been a relative. He had invited the governor of the London Steelyard to Lynn when it had been left in the hands of the Cologne merchants following the arrest of its other Hanseatic residents in 1468 (they alone now enjoyed royal favour and privileges). This was Gerhard von Wesel who could be "loggyd at the Swane, for that is a good place and a secrete and trewe to Dochemen".[9] The Swan or 'La Swanne' was an inn in Grassmarket (Norfolk Street) close to the Tuesday Market Place and Common Staith used by the town's foreign merchants. It had a brewhouse supplied with water from the Kettle Mill on the Gaywood River near the East Gate. The merchant Robert Some was the owner in 1507. To seal a business deal or contract German and English traders would drink beer together in elaborate tankards as was the Hanseatic custom and 'La Swanne' was surely a favoured location.

The Germans had taken over the management of the Lynn kontor by August 1476 when the town council reached an agreement with the Easterlings at the 'Stileyerd'. For long Hanseatic traders in England were allowed to retail goods and fix their own prices (except food) but new local regulations were introduced in 1476:

> Item, on the same day, a communication was made with the merchants of the 'Hanza' called Esterlynges, residing at Lenn in le Stileyerd there, of and concerning divers articles concerning commercial intercourse both of English merchants and the aforesaid merchants and especially of and concerning the sale of their merchandise and it is enjoined on the aforesaid merchants by the whole council of the town that from now on they shall not sell their merchandise by retail except by the last and half last and by the hundred and half hundred. And also that they sell reliable merchandise, under penalty of forfeit of their defective merchandise.[10]

Not unlike today, the usefulness and quality of German goods were recognised in medieval London, and no doubt in Lynn too. Although the town council was almost certainly glad to see the Hanseatic traders back in Lynn to boost its economy, there was clearly a desire to restrict their retailing probably to protect

Lynn shopkeepers. The mayor could view the new German trading post from the Town Hall on the Saturday Market Place! In imitation of the London Steelyard the Hanseatic kontor at Lynn was sometimes called 'the Steelyard'. Hillen quotes from the churchwardens' accounts that 60 yards of "the street of the church sid (side) agaynst the stylyerd" were repaired in 1591.[11]

English provincial kontors were supposedly under the supervision of the London Steelyard which was itself managed by the periodic Hanseatic assembly. The four great kontors of Bruges, London, Bergen and Novgorod were allowed to send envoys to these important assemblies of the German

An artist's impression of the Trinity Guildhall circa 1450.

From: Harrod, H., Report of the Deeds and Records of the Borough of King's Lynn (King's Lynn 1874).

towns. At Lübeck in 1476 the London envoys claimed that the English provincial kontors should "remain subject" to the Steelyard "in accordance with old custom".[12] Each had been despatching its alderman to London to agree regulations for running their establishments. These smaller trading posts were also required to pay the Steelyard an annual tax called Schossgeld for its upkeep. Boston had a reputation for asserting independence from London because of its close ties with Bergen but seems to have made a concessionary annual payment of £5.

II

Fragments of the original waterside premises inherited by the Germans in the Norfolk port were possibly incorporated in the building of the new trading post around 1480: "All the Steelyard buildings date from the years after 1474 when the German merchants were re-granted their special privileges in Lynn and obtained licence from the town to erect a Steelyard".[13] Its layout or plan may have been typical of the smaller Hanseatic kontors across northern Europe. The street range overlooking St Margaret's Priory Church was remodelled around 1670 and again in the 1750s. The original frontage was probably a jettied timber framed and brick structure similar to the adjacent Hampton Court. Parts of the original medieval wall were found behind the 18th century plaster (1969-71). The double-headed eagle of the German Hanse may have adorned the main entrance as it did at the London Steelyard. Here the living quarters, counting house and possibly ground floor shops of the small Hanseatic community had been located. Commissioning ships and organising cargoes as well as general kontor management kept its German occupants busy.

Two warehouses about 100 feet long run from the street range westward to the Great Ouse enclosing a narrow courtyard. Although of different size and construction, they had the same kind of crown post roof, elements of which remain, indicating a late 15th century building date. The southern range of two storeys is timber framed and jettied onto St Margaret's Lane (but with a flat brick face to the courtyard). It is thought that wattle and daub in the upper storey was replaced by brick infill, and this floor also underbuilt in brick before 1700; both levels underwent some renewal in brick in the 18th century and later. The north range is a brick building of three storeys with visible window openings into the courtyard but the north elevation is blank. Traces of windows were discovered in this north wall in 20th century restoration work (1969-71). In the south wall there is a medieval arched door which may have belonged to an earlier building. Big sash windows at first floor level at the eastern end of the range were inserted in the late 18th century when this part of the warehouse was converted into a salon. The gable ends of the two warehouses abutting the Great Ouse would have had openings, with cranes or hoists for the transit of goods, but later extensions of both ranges have destroyed the evidence.

In close proximity and parallel to the river is a large brick and stone building called Marriott's Warehouse; it has occasionally been assigned 'Hanseatic' associations but it is largely of the late 16th century. At high tide it would have been almost surrounded by water.

At the Hanse House there is no indication that the two warehouses had partitions and were probably long undivided spaces suitable for storing imports and exports. The recognition of individual goods would not have been difficult in what was a relatively small community. Furniture, pitch, wax, iron, fish and amber were amongst the commodities brought by German ships from the Baltic; their skippers loaded English cloth, hides, lead, beer and sometimes cheese. It is likely the Lynn kontor handled imported luxury goods such as silks and pepper (Danzig established direct contact with Portugal by 1500 to boost trade in the latter). The German towns would not have invested in the rebuilding of the property granted by Edward IV unless Anglo-Hanseatic trade had been reasonably buoyant. Indeed, it seems trade was sufficiently brisk to warrant an extension of their Lynn complex around 1500, when its two-storey brick western range was erected. Enough of the original roof remains to suggest an early 16th century build. Thus the long and narrow courtyard was fully enclosed; the modest hall or first floor of this western wing was probably a dining room. On the ground floor its north wall still contains three lights of a six-light window before

An aerial view of the Saturday Market Place.
The Hanse House is the quadrangular complex at the top (second from left).

The southern range of the Hanse House looking west towards the river.

the later extension onto the warehouse range made it internal.

The Norfolk port had recommenced its forward role in Anglo-Hanseatic commerce as the location, for the first time, of an independent German trading post ceded by Edward IV in 1474. It had a degree of political or symbolic significance as the Germans had clearly indicated at Utrecht, though the Lynn kontor was also open for business. It was an important hub of the wider Hanseatic community in England if much smaller than the London Steelyard. English hostility to foreign merchants appears to have been more common in London than the provincial ports. At Lynn there is no hard evidence of Anglo- German relations being strained. Sometimes old "personal feuds surfaced" between English and Hanseatic traders, but the

A medieval doorway in the courtyard (north range) of the Hanse House.

two groups were well acquainted and shared commercial interests.[14] It was not unusual for German and English traders to mix socially in the Wash ports or even in London. Easterlings and their local business partners no doubt enjoyed convivial evenings in their preferred riverside taverns which were often the property of Lynn merchants. No instance of a Hanseatic merchant marrying an English woman has been found for Lynn unlike Boston and York.

Did Hanseatic merchants based in the Wash port have links with local guilds from the late 14th century? No fewer than fifty-nine guilds were established in Lynn by 1389 and fifteen were associated with St Margaret's Priory Church where they maintained altars. Others were attached to the Chapels of St Nicholas and St James as well as the friary churches. The Young Merchants founded in 1362 recruited young men from other towns which may have included those from continental ports. For foreign traders there were obvious commercial and social benefits to be derived by involvement with local guilds, particularly those dominated by Lynn's merchant rulers. Further research may provide some answers. Lynn was the home of a Guild of St Barbara who was the patron saint of Hanseatic traders abroad. She was honoured as a protectress from storms, fever, fire and plague, all being the great enemies of merchants. The Church used by the Germans at the London Steelyard was the nearby All Hallows where some former members were also buried. St Barbara's Day was 4 December when there was a requiem mass there for deceased Hanseatic brothers followed by a banquet in their Guildhall by the Thames.

III

The Anglo-Hanseatic Sea War (1469-73) brought trade between Danzig and Lynn to a halt, but Easterlings sailed back into the Norfolk harbour in late 1474, testimony to the close ties between German and English merchants. Hull was also being revisited by Hanseatic ships, though the city's merchants were now drawn more to the Low Countries than the Baltic. Anglo-Hanseatic commerce at Boston and Ipswich did not recover to any degree. Participation by English east coast ports in the Baltic trade became concentrated in the hands of Lynn men who used both English and German vessels to reconnect with Prussia. The Treaty of Utrecht had re-opened the Baltic and once again English ships and "especially" those from the Norfolk port "made their way to Danzig".[15] It was becoming one of Europe's great seaports connecting East and West. In 1474 there were 403 and in 1490 no fewer than 720 ships arriving in Danzig and most departed the port "loaded with grain and wood".[16] Rye was the main cereal exported to the West. Anglo-Danish relations needed to be good for English vessels to navigate safely from the North Sea into the Baltic, and the truce between the two nations in 1473 benefited Lynn merchants.

Anglo-Prussian commerce post the Treaty of Utrecht was therefore largely channelled through Lynn whose export trade had to a great extent been dependent on the Baltic since the late 14th century. A group or hanse of town merchants who handled this traffic has been identified by Fudge. Particularly noteworthy is Robert Bees who was the "only certain English carrier" in the eastern Baltic in 1475 and 1476, in the vanguard of Lynn's drive to restart trade with Danzig.[17] He is listed as a mercer in the calendar of borough freemen (1472-73) apprenticed to Edward Hamond. Bees had several business partners. With Richard Peper he exported cloth from the Norfolk port in 1484 in a Hamburg cogge whose cargo partly belonged to Danzigers. Bees was one of three Lynn merchants and two from Danzig who exported cloth in 1487 in a vessel of a fellow townsman named John Brekersley. In 1490 and 1491 he was involved with other local merchants in the hire of Prussian ships to transport bulk cargoes from the Baltic to the Wash port. Bees, Peper, Wright, Tyge, Trewe, Brodbank, Harde, Wolle, Brekersley and William Amfles were all Lynn potentiores in the forefront of Anglo-Hanseatic trade. The impressive property portfolios of these merchant rulers, along with their piety and charitable sensibilities, are illustrated in the will of Richard Peper (1527) whose daughter Cecily Some appears later in this chapter. Peper was involved in the fish and cattle trades (meat consumption increased in the 15th century and Lynn's cattle market was large). It was the Amfles family who developed today's remarkably well-preserved Hampton Court in Nelson Street. Robert atte Lathe built the medieval hall house or southern range about 1350 to which was added a brick western warehouse wing parallel to the river probably by Thomas Salisbury just before 1450. A timber and brick street range containing shops was erected circa 1470 by William Anfles whose merchant mark is carved in the right-hand spandrel of the front door frame. Such insignia were needed on casks and bales when traders shared cargo space in ships sailing to the Low Countries or Danzig.

Anglo-Hanseatic trade through Lynn in the 1480s and 1490s was conducted by Hamburg merchants and skippers as well as those from Danzig. The first known governor of the Hanseatic kontor established in the Norfolk town in 1475 was Ludkin Smyth, that long standing Englandfahrer. This Hamburg shipowner was in post before 1505 and had been trading through the Wash port for over thirty years. In 1465 he had imported iron, wood, pitch and chests into Lynn which appears to have been his commercial headquarters. In the 1480s and 1490s Hamburg cogges departed the Norfolk haven with cloth, grain, cheese, rabbit skins and coverlets (bedcovers); they returned with iron, wax, pitch, tar and other Baltic goods. From 29 September 1503 to 28 September 1504 Gras counts 271 shipments in the customs account for the Wash port, with the English responsible for 202 and foreigners for sixty-nine, of which twenty-four were Hanseatic merchants. Hans Lutkeher was one of the latter with wine shipments. Richard Amfles and John Tanne of Lynn are identified as two of the biggest traders. Of the 127 vessels arriving and departing during the year in question "47 were apparently alien and 80 apparently denizen". Amongst the "more unusual" imports were playing tables, aqua vite (brandy?), tankards, drinking pots and "two dozen Gospels of St John valued at a half-penny a piece".[18]

In the last quarter of the 15th century Hanseatic merchants were concentrating their cloth export business in London rather than England's other east coast ports as Fudge shows. Excluding the bursts of activity in 1488-89 and 1492-93, when they exported an impressive number of cloths (777 and 480 respectively) from Lynn, their annual total was only between 100 and 200 in these decades. Lynn's attraction for German traders was now less its supplies of cloth and other commodities but more the markets in the town and its region for Baltic goods. Imports of wax revived after 1474 as demand in England continued at a high level despite great quantities being produced at home. There was also an increase in the variety of consumer goods imported by Hanseatic cogges. Haberdashery, purses, tiles, wooden platters, linen and furniture were amongst them. Fenland lighters took loads up river from Lynn. Its hinterland included Cambridge, a commercial crossroads for a large part of East Anglia, with the city's river link to the Wash harbour of the utmost importance. Its colleges were regularly purchasing merchandise brought from Lynn by boat, including wine, wax, fish, timber, furniture, cloth and, by 1550, Newcastle coal to replace the diminishing reserves of local firewood. A good deal of business was transacted at Stourbridge Fair. It was England's greatest trading mart springing up every September by the Cam on the city's outskirts. Boat traffic between Lynn and Cambridge greatly increased as a result. Booths were arranged in streets accommodating traders from most East Anglian towns and London selling cloth, wool, hops, fish, timber, haberdashery, leather, cheeses, spices, beer, wine and other goods. The travel journals of a 17th century English merchant include an interesting account of Stourbridge Fair. Peter Munday lived in Danzig in the 1640s but in 1639 he was touring southern England. He arrived in Cambridge on 11 September and the next day went a mile down river on a boat to Stourbridge Fair:

> On a plain, in tents and booths, making streets and lanes with their particular names, plentifully furnished with all manner of commodities, especially hops....also wool, cloth, salt fish, tar, plate, brassware, wooden ware, all manner of necessities, even to shops of old boots and shoes, and near forty wine taverns. So, having eaten some of their oysters, which were excellent, and tasted some of their wine and good Lynne beer out of their boats which came from thence, I left the fair and came back to Cambridge that evening by land.[19]

Lynn continued to function as the port of Cambridge into the 18th century and beyond before the railways took commercial traffic away from the Fenland waterways.

For Lynn itself the staple Baltic goods remained essential imports. Timber, pitch, tar and iron were needed for ship building and local rope makers imported Prussian hemp. In the 1490s the royal dockyards purchased cordage from the rope works in the town suggesting a substantial industry. Sails were made in Lynn from imported or home-produced canvas in riverside workshops from the 13th to 19th centuries. Timber from the forests of eastern Europe was also in demand in Lynn and its hinterland for the construction industry. Fir was frequently used in medieval house building for roofs and floors. Imported Baltic wood was also chosen to make coffins in England's east coast towns.

If thirty or more English ships could be found at any one time in Danzig in the first half of the 15th century (thirty-six English vessels had been arrested in Danzig on one occasion in 1429), only twelve had arrived there from England "during the three years following the cessation of hostilities" at Utrecht.[20] Lynn's trade with Prussia continued in short booms and slumps into the 1490s. Just four

Danzig ships arrived in the Great Ouse in the summer of 1495 with bulk freight discharged for export cargoes of cloth and coverlets. There was a marked upturn in business at the commencement of the 16th century as the customs particulars tell. Fudge concludes that the combined Baltic cargoes of German and English traders amounted to 55 per cent of the town's total cloth export trade. Of the Baltic goods unloaded at Lynn in 1503-4, the Danzig chests discussed in chapter two appear on the list, along with rafters, eels and platters. There is no doubt that Lynn merchants were the "main link" to Danzig on England's east coast as shown by the trade statistics.[21]

How many Hanseatic traders were based in the Norfolk port in the years after 1474? In Lübeck customs accounts relating to five English ports (1474-81), Lynn is placed third behind Hull in the number of "handelnden Kaufleute" (forty-one and forty-three respectively), and Ipswich fourth with twenty-three active merchants.[22] It should be noted that the value rather than the quantity of goods passing through Ipswich exceeded the total at Lynn by £28. Boston was fifth in the list with just two German merchants to emphasise that it was no longer an important destination. The source makes it clear that London was the preferred location with seventy-six Hanseatic traders recorded in the capital, though far fewer than before the Anglo-Hanseatic War. Its favourable geographical position vis-à-vis Europe combined with good port facilities and the seat of England's government made it difficult to resist. London's population in 1500 of over 50,000 was much larger than any major provincial port and grew rapidly through the 16th century. Antwerp was also within comparatively easy reach by ship. It had replaced Bruges as western Europe's principal international market for wool, cloth, furs, luxury goods, horses and more. Italian, Spanish, French, German and English traders flocked to its fairs and markets by land and sea. There was an 'English House' in Antwerp by 1474 where London merchants were the dominant group.

IV

The east coast ports to the north of London handled a far smaller share of Hanseatic trade post 1475 than before. Lynn was distinguished by its determination to reconnect with Danzig. A group or hanse of town merchants kept the long sea route between the Wash and Prussia open. Their achievement appears impressive given the international conflict and piracy which disrupted Anglo-Hanseatic trade in the 1480s. In 1481 the new Danish monarch recommenced attacks on English shipping after several years of relative peace between the two nations. A renewal of Anglo-Scottish hostilities seems to have encouraged English warships to plunder Hanseatic vessels as well. Lübeck alleged that the English had attacked several of their cogges in 1481 and 1483 and Prussian ships were assaulted in 1484 and 1485. English kings continued to protect the trading rights of the Germans in their island kingdom. Edward IV died in 1483 and Richard III reconfirmed the Hanseatic franchises in 1484, as did Henry VII in 1486, despite "objections" from merchants in Hull, York, Lynn and London.[23] The English complained about new restrictions on their activities in Hanseatic territories where they were still denied reciprocal trading privileges. In Danzig it seems they were now unable to own houses or trade outside the city.

During the 1480s the English reported attacks by Hanseatic cogges on their own ships in the waters around Iceland and Norway. No doubt that "the chief culprits" were the infamous Hamburg privateers called Pinning and Pothorst "who sailed under

Shodfriars Hall in Boston photographed in August 1939.

Of three storeys, the original building was probably 15th century, and could have been a guildhall. It was restored by Oldrid Scott in 1874 and is the most substantial timber framed structure in the town.

the Danish flag".[24] Hanseatic port towns excluded from the lucrative Bergen fish trade by Lübeck's monopolistic grip had turned to Iceland by the 1470s. Hamburg and Danzig followed the English on annual voyages to trade with the Icelanders. Both Germans and English built wooden booths or shops at certain coastal locations to exchange consumer goods for stockfish. Scissors, soap, kettles, wax, mirrors, combs, gloves and swords added to the staple merchandise (beer, grain, wood and tar) which had been shipped earlier in the 15th century. Such a variety of consumer goods must have transformed the social life of the Icelanders. Lynn ships were amongst the English and Hanseatic vessels engaged in the Iceland trade in the 1480s and 1490s and beyond. From the Norfolk port at least fourteen vessels sailed for Icelandic waters every year in the 1520s with loads of salt for preserving the fish serving as ballast. Hanseatic and English ships in Icelandic waters clashed. Sometimes ships deliberately collided with other vessels in medieval harbours to damage them (and this seems to have happened in Iceland). Although the Germans probably sold the bulk of their catch on the continent, they shipped Icelandic fish to London too. This was not without its hazards and big losses. In the summer of 1476 a Hamburg vessel sailing to London with £600 worth of fish from Iceland ran aground near Hartlepool and was "attacked and destroyed by bandits".[25]

English merchants continued to encounter difficulties in Norway. In 1481 men from the Wash ports were again criticised by the Norwegian king whose ministers sent a letter to the mayors of Lynn and Boston. There had been incidents in the waters around Bergen, including attacks on merchant ships, but "perverse people" rather than specific groups were censured. The English were welcome in Norway provided they traded peacefully and lawfully. Their vessels lost a few years before were attributed by the Norwegians "to evil plunderers and pirates" who had also taken their own ships and vigilance against such sea robbers was promised. The King's council in Bergen supported the Icelanders who accused the English fishermen of serious crimes and taking away their livelihood. It warned the Lynn and Boston authorities that "such evils" would not be tolerated but "dealt with firmly".[26] The Dutch from Kampen and Daventer had also established a community in Bergen despite Lübeck's attempt to shut them out.

The Anglo-Danish Treaty of 1490 concluded several years of hostilities between the two nations when some Lynn ships had been seized sailing into the Baltic. Hanseatic privateers serving the Danish King were blamed. At the Anglo-Hanseatic conference at Antwerp in 1491, to settle demands tabled by both sides for damages for losses at sea in the 1480s, Lynn alone submitted claims against the German towns "for losses totalling £2,308 in thirteen incidents since 1485".[27] This indicates how the Norfolk port was indeed prominent in England's Baltic trade. No real progress was made on this key compensation issue but the two sides had partially mended relations to allow the peaceful resumption of international trade. The confirmation of both Hanseatic trading rights in England and English access to Prussia temporarily satisfied English and German delegates.

V

What had been happening in England's other east coast ports since 1474? The Lübeckers had deserted Boston by 1469 and its harbour was silting badly. The final surge of Hanseatic trade in the Lincolnshire port was in 1491-92. It was the Danzigers rather than the Lübeckers who moored their cogges in the Witham, importing Icelandic fish and iron, wood, tar and bowstaves from the Baltic. Out of Boston the Germans had taken small amounts of English cloth which had a ready sale in Prussia. Leland indicates that there had been a significant number of Germans living in the town where they had apparently founded the Franciscan friary and "many Esterlinges" were buried there. They kept "a great house and course of merchandise" at Boston until a local man killed one of them in the reign of Edward IV resulting in the departure of the Germans "and syns the towne sore decayed".[28] When Leland wrote around 1530 the kontor remained but was unoccupied. It was apparently located just to the south of the town centre on a bend in the Witham (the riverline has changed since 1500). In 2018 the Boston Hanse Group won support from the Heritage Lottery Fund to undertake an archaeological excavation to establish its exact location.

The withdrawal of the Lübeckers from Boston was a major factor in its decline as an international port. Yet the Germans insisted on the return of their Boston kontor in the Treaty of Utrecht (1474); the Bergenfahrer authorised their secretary, Christian de Ghere, to assist in the negotiations for taking repossession of it. There was a meeting at Lynn in June 1475 when de Ghere and probably the Bergenfahrer Arnold Block met Hermann Wanmate and Arnd Brekerfeld to make arrangements for taking over the Boston kontor. Also present were Wilhelm Calbent and Kerstyn Yssel who were to be responsible for its safe keeping and maintenance. It was an old house with ten rooms and seven chimneys with an associated rear building in which there were eleven booths. The kontor was described as "right dilapidated" and needed a good deal of repair to secure it against winter weather of 1475-76.[29] It could not have been used for several years. In 1481 the property and its wharf were again in such a state of disrepair that Lübeck granted the Bergenfahrer connected to Boston £20 to cover necessary work. In 1505 the London Steelyard paid for further repairs to its Lincolnshire outpost, and requested Lübeck to encourage the Bergenfahrer to return, but they had abandoned it. It seems that the Germans repaired the kontor again before they sold it. In 1660 "a messuage called the Steelyards" and four acres of land were purchased by the town council from a Mr Earl, but "the materials of the Steelyard building" were acquired by Francis Ayscough for £120 in 1693.[30] It had presumably been demolished.

Cloth manufactured in Suffolk and Essex was exported to Europe through Ipswich and Colchester in the 15th and 16th centuries (the two harbours belonged to the same customs jurisdiction). Southern Suffolk was now the chief centre of English cloth production. Lavenham, Hadleigh, Bury St Edmunds, Long Melford, Sudbury and Colchester (Essex) were the hubs of an expanding industry. Until the 1470s the lion's share of cloth exported from Ipswich and Colchester was in German hands, mainly those of Cologne merchants from London. They were attracted to these neighbouring east coast havens because of their proximity to London and the Low Countries. The Hanseatic traders exported finished and unfinished cloth (some from the West Country via London) including the popular coloured Suffolk cloth to Prussia. There appears to have been a Hanseatic kontor at Ipswich in the parish of St Mary at Quay used for storage and business. William Sabyn (1491-1543) was a prominent local merchant and royal naval officer whose will refers to his premises called the 'Stillyarde'.[31] It was located adjacent to the Blackfriars in today's Foundation Street. German merchants in Ipswich lodged in the inns by the waterside. Colchester in Essex was also the location of a Hanseatic kontor or branch office which handled as much merchandise as the Suffolk town. Colchester and Ipswich were in effect outports of London and offered extra facilities for traders based at the Steelyard on the Thames. In the 1440s Cologne merchants had been responsible for over 50 per cent of the cloth exported from Ipswich and were major dealers in in fish and wine. Dutch and Spanish men were also involved in its wine and fish trades. When the Germans decamped from Ipswich and Colchester in the 1470s both ports suffered a setback, though local traders now had more opportunities. Wool going out of Ipswich to the continent showed an upturn in the late 1480s and early 1490s, before falling away, but it exported more and more cloth. Bulk imports from the Baltic were still landed in both Colchester and Ipswich in the early 1490s, including wax, fish, iron and timber, with Hamburg men exporting some cloth in return. Suffolk clothiers now organised the making and marketing of cloth and sold much of their product to London merchants for export.

Yarmouth (Blakeney and Dunwich were in its customs district) was clearly experiencing economic problems at the commencement of the 15th century when powerful advocates around the King led to wool being diverted from other ports for export from there (1404-06). Lynn was adversely affected. A petition from the merchants in several English towns to rescind the royal order to make Yarmouth a staple port was granted by Henry IV. Yarmouth remained a destination for Hanseatic ships, particularly from Hamburg, with timber, flax, pitch, iron and fish imported in the 15th century. As Yarmouth was the headquarters of the English herring fishery the import of fish by German merchants represented serious competition! The annual autumn herring fair had been the town's biggest commercial event since the 14th century.

The German kontor at Yarmouth was apparently a modest affair, managed by Hamburgers, but they closed it in the early 15th century. The trading post was almost certainly located on the South Quay. The Hanseatic merchants declined an invitation to re-open it in 1416. They had allowed themselves to become involved with a corrupt customs official and no doubt wisely refused to return. Lloyd describes this as a "calculated withdrawal" by the Hamburgers who had been "the mainstay" of Hanseatic trade at the Norfolk port which consequently suffered a setback.[32] Their cogges continued to visit Yarmouth but the port authorities were in dispute with the Germans in the 1440s over the payment of local tolls. Its attraction owed much to the fact that it was the outport of the textile manufacturing city of Norwich whose merchants exported cloth from the 14th to the 18th centuries. Today's Dragon Hall in King Street was built by Robert Toppes in the 1420s as a riverside business centre. In the impressive upper hall foreign merchants could inspect the best Norfolk cloths and English dealers buy the latest consumer goods from the continent. The Germans must have been amongst the trading partners Toppes welcomed. The city council had built a hostel for the accommodation of such foreign merchants on the market place.

Hanseatic interest in Yarmouth was limited by the 1480s and 1490s when only a few Danzig and Hamburg ships visited the town whose harbour was also silting up. Vessels from the same German cities were intermittently at Cley and Blakeney on the north Norfolk coast in the late 15th century, but only modest amounts of cloth and forest products were handled. Around 1490 Sir John Paston received a consignment of Rhenish wine (ten gallons) "of the best" and fifty "orrygys" at Cley, from Lumen Henrikson, who was no doubt a Hanseatic skipper.[33] In 1457 German merchants had hired a Blakeney ship to carry cloth and other goods from Boston to Bergen, though this was probably a rare occurrence. St Margaret's Church at nearby Cley may have been a refuge for Hanseatic traders when on the north Norfolk coast as suggested by ship graffiti.

VI

Trade routes criss-crossing Europe's seas were followed in the 16th and 17th centuries by artists and musicians who sometimes acted as messengers. A Lübeck violinist travelled to London around 1620 for example. English musicians lived and worked in Hamburg. Touring companies of English actors also paid visits to Hanseatic towns before 1650. Cultural influences were naturally transmitted by Hanseatic merchants living in England in the 16th and 17th centuries.

In the 1520s and 1530s north Germans were 'importing' into England the reformed and dynamic Christian faith called Lutherism. They smuggled forbidden Bibles or Lutheran works into London and almost certainly other east coast ports. The earliest known society of English Lutherans originated around 1520 in Cambridge which was closely connected to Lynn. In 1526 Henry VIII received disturbing reports about the outlawed Lutheran texts in the London Steelyard; Thomas More rummaged it but nothing was found (three German merchants were nevertheless arrested there). The English Reformation engineered by Thomas Cromwell, the King's chief minister in the 1530s, allowed Henry VIII to divorce Catherine of Aragon and placed the German merchants in a much brighter light. The King became the head of the English Protestant

Aerial view of the Hanse House showing its quadrangular character and extent by the Great Ouse.

The courtyard of the Hanse House looking east to the street range as it appears today.

The doorway of Hampton Court (Nelson Street) with spandrels showing the merchant mark of the Amfles family.

A graffiti ship from St Margaret's Church at Cley-next-the-Sea in North Norfolk visited by Hanseatic merchants. It appears to be a cogge from the first half of the 15th century; it is one of over twenty such graffiti in the building.

Church as Cromwell presided over the dissolution of over 900 religious houses to boost his master's wealth. Hans Holbein, that gifted immigrant German artist, was soon painting royal portraits, alongside those of the merchants of the London Steelyard.

It is possible that merchants from Hamburg and other Hanseatic cities had openly displayed their Lutheran proclivity in Lynn before London. Some disillusion with the Church of Rome in the Norfolk town is perhaps suggested by an anonymous local writer who showed great interest in the European Reformation. He talked of Luther before any other contemporary English chronicler: "In this yere (1518) leutor wrot to leo the byshop of rome consarnyng pardons and other matters of relygyon for which cawse he was proclaimed (trator) heretycke but by the mantynance of the duke of Saxton he preched and wrot styll agaynst the pope".[34] Small editions of individual books of the Bible were being printed in Low German by 1523 and may have been brought by Hanseatic merchants to Norfolk. Luther had hung up his theses at Wittenburg in late 1517 and Lynn's association with the seaports of the Netherlands and Germany exposed it to the religious "wind of change" in Europe. In 1530 Bishop Nix of Norwich wrote his famous letter complaining about the reading of "erroneous books in English" in his diocese of which Lynn would doubtless have had its share. For 1538 our chronicler uses the phrase "pylgiymes and Idolytre forbyden" when telling of the dissolution of the Lynn friaries which had once been popular with local and German merchants. The closure of Walsingham's shrine brought to an end the flow of pilgrims who had landed at Lynn after long sea journeys to trek the twenty-three miles to 'England's Nazareth'.

VII

English economic expansion by 1500 was largely driven by cloth exports to Europe. The growth of the manufacturing districts in Yorkshire and the West Country as well as East Anglia was fuelled by the wealth generated by overseas commerce. But Bristol, Southampton, Hull, Ipswich, Yarmouth, Boston and Lynn saw their share of the national cloth export trade fall as London's rose. The Wash ports lacked the industrial hinterlands of other provincial ports and lost more of this traffic as a result. Some Suffolk cloth continued to reach Lynn from Bury St Edmunds by road and river, but the level of cloth exports from the Wash port fell away, to no more than thirty a year by 1529 "when they virtually ceased".[35] London was now the source of most of the cloth purchased by Hanseatic merchants whose share of England's total cloth exports was an impressive 25 per cent or more in the 1530s. Yet Lynn persisted with its Prussia connection and some cloth was still being despatched to Danzig in the 1530s.

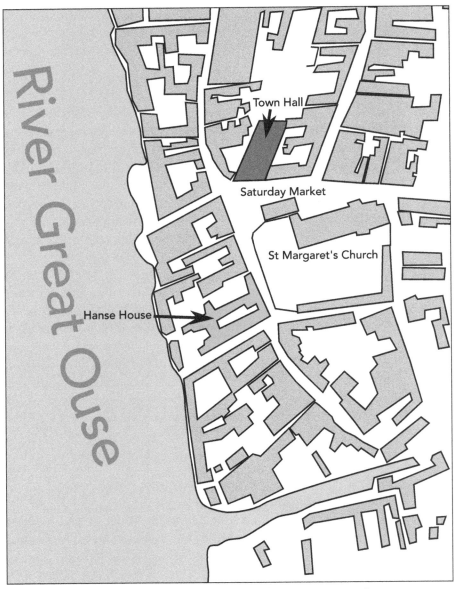

Plan of part of the town in 1830 with the Hanse House in red.

The destructive impact of international conflict on Anglo-Hanseatic commerce was again illustrated by the sea war between Denmark and the Wendish towns which erupted in 1510. Lübeck ships blockaded the Sound and seized vessels from the Low Countries, England and even Danzig. Trade (particularly English cloth exports) recovered after 1511 when Danzig secured exemption from the blockade and bottoms from England and Hamburg. From this episode sprang the Stralsund affair. A Lynn ship belonging to Christopher Brodbank and Nicholas Bateman was taken by privateers sponsored by

Stralsund on the return voyage from Danzig. English demands for the return of the vessel were ignored as Lynn's Baltic trade was further interrupted. To the English this was a simple act of piracy elevated from minor to major significance in Anglo-Hanseatic politics when Cardinal Wolsey took up the case in 1516. As Henry VIII's chancellor he no doubt sensed a good opportunity to discredit the German Hanse whose commercial privileges grated on a burgeoning English nationalism. In 1517 Stralsund attempted to resolve the matter by sending an envoy to London. Wolsey rebuffed him. The Cardinal ordered the London Steelyard to pay damages to the Lynn men, but its governors opted for another hearing at the Star Chamber (a closed court meeting at Westminster). There, in June 1519, Wolsey dismissed the defence case resubmitted by the Germans and awarded the Lynn merchants £500 in compensation. Fudge notes the Germans gave the money "under duress" and only then handed over "all £500 of it in a sealed leather bag".[36] To the Hanseatic towns the Cardinal's verdict came as no surprise!

In the first two decades of the 16th century Hull and Newcastle retained trading links with Hamburg and Danzig, but Boston was no longer attracting Hanseatic ships, and few visited Ipswich. The commercial intercourse between Lynn and Prussia continued through the reign of Henry VIII and Fudge describes this activity as "a presence maintained".[37] It had been disrupted when the Danes closed the Sound to Hanseatic ships in the early 1520s before the traffic resumed. By 1530 Lynn's Baltic trade was firmly in English hands with a local group or hanse dispatching a few vessels to Danzig most years: three in 1531, four in 1536, two in 1537, three in 1538, at least six in 1540, two in 1541 and three in 1542. Small amounts of cloth were augmented by rabbit pelts, lambfells, lead and French salt re-exported from the Wash harbour. Ships undertook the long voyage eastward together, departing Lynn in April or May, and returning from Danzig in July or August every year. Wax, pitch, tar, timber, chests, tables, flax and fish were imported from the Baltic by the Norfolk men who sometimes hired Hanseatic carriers. Amongst the dozen or more Lynn merchants and shipowners engaged in the Prussia trade was the widow Cecily Some who sent cloth to Danzig and grain to the Low Countries and Iceland. Yarmouth, Ipswich and Norwich venturers were likewise involved in Baltic commerce and sometimes used the port of Lynn to access Danzig. Few Danzig cogges now had England's east coast ports as destinations (its merchants complained about exorbitant duties on lead shipments) and Fudge concludes that Hanseatic activity at Lynn had become "marginal and intermittent".[38]

When Henry VIII waged war on France and Scotland in the 1540s a royal proclamation drove much of the English merchant fleet into the campaign and German ships were also requisitioned. Lynn's Prussia trade was again brought to a halt and slow to restart when the war ended in 1546. Its merchants continued voyages to Danzig into the 1550s and 1560s, but only a few ships were commissioned which returned with the usual Baltic goods. In 1557 just one vessel departed Lynn to Hamburg with a cargo of cloth and saffron. Now German cogges and sailors were rarely seen in the Wash port. Traders from the Baltic or Easterlings had preferred "to frequent the small English outposts" like Lynn, Boston and Hull and did not sail to the English capital "in great numbers" until the concentration of overall trading in London began "to increase".[39] London was more and more re-exporting foreign merchandise to provincial ports by coaster as the latter lost overseas trade. An account of the custom and subsidy on all goods (save wool, woolfells and hides) exported or imported by home and foreign merchants at Lynn, from 29 September 1549 until 13 June 1550, is revealing. Grain rather than cloth was now the principal export, along with a variety of other goods, including lead, coal, butter, fish, linen, men's shoes, horseshoes and creamery wares. Hops, salt, iron and wine were the principal imports. Amongst other merchandise unloaded at Lynn were timber, pitch, soap, millstones, rosin, cork, hair, brown paper (for wrapping?), horns, fans, jars and figs. The total number of shipments was thirty-five, of which twenty-one were handled by English and fourteen by alien traders, but "the Hanseatic merchants apparently not being represented at all".[40] This was a sign of the times as London had become the preferred destination for the cogges from the German North.

What of the Lynn kontor? In 1565 the town's mayor referred to "the wonted repaier of merchant straungers is lately with drawn" which may have meant Germans from the Hanseatic towns.[41] Since the early 16th century it was apparently "little used" and by the 1560s the Hanseatic traders had almost certainly departed.[42] The kontor was leased to a succession of local merchants (with the tenant responsible for repairs) but the Germans reserved the right to terminate the lease, with compensation, should they wish to restart business at Lynn. In 1571 it was occupied by Robert Daniel on a twenty-one year lease at only £3 a year (he used the warehouses to store imported salt), but by 1577 it was in the hands of other local merchants. The alternatives for the Hanseatic community were mounting subsidies for the repair and maintenance of an empty property or selling the trading post. In 1567 the London Steelyard told Lübeck that its annual expenses amounted to £800 sterling "and that other sums no less high had to be expended by it in maintaining the factories at Lynn and Boston".[43] This seems an enormous sum, and underlines the need to find tenants for such deserted kontors, particularly when their neglect could mean repossession by the English Crown. The Hanseatic merchants in London had been paying for the upkeep of the Lynn and Boston trading posts as well as their Steelyard. But the Hanseatic towns meeting in Lübeck assemblies were also expected to contribute to the costs of running foreign kontors.

Although Hanseatic skippers were no longer calling at Lynn in the 1570s and 1580s, its coastal and overseas trades were rapidly expanding, particularly the coal and corn traffic between the Wash and Newcastle. The great importance of supplying corn to London was also highlighted in 1565 when Cambridge University petitioned the King's council to stop the transport of corn from Cambridge via Lynn insisting it was "to the pinching of poor scholars' bellies".[44] The university was firmly rebuffed and reminded that grain from the eastern counties was essential to feed the City. England's Baltic commerce was also undergoing a resurgence in the 1570s and 1580s, with ships sailing to Danzig and Elbing (Eblag), and Lynn merchants were "in the forefront of this development".[45] They imported impressive quantities of naval stores (pitch, tar, iron, flax and timber) as well as "Danske" rye, especially when there were food shortages in England as in 1586. With Danzig and Elbing as destinations these Norfolk traders loaded their ships with Suffolk cloth, leather, lead and rabbit skins. Such was the wealth generated by Lynn's coastal and foreign commerce that its merchant fleet kept increasing and "a major rebuilding of medieval town houses was taking place from around 1560".[46]

VIII

The Hanseatic towns did not return to their Lynn trading post after the 1560s, despite the economic growth enjoyed by the town in the 1570s and 1580s, but its retention suggests that this remained an option. By August 1639 it was leased for twenty-one years to William Wormell, citizen and vintner of London, by Marcus Brandt, Conradt Strydholtz and Paul Vandar Vellen of the London Steelyard. William was taking over the lease from his father, Bartholomew, the prominent Lynn merchant. The property is described as a mansion house in Lynn, called the 'Stilliard howse', in the occupation of Bartholomew Wormell, and Stephen Jackson before him, together with all shops, cellars, vaults, warehouses and solars. Bartholomew's son William was to be responsible for the repair of the entire premises including "the bridge" which may have been a link between two of the buildings at first floor level.[47] The street range appears in Henry Bell's drawing of around 1680 of St Margaret's Priory Church from the south. It shows a town mansion in the architectural style of that period. During restoration work in this east wing (1969-71) a late 17th century fireplace and chimney were found as well as evidence of living rooms being extended into the warehouse ranges. It seems that the medieval street elevation was rebuilt by the Germans to ensure this large house remained an attractive asset.

A rare reference to the Lynn kontor in the Hall Books (Corporation proceedings) can be found in December 1722. A letter had been sent to the mayor "from the Hans Towns of Lübeck, Bremen and Hamburgh relating to

The southern part of the Lynn waterfront from the west in 1731 had changed little since 1500.
The Hanseatic kontor (behind far-right ship) was still in German ownership.

their house in this Towne late in Mr Alderman Awborne's use".[48] The town clerk was ordered to prepare an answer, to be stamped with the mayor's seal of office, and despatched to Mr Hopman who was their agent in London. Nothing is revealed of the contents of the letter, or the reply, but it is likely that the Germans were concerned that the property was neglected. If so, a solution was

St Margaret's Priory Church as engraved by Mackworth circa 1745 but a reproduction of Henry Bell's drawing of the 1670s.
The Hanse House must be the building on the left with the street range apparently remodelled in Bell's time.

soon found. In 1723 Daniel Scarlett (mayor 1718-19) leased it for forty-one years and agreed to repair "all that pile or reach of buildings, warehouses and chambers" on either side of the courtyard running "westward" from "the capital messuage".[49] He was a merchant who traded with Scandinavia and Hamburg but died in 1726 and his widow Sarah passed the lease to Martin Sandiver in 1728. In turn, he transferred it in 1732 to Edward Everard, an important Lynn brewer and merchant apprenticed to Daniel Scarlett in 1714. It was Everard (1699-1769) who purchased the property on Bullstake Street (now St Margaret's Place) from the Hanseatic towns in 1751 for £800. Described as a messuage with warehouses, wharfs, shops, cellars, outhouses, vaults, yards and gardens, he rebuilt the Jacobean street range in the form of the fine Georgian house seen today. The building had been known as 'Allemayne Mansion' or 'Stileyard House' before 1751 but may have been called 'St Margaret's House' soon after.

George II (1727-60) was England's king when the property was sold by the German Hanse whose now somewhat dormant members included Hanover. His Majesty's envoy to the 'Hans Towns' in 1751 was Sir Cyril Wych whose principal 'station' seems to have been Hamburg. He was Lord of the Manor of Gaywood near Lynn and may have been involved in the acquisition of 'Allemayne Mansion' by Edward Everard. The transfer deed bears the seals of the mayors and senators of Lübeck, Bremen and Hamburg, dating from the 4, 12 and 19 February 1751 respectively. These urban rulers were known as the merchants "of Almayne of the Teutonic Hanse Towns" acting through their London attorney, Martin Eelking, who probably took the legal document to and from north Germany.[50] So ended Lynn's long and special partnership with the Hanseatic cities, though shipping between the Wash ports and north German harbours continues to this day, and most are members of the New Hanse founded in 1980.

Notes

1. Palliser, *The Cambridge Urban History of Britain*, 654.
2. Harrod, H., *Report on the Deeds and Records of the Borough of King's Lynn* (King's Lynn), 11.
3. Lloyd, *England and the German Hanse*, 277.
4. Friedland & Richards, *Essays*, 106.
5. Purcell, D., 'Der hansische "Steelyard" in King's Lynn, Norfolk, England', in *Hanse in Europa: Brücke zwischen den Märkten 12-17 Jahrhundert* (Köln 1973), 109.
6. Fudge, *Cargoes, Embargoes and Emissaries*, 109.
7. Jörn, N., 'With money and blood': *Der Londoner Stalhof im Spannungsfeld der englisch hansischen Beziehungen im 15.und 16. Jahrhundert* (Köln 2000), 409.
8. Friedland & Richards, *Essays*, 103.
9. Slater, F.R., 'The Hanse, Cologne and the crisis of 1468', *Economic History Review* (January 1931), 99.
10. Alban, J., 'The Hanse in Norfolk Records', A paper read at the Hanseatic History and Archaeology Forum in King's Lynn (2009), 6.

11. Hillen, *History of the Borough of King's Lynn*, 176.
12. Jörn, 'With money and blood', 409.
13. Parker, *The Making of King's Lynn*, 115-117.
14. Fudge, *Cargoes, Embargoes and Emissaries*, 159.
15. Ibid., 170.
16. Keyser, *Die Baugeschichte der Stadt Danzig*, 355.
17. Fudge, *Cargoes, Embargoes and Emissaries*, 88.
18. Gras, *Early English Customs System*, 647.
19. Pritchard, R.E. ed., *Peter Munday: Merchant Adventurer* (Oxford 2011),152.
20. Postan, *Medieval Trade and Finance*, 286.
21. Fudge, *Cargoes, Embargoes and Emissaries*, 158.
22. Jörn, 'With money and blood', 410.
23. Fudge, *Cargoes, Embargoes and Emissaries*. 90.
24. Lloyd, *England and the German Hanse*, 238.
25. Fudge, *Cargoes, Embargoes and Emissaries*, 91.
26. Alban, *The Hanse in Norfolk Records*, 5.
27. Lloyd, *England and the German Hanse*, 285.
28. Thompson, *History of the Antiquaries of Boston*, 62.
29. Jörn, 'With money and blood', 408.
30. Thompson, *History of the Antiquaries of Boston*, 247.
31. Grimwade, P,, *Ipswich: A Hanseatic Port* (Ipswich Maritime Trust 2019), 18.
32. Lloyd, *England and the German Hanse*, 163.
33. Gardiner, J. ed., *The Paston Letters 1422-1509 AD* (Edward Arber 1872-75), 364.
34. Richards, P., *King's Lynn* (Chichester 1990), 92.
35. Lloyd, *England and the German Hanse*, 277.
36. Salmon, P., & Barrow, T., eds., *Britain and the Baltic: Studies in Commercial, Political and Cultural Relations 1500-2000* (Sunderland 2003), 7.
37. Ibid., 18.
38. Ibid., 9.
39. Jörn, 'With money and blood', 350.
40. Gras, *The Early English Customs System*, 624.
41. Williams, *The Maritime Trade of the East Anglian Ports*, 98.
42. Jörn, 'With money and blood', 412.
43. Zimmern, *The Hansa Towns*, 341.
44. Lee, J.S., *Cambridge and its Economic Region 1450-1560* (University of Hertfordshire Press 2005), 106.
45. Williams, *The Maritime Trade of the East Anglian Ports*, 106.
46. Parker, *The Making of King's Lynn*, 79.
47. NRO, 'With Ships and Goods and Merchandise', 14.
48. King's Lynn Borough Archive Hall Book no.10, 1684-1731 [KL/C7/12].
49. NRO, 'With Ships and Goods and Merchandise', 14.
50. Ibid., 13.

Conclusion

This study has hopefully highlighted the significance of the Wash ports in Anglo-Hanseatic history. Lynn's association with the German Hanse bridges the 13th to 18th centuries, or around 500 years, though the heyday for both was the 14th and 15th centuries. Its overseas trade was largely with the major Hanseatic port towns of northern Germany when Lynn was in England's urban premier league. It experienced relative decline after 1750 due to the absence of an expanding industrial hinterland which boosted Hull and Newcastle. However, Lynn's international and coastal trades were still considerable in 1751, the year the German Hanse sold its kontor in the Wash haven.

Lynn's broad hinterland which embraced some of the wealthiest counties in medieval England via the Great Ouse river system, combined with its position on the east coast facing the North Sea and Baltic beyond, attracted German merchants. Lübeck and Hamburg men had footholds in the town by the 1260s, which may have been their headquarters in England, possibly before Henry III granted them commercial liberties and their own hanses in London (1266). Boston had simultaneously emerged as an equally important destination for Hanseatic traders drawn to its growing international summer fair where the best English wool was sold.

Danzig had become Lynn's main Hanseatic trading partner by the 1380s as the rapidly developing English cloth industry drove native merchants to build bigger ships and seek new European markets. The Norfolk port was in the vanguard of their commercial thrust to the East. Baltic traders constituted its most numerous and dynamic hanse with their vessels carrying mainly cloth for valuable return cargoes. Prussian fears that the English were taking control of their homeland's economy sparked hostility, but Lynn and Danzig merchants formed business partnerships, and the Teutonic Knights promoted trade with the West. Traders involved in Anglo-Hanseatic commerce needed international peace and cooperation.

Hanseatic towns did nevertheless turn more protectionist from the 1380s as English and Dutch penetration of the Baltic began in earnest. English merchants also became increasingly resentful of the trading rights their kings had granted the Germans at home and demanded reciprocity in the East. Trade was moreover often disrupted by piracy and international conflict involving Denmark, Holland, England, France and the Hanseatic towns. English monarchs were frequently unable to control the piratical activities of their own countrymen too.

English medieval kings spent much of their time and money fighting the French but realised Anglo-Hanseatic commerce was in the national interest because of the significance of Baltic goods and food imports. Bad harvests at home were particularly alarming. So many rich German merchants based in the English capital were also a convenient source of revenue and loans for warrior kings forever cash strapped. To settle damaging disputes English monarchs despatched embassies to Prussia and the Hanseatic towns whose own envoys were likewise received in London, though the resulting treaties failed to secure lasting peace. Lynn merchants were involved in this international diplomacy being recognised by English kings as experts in Anglo-Prussian trade and politics. England's seaborne commerce with the Baltic was more modest in the 1450s and 1460s than previously but its merchants maintained a presence in Prussia. They were also active in Norway and Iceland which engendered conflict with the Hanseatic towns and Denmark throughout the 15th century.

Hawks in both English and Hanseatic governing camps jogged their respective chieftains into the destructive Sea War (1469-1473) which was triggered by Danish action against ships from Lynn and other east coast towns. The Treaty of Utrecht brought hostilities to an end (1474). For the Germans a high priority in the peace settlement was the grant by Edward IV of a new trading post at Lynn as well as repossession of the London Steelyard and Boston kontor. Their success in acquiring the freehold of these properties in the three English towns which had figured so prominently in Anglo-Hanseatic affairs was a political coup. There was naturally a commercial side to the diplomatic coin demonstrated by the return of Lynn traders to the Baltic and Danzig merchants to Lynn. Yet England's east coast ports lost Hanseatic trade to the capital city. London's Steelyard was back in business but its continental gateway was the Low Countries and Antwerp rather than the Baltic. The Bergenfahrer from Norway had already deserted Boston which did not recover its international commerce after 1474.

England's east coast ports north of London accounted for a considerable slice of England's medieval foreign trade and the Wash ports were particularly involved with the German Hanse. It can be argued that Lynn and Boston warrant more attention in the making of Anglo-Hanseatic history between 1250 and 1550. Lynn was a prominent player. Its merchant rulers were amongst the foremost members of the growing urban bourgeoisie which was accumulating wealth and power in medieval England. The Hanse House by the river Great Ouse is, moreover, the sole surviving kontor established by the German Hanse in England and embodies Lynn's Hanseatic associations Past and Present. A short history of this nationally significant waterside historic complex post 1751 seems therefore appropriate.

Postscript—Lynn's Hanse House since 1751

Following the purchase of 'Allemayne Mansion' from the Hanseatic towns in 1751, Edward Everard rebuilt the street range of nine bays in classical style. Almost certainly in the 1790s, his son Edward (1739 – 1819) extended the family home by converting part of the northern warehouse range into a salon. He had several daughters whose parties there would have included likely marriage partners in members of the rural and urban gentry. The two warehouses running down to the river were granaries and the courtyard between them probably a garden. The Everards extended the northern warehouse range by the erection of a brick maltings to supply their nearby brewery in Baker Lane. There was a malting kiln with an oven beneath and a pyramidal roof (it was still in operation in the 1930s). A late 18th century brick extension of two storeys also abuts the west end of the southern warehouse range. The Everards sold all their business interests in Lynn in 1861 and moved out of the town into the west Norfolk countryside.

The Everards had a partner in the first half of the 19th century called John Prescott Blencowe (1778-1840) who emerged as the firm's "leading spirit".[1] He inherited St Margaret's House and its granaries following his marriage to Pleasance Everard in 1799. Blencowe was mayor in 1817 and 1825. He went into partnership with his brothers-in-law, involved in brewing and shipping, before the acquisition of the 'Bagge & Bacon Bank' in King Street in 1826. Blencowe and five members of the Everard family had raised £6057 to buy the business; he is listed in a local directory for 1836 as a banker living at St Margaret's House. John and Pleasance had eleven children, of whom only one daughter married, and several were living in the same house in

John Prescott Blencowe (1788-1840) lived at the Hanse House.

Oil on canvas by Samuel Lane (1780-1859).

nearby Nelson Street by 1845. In 1892 the surviving children put up a window in memory of their parents in the nave of St Margaret's Priory Church.

In 1862 James Towell leased the malting kiln and associated granaries from the Blencowe family, but W.H. Garland appears as the main tenant in 1871. H.S and J.L Marriott had succeeded him by 1878 when they were operating the maltings and granaries now owned by William Burkitt. Born in Chesterfield in 1825, he became a prominent local corn merchant, residing in Queen Street and later the Tuesday Market Place. Burkitt was one of the town's chief citizens and twice mayor. When he died in 1906 his nephew William Burkitt inherited St Margaret's House and leased the property until his death in 1920.

Residents of St Margaret's House must have tolerated high levels of dust and noise emanating from the adjacent granaries and maltings. The lawyer and town clerk, Edward Swatman, was there in 1861 with his wife, Mary, and eight children aged from two to seventeen. Two nurses, a housemaid, a cook and a kitchen maid were employed by the family. By 1881 a day and boarding school for girls had moved to St Margaret's House, with Margaret and her German born husband, August Goebbels, the twin principals. At least fifteen female boarders aged between twelve and sixteen with two servants are recorded there in the 1881 census. Goebbels visited the homes of some local bourgeois families by bicycle to teach German to the children, although he apparently had little English. Following the death of his wife in 1886, Goebbels transferred the school to the Reverend Brereton, who was soon to establish the Girls' High School in King Street. In 1891 St Margaret's House was occupied by the surgeon Henry Allinson and his wife, Lydia, who were aged thirty-five and thirty-six respectively. He was also paying poor rates for a stable and a warehouse. A coachman, a housemaid and a cook constituted their domestic staff. Henry and Lydia Allinson were still living in the house in 1901 but had gone by 1903.

Between 1908 and 1914 a room in St Margaret's House was used by the West Norfolk Masonic Lodge which had been founded in 1906 mainly for district farmers. The new lodge was accommodated by the householder who was probably a member. A retired Norfolk famer and his wife, with their two daughters, are listed (with ages) in the 1911 census: Thomas Anthony (65), Emma Anthony (50), Ellen? (29) and Gladys (22). There were also three boarders called Joseph Guinness (33), Anthony Poole (18) and Wilfred Black (21). The household of eight persons was completed by servant girl Edith Skipper (18). With twenty-one rooms in the house there was adequate space for lodgers to supplement the Anthony family's income. Joseph Guinness was paying seven shillings a week for his furnished bedroom and sitting room in 1912. In 1913 St Margaret's House had new owners named Henry and Alice Target, aged sixty-eight and forty-nine respectively; he was a bookseller. Following the outbreak of the Great War, in August 1914, their lodgers were British army personnel, including several officers and men who had been billeted. In December 1915 a mysterious death occurred in the house. Lieutenant Albert Benedict, aged thirty-four, was found in his bedroom suffering from a gunshot wound to the head and died later that day. A service revolver was found on his bedroom floor. At the inquest at the nearby Town Hall the jury returned a verdict of accidental death (Benedict is buried in Hardwick Road Cemetery in Lynn).

In the 1920s and 1930s the former Hanseatic complex belonged to the corn merchant, Frank Rust Floyd, who lived in St Margaret's House with his family. The late 18th century salon (built into part of the northern warehouse range) was being used as a drawing room, abutting the granary to the west. In that part of the house on St Margaret's Lane the kitchen and an office were on the ground floor and living accommodation above. The dining room and a small study with 'a blue room' were in the street range overlooking the Church. Gillian Floyd also remembers that several teachers found lodgings in her grandfather's grand residence. Frank Rust Floyd was interested in the Hanseatic League and welcomed to St Margaret's House local groups on town tours. He had been Lynn's mayor in 1911. By 1944 the warehouses and maltings had already been leased and Mr Floyd died in 1948 aged ninety-four. Both World Wars in the 20th century impacted adversely on the Floyds and other merchants dependent on Lynn's seaborne trade with Germany and Europe.

The courtyard of the Hanse House in the 1930s looking west with the river beyond.

The Hanse House (centre) from West Lynn in 1907. Its Georgian maltings can be detected. The large building (left) is Marriott's Warehouse built circa 1580 by a Lynn merchant.

A drawing of the 18th century extension of the northern range of the Hanse House in 1937 when operating as a maltings.

In 1945 'The Society for the Protection of Ancient Buildings' (SPAB) undertook a survey of the town for the local authority which highlighted its remarkable collection of historic buildings. Lynn's series of warehouses or commercial buildings of medieval and Tudor construction was "unrivalled in England" and a special study recommended. The Society's survey refers to the warehouses attached to St George's Hall and Clifton House "but of equal interest are the old Steelyard buildings" at Messrs Floyd's premises in St Margaret's

Place which were "a fine example of merchant's house and warehouses combined".[2] The report was published by the Borough Council of King's Lynn. The Society recognised with "great satisfaction" its sense of responsibility shown for "the preservation of the many historic buildings" which gave "this ancient town its exceptional individuality and distinction".

In April 1947 the warehouses were leased by a local corn merchant who wanted to undertake some external construction work. The Town Hall informed him that an inspection of historic buildings had to be undertaken by the Ministry of Works before it authorised any alterations. At the same time a Lynn estate agent approached the Borough Council on behalf of the owners of St Margaret's House to lease the property for

St Margaret's Priory Church viewed from the east or street range of the Hanse House.

offices. This involved a change of use because it was scheduled for housing but to convert nineteen rooms for flats would be too costly. The Town Hall was offered first refusal if permission were granted. It decided against leasing St Margaret's House for offices after investigating the proposal. No official objection was made to the change of use. In June 1947 the Borough Council received enquiries from both the Ministry of Health and Norfolk County Council about establishing offices in the building. Town councillors insisted that part of the property abutting on St Margaret's Lane should remain residential, perhaps for a caretaker and his family, which reflected the urgent need for housing after 1945.

In 1947 Norfolk County Council took a lease of twenty-one years on the historic complex and set up its Western Area Education and Planning Departments in St Margaret's House, despite parts of the warehouses being in a poor condition. A Mr John Stokeley was also a resident. In January 1968 the Borough Council considered its future for museum purposes but deferred a decision pending deliberation by Norfolk County Council. The latter commissioned the Norwich architect, Donovan Purcell, to report on the state of the property and write a feasibility study. He demonstrated that St Margaret's House and warehouses could be sympathetically converted into the Western Area headquarters of Norfolk County Council, thus preserving nationally important historic buildings at the same time. This became the preferred option partly, no doubt, because the restoration project would be assisted by the Historic Buildings Council for England. The County Council purchased the property for about £11,000 in 1969 and, by 1971, the work was complete. The cost was £130,000. Rotten roof trusses (most beams were of oak) were replaced and 80,000 old tiles procured to remake the roof. The modern cement was removed from the courtyard walls to reveal the medieval brick. In April 1972 'St Margaret's House and Hanseatic Warehouses' were opened for view to the public and listed grade one in the same year. Other County Council departments had moved there by 1973, including Highways and Smallholdings, Weights and Measures and The Registry Office (births, deaths and marriages). The interior had been divided up by partitions into offices which masked much earlier fabric. New or modern fenestration was also installed in the two warehouses and shorter west range. The Georgian character of the street range has fortunately survived (the sandstone flags in the hall, fenestration, floors and staircase).

Since the County Council sold the property in 2011 the new owner has removed the office partitions (installed 1969-71) to open up the two warehouse ranges. An undercroft wine bar and a bistro occupy part of the northern warehouse range and the Georgian maltings respectively. The Rathskeller (the bistro) has a direct link with the Hamburg Suite used for a variety of functions in what is the best-preserved section of the northern warehouse. Here the German merchants stored their wax, pepper, pitch, amber and furs. On the attic floor above is the Lutkyn Room (named after the first known governor of the Hanseatic kontor) available for board meetings and receptions. The upper storey of the short west wing of the complex overlooks both the river and courtyard and probably served as a dining hall circa 1500. It has been licensed for civil marriages since 1972 when named the Hanse Suite. Adjacent there is a fine Tea Room which shares the first floor of the southern warehouse range with an apartment. On its ground floor along St Margaret's Lane are located the Citizens' Advice Bureau and offices. Two attractive apartments can be found on the first and attic floors of the Georgian street range with more offices on the ground floor. The courtyard itself is a pleasant summer meeting place where musicians sometimes perform and parties are held. Hanse House has been the prime venue for activities one weekend every May when the town celebrates its Hanseatic associations Past and Present. On 19 March 2019 the completion of the restoration work undertaken by the new owner was marked by a talk and reception with a plaque unveiled in the new riverside porch. In the adjacent lobby of the western range can be found a splendid model by Mr Fred Hall of how the Hanse House would have appeared at the commencement of the 16th century.

Notes

1. Thew, J.D., *Personal Recollections* (King's Lynn 1891), 44.
2. Society for the Protection of Ancient Buildings, *Report and Survey of the Buildings of Architectural and Historic Interest prepared for the Corporation of King's Lynn* (King's Lynn 1945), 18.

Picture credits

Archiv der Hansestadt Lübeck 136 (bottom).

Armand Colin (Paris) 6.

Ashton, R. 75, 81, 169 (top).

Author's collection 8, 39, 58, 105, 142, 143, 156, 164, 184 (top).

Barrett, J.C. 26.

Borough Council (King's Lynn and West Norfolk) LRPS 04/13719C 181.

bpk Berlin/Gemäldegalerie, SMB/Jörg P. Anders 37.

Cann, R. 118.

Champion, M. 170 (bottom).

Elevated Photography Co. Ltd. 88.

Elfleet, K. front cover, 169 (bottom).

Floyd, G. 183, 184 (bottom).

Gifford, A. 12, 159. 185.

Grassmann, A. 23 (top).

Heritage Lincolnshire 136 (top).

Historic England © 85.

Howling, B. 3, 27.

King's Lynn Minster 60.

Knights, P. 144.

Lee, K. viii, 122, 133, 172.

Lynn News 152, 158 (top).

Malbork City Hall (Poland) 16.

Museen für Kunst und Kulturgeschichte der Hansestadt Lübeck 57.

Museum of Gdansk 91, 93.

Nockolds, J. 92.

Norfolk Medieval Graffiti Society 170 (bottom).

Norfolk Museums Service (Lynn Museum) 53, 61, 86, 97, 111, 154, 176.

Norfolk Record Office (King's Lynn Borough Archive) 89.

Parker, V. 48.

Richard Kay publications (Boston) 65, 77.

Richards, S. 110, 125.

Society of Antiquaries of London 115, 145.

Society for Medieval Archaeology 54.

Thorney Abbey Churchwardens 24.

Tuck, J. 55, 58, 81, 124, 146, 170 (top).

Usher, M. 62.

Victoria and Albert Museum 87

White, S. 158 (bottom).

Wilkins, R. 59, 128.

Bibliography

Alban, J.,
'The Hanse in Norfolk Records'. A paper read at The Hanseatic History and Archaeology Forum in King's Lynn (2009).

Allison, K.J. ed.,
The Victoria County History of York East Riding, Vol. VI: Beverley (Oxford University Press 1989).

Amor, N.R.,
Late Medieval Ipswich (Woodbridge 2011).

Anderson, G.H.,
Précis of the Lynn red book records [n.d].

Ayers, B.,
The German Ocean: Medieval Europe around the North Sea (Equinox Publishing 2016).

Bale, A.,
The Book of Margery Kempe (Oxford 2015).

Bange, B.,
Lisa von Lübeck: Das Hanseschiff des 15. Jahrhunderts (Hamburg 2005).

Barron, C.M. & Sutton, A.F.,
The Medieval Merchant (Shaun Tyas 2014).

Barrow, T. & Salmon, P.eds.,
Britain and the Baltic: Studies in Commercial, Political & Cultural Relations (University of Sunderland Press 2003).

Bates, D. & Liddiard, R.,
East Anglia and its North Sea World in the Middle Ages (The Boydell Press 2013).

Beardwood, A.,
Alien Merchants in England 1350-1377 (Cambridge, Mass. 1931).

Bekemans, L. & Beckwith, S. eds.,
Ports for Europe (Bruges 1996).

Berggren, L., Hybel, N., Landen, A. eds.,
Cogs, Cargoes and Commerce: Maritime Bulk Trade in Northern Europe 1150-1400 (Toronto 2002).

Bonney, M.,
'The English medieval wool and cloth trade: new approaches for the local historian', *The Local Historian* (February 1992).

Biernat, C. & Cieslak, E.,
History of Gdansk (Gdansk 1988).

Bjork, D.K.,
'Piracy in the Baltic 1375-1398', in *Speculum*, vol.18 (Cambridge Mass. University Press 1943).

Brand, H., The German Hanse in *Past & Present Europe* (Groningen 2007).

Braudel, F., *Civilisation & Capitalism 15th-18th Century Volume 3* (London 1984). .

Carus Wilson, E.M., 'The Medieval Trade of the Ports of the Wash', *Medieval Archaeology* (1962-3).

Carus Wilson, E.M., *Medieval Merchant Venturers* (London 1967).

Carus Wilson, E.M., 'Die Hanse in England', in *Hanse in Europa: Brücke zwischen den Märkten 12-17 Jahrhundert* (Köln 1973).

Champion, M., *Medieval Graffiti* (London 2015).

Chisholm, M., *Anglo-Saxon Hydraulic Engineering in the Fens* (Shaun Tyas 2021).

Clarke, H. & Carter, A., *Excavations in King's Lynn 1963-1970* (London 1977).

Colvin, I.D., *The Germans in England 1066-1598* (London 1915).

Cowan, A.F., *The Urban Patriciate: and Venice 1580-1700* (Cologne 1986).

Cunningham, W., *The Growth of English Industry and Commerce* (Cambridge 1922).

Cushing, P., 'New Information about Cogs: Medieval Naval Logistics from an Eyewitness Crusade Chronicle', *Avista Forum Journal* (Fall 2010).

D'Haenens, A., *Europe of the North Sea and the Baltic: The World of the Hanse* (Antwerp 1984).

Dollinger, P., *The German Hansa* (MacMillan 1970).

Dunlop, J.K., *Hamburg 800-1945 A.D.* (Hamburg 2021).

Foister, S., *Holbein in England* (Tate Publishing 2006).

Foister, S., *Holbein & England* (Yale University Press 2004).

Friedland, K., *Die Hanse* (Stuttgart 1991).

Friedland, K., *Lectures 1970-2009* (Kiel 2010). A private collection presented to the author.

Friedland, K. & Richards, P.eds., *Essays in Hanseatic History* (Dereham 2005).

Fudge, J., *Cargoes, Embargoes and Emissaries: The Commercial and Political Interaction of*

England and the German Hanse 1450-1510 (University of Toronto 1995).

Gaimster, D.,   *German Stoneware 1200-1900* (British Museum Press 1997).

Villain-Gandossi, C.,Busuttil, S. & Adam, P. eds., *Medieval Ships and the Birth of Technical Societies, Volume 1* (Malta 1989.

Gardiner, J., ed., *The Paston Letters 1422-1509 AD* (Edward Arber 1872-1875).

Gauert, H., *Die Geschichte der plattdeutschen Sprache* (Hamburg 2017).

Gies, J. & F., *Merchants & Moneymen; The Commercial Revolution 1000-1500* (London 1972).

Giles, K. & Clark, J., 'St Mary's Guildhall, Boston, Lincolnshire: the archaeology of a medieval public building', *Medieval Archaeology* (2011).

Goodman, A., *Margery Kempe and Her World* (London 2002).

Gottfried, R.S., *Bury St Edmunds and the Urban Crisis: 1290-1539* (Princeton University Press 1982).

Grimwade, P., *Ipswich: A Hanseatic Port* (Ipswich Maritime Trust 2019).

Graichen, G. & Hammel-Kiesow, R., *Die Deutsche Hanse* (Hamburg 2011).

Gras, N.S.B., *The Early English Customs System* (Harvard University Press 1918).

Gras, N.S.B., *The Evolution of the English Corn Market* (Harvard University Press 1915).

Grassmann, A. ed., *Lübeckische Geschichte* (Lübeck 1997).

Greif, A., *Institutions and the Path to the Modern Economy* (Cambridge 2006).

Harreld, D. J. ed., *A Companion to the Hanseatic League* (Brill 2015).

Harris, J., *Moving Rooms* (Yale 2008).

Harrod, H., *Report on the Deeds & Records of the Borough of King's Lynn* (King's Lynn 1874).

Henn, V., 'The German Hanse and its Kontors'. A paper read at The Hanseatic History & Archaeology Forum in King's Lynn (2009).

Hicks, M., *Warwick the Kingmaker* (Blackwell 2002).

Hillen, H., *History of the Borough of King's Lynn* (EP

	Publishing 1978).
Hingeston, F. C. ed.,	*The Chronicle of England by John Capgrave* (London 1858).
Hooton, J.,	*The Glaven Ports: A Maritime History of Blakeney, Cley and Wiverton in North Norfolk* (Blakeney 1996).
Huang, A.,	'1358-1669: 300 Years of Hanse Assemblies —their End and Heritage'. A paper read at the Hanse Festival in King's Lynn on 11 May 2019.
Hundt, M. & Lokers,J. eds.,	*Hanse und Stadt* (Lübeck 2014).
Hutchinson, G.,	*Medieval Ships and Shipping* (London 1994).
Hybel, N.,	'The Grain Trade in Northern Europe before 1350', *The Economic History Review, LV* (2002).
Ingleby, H. ed.,	*The Red Register of King's Lynn* (King's Lynn 1922). Two volumes transcribed from the Latin manuscript.
Jacob, E.F.,	*The Fifteenth Century 1399-1485: The Oxford History of England* (Oxford 1985).
Jahnke, C.,	'Überlegungen Zur Entwicklung des Hansebegriffes und der Hanse als Institution resp. Organisation', in *Hansische Geschichtsblätter* (Trier 2013).
Jahnke, C.,	*A Companion to Medieval Lübeck* (Leiden 2019).
Jansen, V.,	'Trading Places: Counting Houses and the Hanseatic Steelyard in King's Lynn', in J. McNeill, ed., *King's Lynn and the Fens* (Leeds 2008).
Jenks, S.,	*England, die Hanse und Preussen: Handel and Diplomatie 1377–1474, Volume 1* (Köln 1992), .
Jenks, S.,	'A Capital without a State: Lübeck capat tocius hanze', in *Historical Research 65* (1992).
Jörn, N.,	'With money and blood': Der Londoner Stalhof im Spannungsfeld der englisch-hansischen Beziehungen im 15.und 16. *Jahrhundert* (Köln 2000).

Karlsson,G.,   *A Brief History of Iceland* (Reykjavik 2010).

Kerling, N.J.M.,   *Commercial Relations of Holland and Zeeland with England from the late Thirteenth Century to the close of the Middle Ages* (Leiden 1954).

Keyser, E.,   *Die Baugeschichte der Stadt Danzig* (Köln 1972).

Kiedel, K.P. & Schnall, U. eds.,   *The Hanse Cog of 1380* (Bremerhaven 1985).

Lappenberg, J.M.,   *Urkundliche Geschichte des Hansischen Stahlhofes zu London* (Osnabrück 1967).

Lee, J.S.,   *Cambridge and its Economic Region 1450-1560* (University of Hertfordshire Press 2005).

Lindberg, E.,   'Club Goods and inefficient institutions: why Danzig and Lübeck failed in the early modern period', *The Economic History Review* (August 2009).

Lloyd, T.H.,   *Alien Merchants in England in the High Middle Ages* (Brighton 1982).

Lloyd, T.H.,   *England and the German Hanse 1157-1611* (Cambridge 1991).

Lloyd, T.H.,   *The English Wool Trade in the Middle Ages* (Cambridge 1977).

Mackerell, B.,   *The History and Antiquity of the Flourishing Corporation of King's Lynn in the County of Norfolk* (Norwich 1737).

Maddock, S.,   'Neighbours, nuisances and night-walkers in early fifteenth-century Lynn', in The Annual: *The Bulletin of the Norfolk Archaeological and Historical Research Group*, no. 24 (2015).

Mardle, J.,   'King's Lynn and the Hansa', in *St Margaret's House and Hanseatic Warehouses, King's Lynn* (Norfolk County Council 1972).

MacGregor, N.,   *Germany: Memories of a Nation* (London 2014).

McGrail, S. ed.,   *The Archaeology of Medieval Ships and Harbours in Northern Europe* (Greenwich 1979).

Möller, C.,   *Von Frieden und der Hanse* (Osnabrück

	2006).
Mortimer, I.,	*1415: Henry V's Year of Glory* (London 2010).
Moyle, F.,	*The King's Painter: The Life and Times of Hans Holbein* (Head of Zeus Ltd. 2021).
Murray, J.M.,	*Bruges, Cradle of Capitalism 1280-1390* (Cambridge 2005).
Naish, J.,	*Seamarks* (London 1985).
Nash, E.G.,	*The Hansa: Its History and Romance* (London 1929).
Nicolle, D.,	*Forces of the Hanseatic League: 13th—15th Centuries* (Osprey Publishing 2014).
Nightingale, P.,	Review of 'The Overseas Trade of Boston in the reign of Richard II', by S.H. Rigby, in *Economic History Review LIX* (2006).
Norfolk Record Office	'With Ships and Goods and Merchandise: King's Lynn and the Hanse'. A guide to an exhibition of facsimile documents from King's Lynn and Norwich (NRO 1998).
Norris, M.W.,	*Monumental Brasses: The Portfolio Plates of the Monumental Brass Society 1894-1984* (Boydell Press 1988).
North, M.,	*From the North Sea to the Baltic: Essays in Commercial, Monetary and Agrarian History, 1500-1800* (Variorum 1996).
Ormrod, W. & Lambert, B. & Mackman, J.,	*Immigrant England 1300-1500* (Manchester 2019).
Owen, D. ed.,	*The Making of King's Lynn: A Documentary Survey* (London 1984).
Owen, D. ed.,	*William Asshebourne's Book* (Norfolk Record Society 1981).
Palliser, D.M. ed.,	*The Cambridge Urban History of Britain 600—1540* (Cambridge 2000).
Panayi, P. ed.,	*Germans in Britain since 1500* (London 1996).
Parker, K. M.,	*Lordship, Liberty and the Pursuit of Politics in Lynn 1370—1420* (unpublished UEA PhD thesis 2004).
Pettegree, A.,	*Brand Luther* (Penguin Books 2016).
Parker, V.,	*The Making of King's Lynn* (Chichester 1971).

Pickvance, C.G.,	'Medieval domed chests in Kent: a contribution to a national and international study', in *Regional Furniture*, vol 26 (2012).

Postan, M.M.,	*Medieval Trade and Finance* (Cambridge 1973).

Postan, M. M. & Power, E. eds.,	*Studies in English Trade in the Fifteenth Century* (London 1933).

Postel, R.,	'The Hanseatic League and its Decline'. A paper read at the Central Connecticut State University, New Britain, CT, 20 November, 1996.

Pritchard, R.E. ed.,	*Peter Munday: Merchant Adventurer* (Oxford 2011).

Proost, M.,	*Die Bedeutung der Stadt Emmerich während der Hansezeit* (Münster 1964/5). A copy from the Stadtarchiv Emmerich.

Pullat, R.,	*Brief History of Tallinn* (Tallinn 1998).

Purcell, D.,	'Der hansische "Steelyard" in King's Lynn, Norfolk, England', in *Hanse in Europa: Brücke zwischen den Märkten 12-17 Jahrhundert* (Köln, 1973).

Reder, D. & Virnich, C-J.,	*350 Years of the Hamburg Chamber of Commerce* (Hamburg 2015).

Richards, P.,	*King's Lynn* (Chichester 1990).

Rigby, S.H. ed.,	*The Overseas Trade of Boston in the reign of Richard II* (Woodbridge 2005).

Rigby, S.H.,	*Boston 1086–1225: A Medieval Boom Town* (Society for Lincolnshire History and Archaeology 2017).

Rogers, A.,	*Noble Merchants* (Bury St Edmunds 2012).

Roskell, J. S., Clark, L. & Rawcliffe, C.,	*The House of Commons 1386–1421 Volumes I, II & III.* (Stroud 1992).

Ross, C.,	*Edward IV* (Los Angeles 1974).

Salter, F.R.,	'The Hanse, Cologne and the Crisis of 1468', *The Economic History Review* (January 1931).

Salzman, L.F.,	*English Trade in the Middle Ages* (Oxford 1931).

Schildhauer, J.,	*The Hansa: History & Culture* (Leipzig 1985).

Schulz, F., *Die Hanse und England* (Darmstadt 1978).

Scott, T., *Society and Economy in Germany 1300-1600* (Basingstoke 2002).

Secretan, V., *Bryggen: The Hanseatic Settlement in Bergen* (Bergen 1982).

Sharp, B., *Famine and Scarcity in late Medieval and early Modern England* (Cambridge 2016).

Simon, U., *Simon von Staveren: Ältermann der Deutschen oder 'King's merchant'?* (Hamburg 2012).

Simpson, G., 'The Pine Standard Chest in St Margaret's Church, King's Lynn, and the Social and Economic Significance of the Type', in J.McNeill ed., *King's Lynn and the Fens* (Leeds 2008).

Sobecki, S., 'The writyng of this tretys': Margery Kempe's son and the Authorship of Her Book, in *Studies in the Age of Chaucer*, 37 (2015).

Spufford, P., *Power and Profit: The Merchant in Medieval Europe* (London 2002).

Society for the Protection of Ancient Buildings *Report and Survey of the Buildings of Architectural and Historic Interest prepared for the Corporation of King's Lynn* (1945).

Sternfeld, F. ed., *European Hansemuseum Catalogue* (Lübeck 2016).

Swinden, H., *The History and Antiquities of the Ancient Burgh of Great Yarmouth* (Yarmouth 1772).

Taylor, W., *The Antiquities of King's Lynn* (Lynn 1844).

Thew, J, D., *Personal Recollections* (Lynn 1891).

Thompson, P., *The History of the Antiquities of Boston* (Boston 1856).

Tipping, C., 'Cargo Handling and the Medieval Cog', in *The Mariner's Mirror* (February 1994).

Toulmin Smith, L., *Expeditions to Prussia and The Holy Land made by Henry Earl of Derby in the years 1390-1 and 1392-3* (Camden Society 1894).

Tracy, C., *English Medieval Furniture and Woodwork* (London 1988).

Ungar, R.W., *The Ship in the Medieval Economy 600—*

	1600 (London 1980).
Urban, W.,	The Teutonic Knights: A Military History (Greenhill Books 2003).
Veale, E.M.,	The English Fur Trade in the Later Middle Ages (Oxford 1966).
Ward, R.,	The World of the Medieval Shipmaster (Woodbridge 2009).
Warner, G. ed.,	The Libelle of Englyshe Polycye: A Poem on the Use of Sea Power 1436 (Oxford 1926).
Westerdijk, P.J.,	De Scheepvaart en Handel van Vlaadingen in de Late Middeleeuwen Voornamelijk op Engeland (Vlaadingen 1986).
Westholm, G.,	Hanseatic Sites, Routes and Monuments (Gotland 1996).
Williams, N.J.,	The Maritime Trade of the East Anglian Ports 1550–1590 (Oxford 1988).
Williamson, T.,	England's Landscape: East Anglia (English Heritage 2006).
Wolf, N.,	Holbein (Taschen 2004).
Wubs-Mrozewicz, J. & Jenks, S. eds.,	The Hanse in Medieval and Early Modern Europe (Leiden 2013).
Zimmern, H.,	The Hansa Towns (London 1899).

Selected Primary Sources

The National Archives (TNA):	E122/97/4,E122/94/14, E122/93/22, E122/94/16, E122/94/2.
	Exchequer: King's Remembrancer: Particulars of Customs Accounts (reference E122).
Harrison, R. ed.,	The Chancery Rolls in so far as they refer to King's Lynn: vol.I, The Patent Rolls 1258-1327 (King's Lynn 1992); vol. II, The Patent Rolls, 1327-1377 (King's Lynn 1993); vol III, The Charter Rolls 1204-1415 (King's Lynn 1993); vol. IV, The Close Rolls, 1256-1377 (King's Lynn 1994); vol. VI, The Chancery Rolls, 1377-1399 (King's Lynn 1999).

The Patent Rolls and the Close Rolls are key sources for the study of English medieval government created in the Royal Chancery (at first the Crown's secretariat). The Letters Close are private and formal communication whereas the Letters Patent are public communication of the royal will.

King's Lynn Borough Archives.

The Hall Books contain minutes and memoranda of proceedings at congregations of the Mayor and Community of Lynn from the 14th century. The volumes used in this study listed below.

Translation by Holcombe Ingleby of King's Lynn Corporation minutes book 1, 1422-1450 (Hall Book 1422-1429, 1450, KL/C7/2). Typescript, 1924.

Translation and transcript by Holcombe Ingleby of King's Lynn Corporation minutes book III, 1497-1544 (Hall Book 1497-1543, KL/C7/5). Typescript, 1923.

Transcript by Holcombe Ingleby of King's Lynn Corporation minutes book IV, 1544-1570 (Hall Book 1543-1569, KL/C7/6). Manuscript, 1924.

Hall Book no 1, 1431-1450 [KL/C7/3].

Hall Book no 2, 1453-1497 [KL/C7/4].

Hall Book no.10, 1684-1731 [KL/C7/12].

A Calendar of the Freemen of Lynn 1292-1836 (Norwich 1913). Compiled from the Records of the Corporation of that Borough by permission of the Town Clerk.

Norfolk Record Office

Records of the King's Lynn Poor Law Union, St Margaret Ward Overseers Rate Books, 1865 and 1885 [C/GP 13/429 and 494].

Valuation Lists, 1905 supplemented to 1912 [C/GP 13/562].

Registers of Duties on Land Values, King's Lynn Division, Stonegate Ward, 1910 [P/DLV 1/242].

Historical Manuscript Commission

The Manuscripts of the Corporations of Southampton and King's Lynn [Eleventh Report, Appendix Part III]. London 1887.

Index